THE STORY OF AMERICAN PAINTING

SERIES IN AMERICAN STUDIES

Editor-in-Chief: Joseph J. Kwiat
PROGRAM IN AMERICAN STUDIES
UNIVERSITY OF MINNESOTA

THE STORY

OF

AMERICAN PAINTING

THE EVOLUTION OF PAINTING IN AMERICA

FROM COLONIAL TIMES

TO THE PRESENT

By CHARLES H. CAFFIN

With a New Introduction by
STUART LEVINE
THE AMERICAN STUDIES DEPARTMENT
UNIVERSITY OF KANSAS

JOHNSON REPRINT CORPORATION

NEW YORK AND LONDON

1970

FERNALD LIBRARY
COLBY-SAWYER COLLEGE
NEW LONDON, N.H. 03257

ND
205
C 2

The edition reproduced here was originally
published in 1907

© 1970 by Johnson Reprint Corporation
All Rights Reserved

Library of Congress Catalog Card Number: 79-107852

. 081

Printed in the U.S.A.

INTRODUCTION

In a book printed in 1901, six years before he published *The Story of American Painting*, Charles Caffin found himself in a curious logical bind. He was writing about the potentialities of photography as a fine art, and had been arguing that photographers should not try to imitate painters or engravers, but should rather build their art upon the idiomatic techniques and procedures of their own medium. Yet a given photograph which looked much like a good etching pleased him very much. So he wrote:

> Well, to myself, the print . . . conveys every impression of an etching, having the beautiful characteristics that one looks for therein: spontaneousness of execution, vigorous and pregnant suggestiveness, velvety color, and delightful evidence of the personal touch. There is nothing sacred or even desirable in the mere process of etching upon copper apart from its results. If similar results can be obtained some other way, and the artist chooses to adopt it because he finds it easier or more convenient, what concern is it of ours? Surely none. I may have thought or written otherwise in the past. Let me admit conversion. The fact is, in this new art critics and photographers alike are feeling their way—they to expression, we to judgment.[1]

Charles Henry Caffin (1859–1918) may not have been the most learned art critic of his day, but surely he was among the most open-minded, the least frightened by what was new in as turbulent an era as the visual arts have known. Oxford-trained, he had come to America in 1892 as a consultant for the World's Columbian Exposition in Chicago; by 1897 he was a permanent resident of New York City, engaged in a career which included lecturing, newspaper and magazine criticism, and authorship of a herd of art-appreciation books, some of them gathered from his regular journalistic columns.

---

[1] *Photography as a Fine Art: The Achievements and Possibilities of Photographic Art in America* (New York: Doubleday, Page & Company, 1907), pp. 108–110.

One is tempted at first to write him off as a naive believer in the "uplifting" qualities of art, or even as simply a commercial practitioner of art appreciation, a prototypical turn-of-the century preacher of "Onward and Upward with the Arts." A closer look at his work, though, reveals originality and intellectual courage, as well as an extremely valuable pragmatic familiarity with the day-to-day world of galleries, shows, and young artists which one would be less likely to find in a more academic writer.

His book on photography will serve to introduce his characteristic methods and attitudes. Cut away from its illustrations, *Photography as a Fine Art* seems a very modern book, arguing as it does for freedom and innovation, idiomatic use of the medium, and a new set of standards separate from those of painting. Yet the photographs themselves do look like paintings, charcoals, or etchings, especially the ones he likes best. He lauds Alfred Stieglitz, for instance, for being a pure photographer, yet praises Stieglitz's photos by comparing them to paintings they resemble. And when one looks closely at his logic, holes appear. A photo should look like a photo; "faked effects" are a bad thing (see pp. 30 ff., for instance). Yet doctoring a negative is aesthetically permissible (see p. 17 and elsewhere). The work of Gertrude Käsebier causes even more difficulties. Caffin's impulse always is to find first principles and explain the world in terms of them. Clearly he loves her photographs, but can't make them fit his principles.

Yet the record he leaves is too valuable for us to quibble over his difficulties. This is how a confusing new art looked to a conventionally trained but open-minded critic, and here are the artists he chose to write about, and their work. Are his first principles questionable (". . . the chief beauty in a work of art, be it painting, photograph, or silver salt-cellar, is the evidence of the artist's expression of himself" [90–91])? Is there Anglo-Saxon racist condescension (Indians are "an alien race—one fading from the earth" [p. 105])? Does he praise artists long forgotten, and styles which seem backwaters to us? Such things are in themselves valuable as intellectual artifacts. Our judgment might be wrong, for one thing; for another, as students of periods in the American past we should be trying to see through the eyes of the past. We can learn as much from his errors, indecisions, and attitudes as we can from those of Henry Adams.

He can teach us about ourselves, too, for when we catch ourselves agreeing too wholeheartedly with him, and are struck by how modern many of his attitudes seem, the context brings us up short—he seems outrageously dated a page later, and reminds us that our own attitudes are hardly universal truths, either.

A further strength of Caffin's work needs to be mentioned, one not especially evident in his book on photography but important for an understanding of *The Story of American Painting*. The man was an extraordinarily effective teacher. I know of no books on painting written since which do the job of helping the neophyte to the art to react aesthetically to the paintings of a given age, as well as do the series of volumes which Caffin wrote under the title-pattern "How to Study. . . ."

He succeeds for two special reasons. First, he deliberately limits himself to pairs of paintings, devoting a short chapter to each pair. Though enthusiasm for his subject leads to many such statements as, "I wish we were able to reproduce several other works of this master," he restricts himself for the most part to using the paired works reproduced in each chapter to typify forces at work in the artists' day and place, artistic motivation, technique, and method. The reader has the two works before him; the selections are extremely well chosen; the result is that Caffin's comparisons and contrasts stick in the mind extremely well. If we compare Caffin's "How to Study . . ." books to the standard modern introductory text, H. W. Janson's admirable *History of Art: A Survey of the Major Visual Arts from the Dawn of History to the Present Day* (New York, 1962), we see immediately how well Caffin's pedagogical device works. Janson is his superior as scholar, as prose stylist, and as historian; his book, moreover, is incomparably more inviting than any of Caffin's—generous in format and lavish in its use of half-tone and glossy color plates. But the novice remembers Caffin more clearly because Caffin does less, and focuses so strongly on so few works. I don't mean to imply that the "How to Study . . ." books are skimpy or superficial; they're surprisingly rich. But they are deliberately severe in organization: each small chapter tells what two paintings mean to the author.

Caffin has a sure feel for the condition of the novice "art appreciator"; this is another reason for his effectiveness as a teacher. He knows his readers were not brought up with the masters, so to speak, and so addresses himself to teaching them how to see. I have myself sent students to *How to Study the Modern Painters* (New York, London and Toronto: Hodder and Stoughton, 1914), and as recently as 1941, chapters of his "How to Study . . ." series were assembled and republished as *How to Study Pictures by Means of a Series of Comparisons of the Painters' Motives and Methods* (New York: A. Appleton-Century Company).

Charles Caffin said in *American Masters of Painting*[2] that there was a grain of truth, no more, in art-for-art's-sake (p. 84), and in 1913 published a book designed to argue the opposite point, *Art for Life's Sake: An Application of the Principles of Art to the Ideals and Conduct of Individual and Collective Life*.[3] It's a fascinating document which reflects any number of intellectual currents of its day. The book is racist; it is also pseudoevolutionary in a number of rather naive ways; and, like the present volume, it is sometimes wrong, as when Caffin tells us, in an attack on Mediterranean aristocracy, that the three balls of the Medici "testify to their origin as money-lenders" (p. 31). But in it Caffin tries to think out the implications of optimistic democratic faith, science-as-progress, the cult of onward-and-upward, and so forth, and arrives at the idea that art provides a model of ideals and values.

Most artists and critics react to their milieu; Caffin talks about how he personally reacted, tracing his development from a conversation in his father's study (pp. 45 ff.) to his current feelings. He says that he was taught to believe that man was born to sorrow, but that his own boyish instincts resisted, and that modern science and human progress have since demonstrated that a life of beauty and joy is within human grasp. Education must

[2] *Being Brief Appreciations of Some American Painters* (New York: Doubleday, Page & Company, 1902).

[3] (New York: The Prang Company).

be revised; "Beauty of Life and Living must be put at the head of the curriculum" (p. 57). What he proposed probably can be understood best as part of the tradition of utopias being created by other writers of his day; such a comparison would be worth doing. For our purpose, it's enough to note that beyond all that is transient in the book, Caffin reaches a few positions which sophisticated interdisciplinary study today is just beginning to deal with.

He knows, for example, that the compartmentalization of the arts is peculiar to our culture, though he arrives at his conclusions by courses of reasoning which would appear foolish to a contemporary social scientist. He argues that to view art as an activity separate from other human pursuits is not healthy, and, after a career devoted to propagandizing for elite art, insists that art is where you find it, that any activity which the culture uses for art can be thought of as art. So Caffin concludes that "moving picture shows" are potentially an art form—the earliest statement to that effect I know (pp. 20–21), and one for which he should be honored.

It is part of his more general argument that all human activity can be conducted as art, hence making all life beautiful. The message is deliberately Messianic. He is preaching "the gospel of the New Democracy, based upon the Union of Art and Science" (p. 13); Jesus, not unexpectedly, is Caffin's kind of life-artist (p. 14).

We have no business summarizing the book or discussing it in detail here. Suffice it to say that it is, for all its limitations, a strong testimonial to Caffin's open-mindedness and originality as well as his commitment to his age. *Art for Life's Sake* is an impressive attempt to show that a life devoted to art could teach one to live meaningfully, that, moreover, an art critic could be devoted to the world around him in the same manner as he was devoted to his art. That, indeed, was the message; the world can be treated as art.

II

If we are to evaluate the quality of our own information about the history of American painting, we have to understand something of the process by which a canon was established. Suppose, for example, that we were trying to find the answer to one of those basic cultural issues which properly concern people in American Studies: what kind of an environment has America provided for creative people? Our usual procedure in thinking out our answers to such problems is to review what we know about the histories of the various arts. But what we know is the result of what we have been taught, what we've seen in museums, and what we have read. And who decided that the paintings and painters we know are really the significant ones? Somewhere along the line, did someone define a sociological universe, call it "American painters," and then proceed to take a random sample as a basis for generalization? Obviously not. We look at works which someone in the past has decided were the most significant. This skews our sample immediately, but we still can proceed if we have an idea at least of what was the basis for the selection. One's first impulse is to say, "Why, aesthetic quality, of course," but this frequently turns out not to be the case at all.

In Charles Caffin's case, for example, absolute aesthetic criteria seem less important than a vaguely evolutionary pattern which he apparently had in mind, and this despite the fact that Caffin is very much an aesthetically-oriented art critic, and not primarily an art historian. His subtitle is honestly worded: this book was to show the "evolution" of painting in America. His means of selection is easy to state: what leads to our present taste deserves emphasis; what doesn't, doesn't. Hence in the early pages, John Smibert is dismissed, and we are told that Benjamin West's influence on the styles of young artists is "unfortunate" (p. 11).

The "modern" position he believes in is based upon recognition of the importance of individual expression. Reduced to technical terms, this means that the more painterly the work of a painter is, the more aware the viewer is of paint and brush-strokes on canvas, the more modern the painter. The works of painters which do not reveal this characteristic are considered inferior or at best artistic dead ends, regardless of their intrinsic merit. Caffin gives us a good statement of his position on page 203 of *The Story of American Painting* in a discussion of Alexander W. Wyant. When Wyant was dying, Caffin tells us, he exclaimed, "Had I but five years more in which to paint, even one year, I think I could do the thing I long to." Caffin then says,

> This is the cry of a true artist, one whose soul was set upon that most evanescent intangible quality—expression, while his hands were hampered by a medium comparatively clumsy and hard to manage. To others it will seem that he reached achievement; to himself, conscious of what he longed to do, there remained to the end a royal discontent.

The soulful rhetoric of old-fashioned art criticism which Caffin employs in that paragraph should not hide the fact that the position he states is standard dogma in art courses today. Caffin believes in it fervently, and uses the old rhetoric to serve what he feels are new and permanent truths. It is what makes him unafraid of new things happening in Europe; very early in the century he wrote favorably of Matisse and Picasso. Abstraction meant more expression and less representation, and he approved.

III

We have noted that we generalize on the basis of our knowledge, which in art means the total of our training and our experience. Thus if we look at some of the standard assumptions about the arts in America, or the arts in a democracy, or the arts in a fluid society, or the arts in a capitalist society, and try to determine whether these generalizations are true, we will turn for the most part to what we know about the careers and productivity of the artists who have "made" the standard surveys.

Even this much checking with evidence, of course, is unusual. One can read through a distressing number of discussions of American culture without ever reaching this level of empiricism. Dip into an issue of a contemporary "quality" magazine—and you are likely to find "concerned" articles which assume, for example, that the United States is and has been an extremely bad environment for artists. We too are liable to assume that this is true simply because, on a certain level of sophistication, we have encountered the assumption before. It is preferable to evaluate these generalizations in the light of evidence. What's wrong, of course, is that our evidence itself is unsound. We need much more information than the surveys will give us. At the present writing—1969—everyone is suddenly very much aware of how thoroughly we have omitted the contributions of American Negroes from surveys of all aspects of our national experience, the arts among them. There have been other omissions, equally arbitrary. And the artists for whom we have a great deal of information, because scholarship has been done on their careers, are almost always the same artists who show up in the surveys. The rare enthusiasm for a previously unknown artist is probably the exception that proves the rule. But if we are to understand the whole problem of the artist in American society, we need all kinds of information about the ambience in which artists worked in different periods, and this means all artists, not just the few fortunate enough to have impressed somebody in their own time or sometime thereafter that they were important enough to be included in a survey.

A couple of examples will have to suffice to illustrate the nature of the problem. Any standard history of painting in America stresses portraiture in the seventeenth and eighteenth centuries, largely because there is relatively little else to discuss. Nineteenth-century portraiture is covered, but not in nearly so much depth, even though the century saw hundreds of competent portraitists. We must ignore for the purposes of this illustration the fact that many painters considered portraiture beneath their dignity. What is important is that many more practiced it, but failed to gain a place in the histories. In the twentieth century, portraiture goes on, and on quite a large scale, but is practically unmentioned in the surveys. The reason for this selective coverage, of course, is that the authors of surveys are trying to cover the careers of men they take to be significant in the history of our art; where there was less to discuss, or less that was new, they discussed what there was.

This is not intended to single out art historians for special castigation. Their scheme is reasonable, given the peculiarities of our art history. Similar unintentional distortions occur in the histories of our other arts. John Tasker Howard and Gilbert Chase, our best surveyors of music, cover all manner of "minor" phenomena up to the appearance of the first permanent large professional orchestras and trained professional composers— church music, shape-note music, itinerant music masters, and commercial ballads, for example. They say practically nothing about such matters after, say, 1880, though commercial balladry, for instance, continues on an enormous scale to the present, a scale which might make it seem more important to a student of our culture than concert music.

One of the most valuable things about Caffin is that as magazine and newspaper critic and a man-about-art of his day, he had a very good feeling for the commercial world of art; for what groups of painters, some of them now forgotten, had in common; for what gallery and salesroom life felt like, and for how tastes and fads changed and were created, or as he would have said, "evolved."

We have to pick up a lot of this information by inference in Caffin, because he doesn't consider it terribly important, and assumes that we already know what he is talking about. A passage such as the following is both tantalizing and frustrating:

Until Millet pricked the pretty bubble of misrepresentation, and taught men to study human life as it really is, these fancy idylls of peasant genre, turned out from Düsseldorf or under its influence flooded our American market. Any one who is conversant with the operations of the picture salesrooms knows how large a part they have played in the greater number of collections (109–110).

Unfortunately, we are not "conversant" with salesrooms of his day, and we should be. What he says is very valuable to an understanding of the process of taste development, but the modern reader interested in the problem wants him to spell it all out, and it does not occur to Caffin to do so. He says of the Düsseldorf painters, "their popular appeal may have done much to interest people in pictures, but it certainly postponed for a considerable time a just appreciation of the true nature of pictorial art" (p. 110).

This suggests that Caffin conceives of the art audience as perhaps pyramidal in structure. If we defined its base as "collectors whose tastes have reached only the limited development represented by the kind of painting he characterizes as 'from Düsseldorf,' " and its apex as something like, "people whose collections include impressionist and post-impressionist work," or, perhaps, "works clearly moving in the direction of abstraction," we must conclude that he believed that tastes, to some extent at least, develop.[4] "The true nature of pictorial art," always means, in Caffin, art which is expressive of the individuality of the artist. And this belief in personal expression always means "as opposed to literal or methodical copying of nature." He feels that the mature student of art has grown to this position.

If it seems terribly obvious that tastes develop, it is worth pointing out that most critics of the arts operate with a very different assumption. They write as though their audience were born to its art, so to speak, and had the same tastes as the critic. Anyone whose taste is less well developed is a philistine. That's perhaps an exaggeration; perhaps it would be more accurate to define the critics' intentions in this manner: they assume that their readers at least want to have the very best tastes, and so write from a rather snobbish attitude to give people of unacceptable tastes the cue to what are more acceptable values and attitudes. The snobbery, in other words, is quite deliberate,

[4] Some years ago, the editor did a study of the structure of the audience of another art, concert music, and found that the pyramid really seems to exist. At its base were concertgoers whose tastes had developed as far as the easily accessible high romantic composers—Tschaikovsky, Rimsky Korsakof, and Rachmaninoff, for example, while people at the apex—those with a taste for, let us say, contemporary chamber music, baroque music, and so forth, relatively more esoteric works as they are generally conceived to be, had almost uniformly come to their more esoteric tastes by a process which, at one stage, included the familiar high romantics. That tastes develop was no surprise, though it was good to have detailed information on the process. What was suprising was that snobbery did not seem to be operating very effectively. Most of those surveyed still retained their taste for music "lower" on the pyramid. Indeed, most still retained their taste for popular music and for standard music as well (standard music I defined as "arranged music—the semi-classics, 'standard' older popular songs, popularized classics, background music, mood music, show music, and so forth). ("Some Observations on the Concert Audience," in Hennig Cohen, ed., *The American Cuture: Approaches to the Study of the United States* [Boston: Houghton Mifflin Company, 1968], 296-311. Originally published in *American Quarterly*, XV, 2, pt. 1 [Summer, 1963]).

and may even be said to be present for a good cause; you
pretend that your reader has better tastes than he really does
in order to show him that there *are* better tastes. Caffin himself
sometimes displays this tendency, but just as often he operates
on the assumption that his reader is new to the arts. As an
excellent educator, he seems to have this in his mind more often
than do most writers on art.

If we are to understand the role of the arts in American
culture, we badly need information about the American audience. For earlier times, we must operate from secondary
sources, and it is here that Caffin is again valuable. While it
would be absurd to claim that Caffin provides us with all the
data we need for the art audience at the turn of the century,
there is enough evidence scattered casually in his writings to
make them about the best source we have for a general feeling
for the structure of the art public in his day.

IV

The Story of American Painting is weakest at the start. Like
many students of painting before and since, Caffin is a sad
historian. He accepts, uncritically, every stock generalization
about seventeenth- and eighteenth-century America: New England is bigoted, narrow, and obsessed with sin; the South is
elegant and cultured (pp. 5–9). The Middle Atlantic states,
moreover, seem to have been absorbed by the South and New
England; they are never discussed.

There are simple factual errors as well: he thinks that there
were no painters before Gustavus Hesselius (p. 5) and was no
imaginative literature at all before 1820 (p. 6). His account of
John Singleton Copley is very nearly a total disaster. One finds
errors in both important and unimportant details. The extent
to which Copley trained himself continues to astonish modern
writers, as it should, but Caffin says that all Copley had seen
was work by Smibert and West, and this is simply wrong (p.
12). A few pages later, we find Caffin saying, "Himself of good
family, handsome, brilliant in manner, and early gaining success as a painter, he moved in the best society, and dressed and

lived in style" (p. 18). Doesn't he know that Copley's widowed mother eked out a living selling tobacco to sailors on the wharf in Boston? That Copley has been repeatedly described as "painfully shy"? That Copley became a professional painter in his early teens because he had to, because it seemed a good way to bring some badly needed cash into the family? (Caffin is right, of course, in describing Copley as handsome and in saying that success and skill came quickly—one wants to add, "and at an astonishingly tender age"—and that he then prospered.) One cannot excuse Caffin on the grounds that accurate information about Copley's life was not yet available. It was readily available.

Caffin sees a sharp contrast between Smibert's age and Copley's: New England had suddenly become more liberal. Yet, a few pages later, we are told of how his "artistic spirit" was "curbed by the narrowness of environment" in Boston (p. 21). And the "wrongest" thing in Caffin's book is his concluding sentence about Copley. Remember Copley's personal timidity and his apparently desperate fear of an ocean voyage; remember how uncomfortable and dangerous life became for him and his family after his really very heroic effort to mediate the last great dispute between Loyalists and Patriots before fighting actually broke out in Boston; remember also the bitter unhappiness of his later years in England: "He was the first of a numerous band of American painters who have deliberately chosen to live in Europe, because there they could find an atmosphere more congenial to their art" (p. 22).

Caffin also has an annoying weakness for gratuitous facts. A single example will suffice. Talking about changes in Copley's style during the European trip which preceded his settling in England, Caffin tells us that in Rome Copley "painted the portrait of Mr. and Mrs. Ralph Izard, the former a wealthy planter of South Carolina and his wife, before her marriage a Miss Alice DeLancey of Mamaronack, New York" (p. 21). Social notes from all over. This information serves no purpose whatsoever; it's not even part of a deliberate attempt to show us the social status of Copley's sitters.

It is undoubtedly unfair to pick on Caffin for this sort of

thing; art history and art criticism—not to mention the history and criticism of other fields—have always been guilty of uncertainty of methodology and inconsistency of approach. One writer, speaking of the state of literary scholarship before the promising advent of the New Criticism, called it an "age-old combination of gush and gossip," and one winces at the accuracy of his characterization. It fits too much art scholarship as well. It seems important, then, that what is valuable in Caffin be clearly separated from what is arbitrary, misinformed, or simply wrong, lest this new edition be taken as an authority in areas in which it really has no competence. Caffin can be valuable even when he is wrong, but one has to know what's right to make the judgment.

<h1 style="text-align:center">V</h1>

The matter of expressivity is a case in point. Charles Willson Peale and Copley were not "painterly," so Caffin treats them condescendingly. Hudson River and other popular landscapists, Caffin complains, can tell us "what the scene looks like, but not what it feels like. . . . Apart from questions of technical skill, this is the . . . difference between the earlier landscapes and those of the present day, in which we shall find the expression of a mood in nature to be the painter's aim" (pp. 81–82). Our own predisposition to agree should not blind us to the essential illogic of such arguments. A page earlier, Caffin reproduces Bierstadt's "Yosemite Valley," and says that it "very cleverly represents the facts of the scene, but with a uniform precision of detail that becomes monotonous." True enough. Yet if the Bierstadt in question (p. 80) does not also represent a "mood in nature," then no painting ever did.

Caffin feels more kindly to the men of the Hudson River School than to some of their contemporaries who worked in more ambitious genres; at least, he says, the landscapists reflected national sentiment. Their work, moreover, has a place in his evolutionary scheme: it is the bad stuff we had to grow away from before we could reach genuinely "expressive" landscape painting. We see again how important that word "evolution" in Caffin's subtitle is as a clue to his bias: he will pay most attention to that art which he feels leads to the present. This attitude has helped much of his criticism to weather well; it made him sympathetic to the most revolutionary elements in the painting of his day. But it also inadvertently distorted his survey by leading him to brush quickly over men whose work did not seem to him in the mainstream.

Caffin is quite consistent on this matter, and his feelings coincide so well with standard art critical dogma of our own day that it's tempting to let his position go unchallenged. But it has no more inherent logic than its opposite. Discussing the work of Asher B. Durand, he complains that the painter works patiently and conscientiously to put together "little effects" but fails to grasp the "salient characteristics of the whole or its part." The painting in question is thus not sufficiently expressive of the artist's personality. A footnote in which he apologizes for the quality of the plate of the painting under discussion shows the weakness of Caffin's position:

> This lack of synthesis is much less apparent in the small reproduction than in the larger original, because the photograph and the subsequent half-tone process of reproducing it have tended to compress the details into masses of tone, and have in a way, effected a synthesis (p. 72).

If reducing the original to a print in the book does all this, wouldn't standing a few feet further away from the original have the same effect? Caffin's standard argument about being painterly is all very well, but really, why can't the "kick" in a painting be just as well the artist's skill in figuring out ways to make it seem that he has painted each leaf? Why is "niggling brushwork" (Caffin's favorite phrase for it) of necessity bad? One wonders, if the camera hadn't been invented, whether this ideal would have triumphed, or at least survived in more respectable form. We admire, after all, Dutch interior painters whose brushwork is as "niggling" as anything Caffin discusses.

I'm not arguing that Durand is a greater artist than Caffin thinks he is, though I think that I would argue that Copley is; indeed, given Caffin's general judiciousness and the surprising extent to which his taste coincides with our own, I would guess that he had not seen very much of the best of Copley's works.

It's clear enough from the emphasis in his books and his work as magazine and newspaper art critic that he was most familiar with those American works which he had seen at specific exhibits he went to cover, and with the traditional corpus of European masterworks in which he had been trained before coming to the United States. In arguing about the expressive importance of a painterly approach, he was taking a sound and defensible position. My only point is that we should see it as a culture-bound attitude. He is speaking out of a specific historic time and place, out of the assumptions which an "enlightened" and open-minded critic, unafraid of the new, would make. But the ideas he expressed do not necessarily have the authority of sacred writ; one could construct other aesthetics equally valid.

Within the subculture of the art world, the strength of attitude and prejudice must be very considerable. That Caffin would say such things demonstrates this strength, for he was an original and quite independent thinker, not generally given to accepting dogmas of the art world at face value. Five years earlier, in *American Masters of Painting*, he had looked at precisely the same issue in a chapter on George Inness. Discussing Thomas Cole's influence, he had in effect caught himself in the process of making an overly simple contrast: Cole is just a topographical painter, while Inness produces a sense of intimacy with the landscape. Then, in a remarkable passage, Caffin thinks over what he has said, decides that his judgment is based on arbitrary grounds, and concludes that Cole's path really might have lead, ultimately, to great painting. "Wait a minute," he says in effect, "I've been judging Cole on the basis of my training in European landscape." And then he picks into that training: "We must not forget that our estimate of the functions of landscape painting comes to us from Holland, a country of limited horizons, through France. . . . The so-called classic landscape was grandiloquently superficial," and so we have preferred the intimacy of the French way of seeing nature. "Perhaps too rashly," Caffin concludes; perhaps one could have great landscape that is neither intimate nor superficial (*American Masters*, pp. 5–6).

The principle of selection which Caffin utilizes in his work is nowhere more clearly in view than in his discussions of those artists who seem to him to be important. Because Washington Allston and John Vanderlyn "look backward," they did not thrive in America. (See especially page 65.) Allston and Vanderlyn, moreover, are "cosmopolitan," while the spirit of their age was nationalistic. Hence the painters of the Hudson River School, while technically uninteresting, are at least attuned to their times, and worthy of extended discussion in the "evolutionary" pattern.

One is uncomfortable with his conclusions. The Hudson River people are interesting, and their popular appeal is important to an understanding of their age. Yet Allston, despite his perhaps unreasonable ambitions, did receive the kind of patronage—in the form of what amounted to large grants—which he needed to pursue his ideals over a long period of time. There were businessmen willing to put up a lot of money to let him do his thing; such patronage is, culturally, exactly as important as the popularity of the Hudson River painters in indicating attunement to the times.

Caffin's comparison of Peale, Copley, and Stuart is another excellent example of the operation of his bias. He begins by saying that Stuart's career "stands out in the early chapter of American painting as a single unrelated episode." That's questionable in itself. "Unrelated" to what? Stuart is one of a number of talented Americans who went or was sent by sympathetic businessmen to England for further training; hence his career bears a relationship to those of a number of his contemporaries. He worked with West in London; West also befriended numerous other young American painters. The style he learned was not West's, but in its bravura brushwork reveals close relationship to the style of a whole school of late eighteenth-century British painters, most notably, Sir Joshua Reynolds. Copley's work is also related to Reynolds', both during his colonial period, when he wrote to the more famous artist asking advice, and rather naively and charmingly tried to follow it, and during his English period, when he learned and used Reynolds' technique. The technique of Copley's English work, while different from Stuart's, has the same relationship to the parent school as does Stuart's: you can tell that both painters had been influenced by the technical procedures of English portraiture. So it's unfair to call Stuart's career "unrelated" to forces which affected other Americans.

Stuart seems more important to Caffin because he fits in with an imagined evolutionary tendency toward a more painterly, and therefore, in Caffin's logic, more expressive style. If "progress" equals "painterly," he has to see Stuart as far out of Copley's class. Stuart *is*, of course, in certain senses, especially if one compares mature Stuart to colonial Copley: Stuart simply knows more. But as to who is the more important artist—I think if we get away from Caffin for a moment, we are as likely to decide that Copley is as that Stuart is. The final judgment, of course, is subjective: I am more likely to be moved when I am standing in front of one of the great Copleys than when I am standing in front of even one of the most wonderful of Stuart's portraits; others might feel differently. Our point is that Caffin does not see things this way. He is *sure* that Stuart is better and more important.[5]

Caffin's familiarity with American painters increases as one moves along chronologically. The nearer we get to the present, the more data he has. His conclusions become correspondingly less simplistic. His cultural and historical ideas, however, are liable to remain naive, to some extent, I imagine, because he is an American by adoption, and has perhaps less sense of certain commonalities of experience.

This often creates distortions. On page 166 he is discussing the scarcity of nudes in our painting history, and, after mentioning "long centuries of Puritanical tradition and prejudice," concludes that "The classics, as a mine of poetic thought and concrete ideals, were equally unfamiliar. . . ." Provinciality and ignorance have been with us throughout our history, but no writer familiar with the history of education in this country

---

[5] Indeed, Caffin seems to have a special reverence for Stuart. In *American Masters of Painting* he gives Stuart the last chapter (185–195) and does a virtual whitewash of Stuart's uneven career, playing Parson Weems in an attempt to create in Stuart a figure to be held up as a model to youth.

on any level in the eighteenth and nineteenth centuries would ever claim, as Caffin does, that the classics were underemphasized. Nor should we forget some other facts about American culture in the century before Caffin wrote: the architecture of Greece and Rome was so familiar as to have become a vernacular tradition. Neoclassicism and the romantic association with the democracy of the Greek city-states and republican Rome were so pervasive that they influenced not only architecture but even clothing. And, if we may use "classics" in the other sense of the word, recent scholarship has reminded us of what Caffin should have known, that nineteenth-century Americans were astonishingly familiar with Shakespeare, so much so that the most popular forms of entertainment could assume audience familiarity with Shakespeare, and build upon it in parodies—witness *The Adventures of Huckleberry Finn.*

VI

Yet Caffin's capacity for growth and development is impressive. From time to time, particularly in the early portions of this book, one encounters a passage which tempts one to chuckle indulgently at how dated or stuffy or narrow were the Edwardian critics, only to be brought up short a couple of paragraphs later by evidence of real breadth of judgment. Thus one wonders what jingoist history he had been reading which lead him to call the War of 1812 "The Second War of Independence" (p. 46). But three paragraphs later he is arguing against the nationalist implications of Emerson's "The American Scholar," which strikes him as "a singular combination of fallacy and truth. For in the kingdom of thought, wherein Emerson himself dwells and of which painting is a province, there are no boundaries of oceans or continents, no disabilities of dependence or alienship, but a community of free intercourse" (p. 48).

The Story of American Painting becomes more judicious as it moves along. Making a point about the work of the nineteenth-century artist Chester Harding, the author is careful to insert a modest disclaimer—"so far as I am acquainted with his work" (p. 93). Since Caffin does not seem to have been

very long on information on earlier painters, apologies of this
sort would have been welcome in his treatment of the seventeenth and eighteenth centuries. When he assumed that he knew
the pattern, as he did when he told us, in effect, that obviously
there could have been no painting in Puritan days, he was at
his weakest. Perhaps the complexity which resulted from his
knowing more was part of what makes the latter parts of his
book more thoughtful and valuable.

One wants to praise Caffin for his unwillingness to become
involved in a chauvinistic argument—one to the effect that a
truly American art must grow out of national themes on national soil, or something of this sort. Yet when he summarizes
and generalizes one is very much aware of the bias produced
by his experience and training. The best way to study American
painting, he says, is to examine

> the fermentation which occurred in European art during the
> past century and to trace how American painting gradually
> aligned itself with the foreign movement. So far from its being
> a story of self-sufficient isolation, it has come to be one of com-
> plete identification with the strivings of other countries. For,
> to-day, so far as concerns technical considerations, painting is
> an international art with a free trade in methods, the clearing-
> house of which has become Paris (pp. 86–87).

Caffin is right about Paris in his day, and certainly right
about free trade. The United States had had what might be
called international artists from about the time of Allston; some
would argue that this had been true since the days of West,
with the international "clearing-house" shifting from London,
to Italy, to Germany, and finally to Paris. And if one looks at
the painters with whom Caffin feels most comfortable, the
theory that American painting is a history of adjusting to Europe makes a good deal of sense. But it depends upon which
painters one looks at. If one made the center of one's discussion
of the contemporary (to Caffin) art world, let us say, Winslow
Homer, Thomas Eakins, and Albert Ryder, then clearly no such
simple pattern would emerge.

Still, Caffin's point is well taken; he is still arguing with

Emerson, and his idea is that art has a technical history which transcends national boundary lines; he is quite right.

Caffin discusses those figures of his own period who have seemed most important to more recent writers, though he gives more space to people we have tended to forget. To some extent this is because most of our critics seem to feel that the big men in the history of our art, until about 1950, have tended to be loners, whereas Caffin, writing at the time, assumes that he is witnessing a kind of harvest in which tendencies long maturing in modern art have come to fruition. He wants to tell us about men who represent the first of what he hopes will be a bumper crop. He is impressed with the "loners"—men such as Ryder, Homer, and Eakins—but since they don't fit into his general scheme, he gives them less attention than figures whom he takes to represent, if we may shift metaphors, the mainstream.

Modern critics would expect more to be said, for instance, about Albert Ryder, though they might find Caffin's favorable judgment about right. Caffin does not seem to know about Ryder's mysticism. If he had, he still could not have guessed that mysticism—even downright occultism—would appear to be, seventy years later, as powerful a force in our art history as we have had: Ryder seems today to have been both a spiritual forerunner of much of our best art and also an important direct influence on some of our best painters. But Caffin's error in emphasis—if it really is an error—is more than excusable. He tried to report the art world as it looked to an active art-show goer; he would have felt that he was producing an eccentric picture had he not selected his major examples from what looked to be the going movements.

Caffin's treatment of Whistler provides the necessary contrast; he devotes a full chapter (pp. 285–303) to him, and praises him very strongly. We think him important, too, especially as a forerunner of our own day, and would agree that in his work Impressionism and the Japanese print help move us toward abstraction. Our discussions, however, are not conducted in the same prose:

> We are overmuch drilled from childhood to . . . have little reverence or habit of quiet thoughtfulness, and too soon to lose the

fragrance of our natures in the withering heat of worldliness.
With Whistler, we may do well to enter at times into the tranquil
half-light of the soul, and ponder upon the things of the Spirit
(p. 303).

But curiously, in this case, romantic rhetoric may get closer to
what has been important in Whistler than modern critical
rationalizations about the flattening canvas and the movement
toward abstraction. Whistler *did* talk about soul and spirit,
and so do abstract expressionists. The most powerful movement
in our painting history *was* (and still *is*) shot through mysticism. Its practitioners do not like the tendency among friendly
critics to explain their works in terms of design and composition; their own prose runs rather to what the nineteenth
century would have called transcendent inspiration. Indeed, as
Harold Rosenberg explained in *The Anxious Object: Art Today
and its Audience*,[6] the movements which have followed abstract
expressionism have been in large part a deliberate attack on
such rationalization.

Thus, though Caffin misses the mysticism of Ryder, he senses
it in Whistler, and is most "modern," paradoxically, through
his most old-fashioned prose.

One aspect of his treatment of Ryder may be very important.
Caffin says that Ryder "embroiders every inch of the canvas,
as if his brush were a needle, threaded with brilliant silks or
strands of gold and silver" . . . (pp. 218, 221). Modern critics
see Ryder in rather large masses, and think that he wanted to
give the impression of light radiating from within. Caffin speaks
of embroidery, and says that a weakness of the paintings is that
the radiance is only on the surface (p. 221). Forget for the
moment that the modern writers, through scholarship, know
more about Ryder's intention and his curious methods. Remember instead that we see very little of a Ryder painting; many
have turned almost black by now. Caffin saw them when they
were new. Could he be recording something about what Ryder
looked like to an unbiased observer when his works were fairly
new? Only in a rare and quite complex composition such as

6 New York: Horizon Press, 1964.

"Siegfried and the Rhine Maidens" does a modern viewer see anything that looks like "embroidery." If Caffin is right, perhaps we should rethink our generalizations about Ryder.

Caffin is less surprising in his treatment of Thomas Eakins (pp. 231–233). He praises him strongly, and for pretty much the reasons we do today. Perhaps he's more comfortable with Eakins: he knows where he studied, and so can—perhaps a little too easily—call him a representative of the influence of French realism. Yet we wish he had written much more, or perhaps knew much more, about Eakins, who seems to us very important indeed. Caffin's judgment seems sound:

> . . . here is an instance where a picture may be superior to a mere work of art; . . . there is in Eakins a capacity broader and deeper than that of simply being an artist. He has the qualities of manhood and mentality that are not too conspicuous in American painting (pp. 232–233).

But if that is true, then Caffin's treatment seems skimpy.

Caffin knows the standard big "exhibition machines" of Winslow Homer, from the early "Prisoners from the Front" through the heroic "Life Lines," "Undertow," "Danger," and "Eight Bells"; his list shows how early the canon of Homer's "best" oils was established. He praises them for strength and originality, and does so strongly (pp. 233–237). He doesn't bother to mention the watercolors: those are what are most exciting to modern writers, who are liable to say things as strong as, "Winslow Homer invented twentieth-century watercolor technique." Knowing the market as he did, Caffin should have been aware of how many watercolors Homer was producing, and how well they were selling. We can be perfectly certain that he knew Homer's work in watercolor; *American Masters of Painting* contained a paragraph of praise (p. 80) for them. Perhaps the importance of the medium had not yet become clearly enough established for him to recognize the importance of Homer's accomplishment. There's a good lesson here for us as students of our own culture: one never has knowledge of the future; our estimate of what's important is based on our sense of context, and that in turn is based on the past.

Moreover, his accounts of the forgotten men who looked good to him are invaluable. They seem to have been good painters; their work *was* forward-looking, in technical terms—painterly and "expressive." George de Forest Brush, for example, is discussed at considerable length (pp. 174–181). Caffin dislikes certain characteristics of his work, but Brush obviously seizes his imagination—so strongly that Caffin is willing to waive his usual strictures against literary painters and praise him as a painter of ideas. I dare say few readers have ever heard of George de Forest Brush, but it's worth knowing that a turn-of-the-century critic, forward-looking, scornful of the dead hand of the academy, friend of the innovator, was still so moved by "The Sculptor and the King" (p. 179), a work painted in the mode of Brush's teacher Gérôme, relying for its effect entirely upon the glossy technique and "finish" of the academicians, and upon a sentimental and pseudoarcheological conceit. I suspect, in short, that Caffin is telling us something important about a taste strong enough in the culture to overcome his own critic's standards and our own training. Radical though he is, and suspicious of literary flavor in painting, Caffin will on occasion make an exception. *American Masters of Painting* contains quite a long defense of the storytelling painting, which he uses to justify his praise for Edwin A. Abbey (pp. 83 ff.).

Another man lost to modern critics is Alexander Harrison. From what Caffin says, he was very impressive in his day, a radical and a *plein air* painter of power, quite early for his approach, too. But there is more in him for us than the temptation to see whether one couldn't pick up a few of his works for a song. Our critics tend to devote most of their attention in the period to those Americans whose paintings did not too strongly reflect the big movements on the continent. Caffin, in contrast, often sees American art as French art by Americans. A man like Harrison is just a good Impressionist. Caffin's sense of perspective for his own day is doubtless better than ours.

John La Farge still holds his place in many of our surveys, though he seems less important to us than he did to Caffin. Caffin feels that La Farge is important, and argues from solid evidence, in terms of his own perfectly sensible aesthetic, to show why. The disparity of judgment is important cultural evidence: if we use Eakins instead of La Farge to make a point about the period, we're ignoring the manner in which at least certain well-informed people at the time perceived the art-world. For example: Caffin waxes enthusiastic over La Farge's big religious murals. We pay at best polite attention to them. We assume, indeed, that religious painting has never really flourished in America, and it is routine to conclude in art history courses that this has something to do with the pragmatic national character. Arthur Townsend, in a forthcoming work, argues that we have produced great quantities of religious art, much of high quality. It has generally not made the standard surveys, illustrating again the peculiar biases built into our canon. While I have not seen enough of Mr. Townsend's evidence to be sure that he is right, I have seen enough to feel that Caffin's praise of these La Farge religious murals is closer to the *cultural* truth than our own standard judgment.

The perspective from which Caffin operates is not ours, and the difference should be enlightening. It comes as a surprise to us that his strongest attack on gentility is a part of his chapter on mural painting. (It is, by the way, a scathing attack, one worth reading if you have been taught that all critics at the turn of the century believed in the Genteel Tradition.) We treat murals parenthetically if at all, because we feel that little of major importance has happened in the field in our country. Caffin would agree that little has happened—our muralists, he says, "have not yet risen to the occasion" (p. 330). But his anger and his perception of "the occasion" are different: the American condition seemed to him made for mural painters. America had "grandeur," "a virility, not without its flavour of brutality," a "gilded" leisure, and deep racial (!) pride (p. 331). Moreover, there was all manner of patronage and opportunity available: "Nowhere do conditions, present and past, offer more abundant suggestions to the imagination, and nowhere are mural painters receiving so much encouragement of opportunity" (p. 330). We think of murals as an art form which flourished in the European past, in revolutionary Mexico in our own day, and only under intense government support and for a brief and not entirely distinguished period during the days of the WPA in the 1930's in our own country; it simply wouldn't occur to us to think of the United States as a place ripe for a great school of muralists. Yet it felt that way to Caffin, and he knew the market. His perspective is priceless.

Caffin shows us other cultural facts as well. There are certain characteristics in the styles of a period which generally go unmentioned, but which show up in the works of disparate artists; Caffin's book enables us to see some of them. Vaguely-painted passages are fashionable, though Caffin never says so: his plates tell us. Certain characteristic handlings of line appear in painters as different as Homer—whom we think of as important—and Abbott Thayer, who looks to us dated. Thomas Dewing's "The Spinet" (p. 188) reminds us of Eakin's paintings of lady musicians in more ways than subject matter. Anyone who has had publication-design work done by professional commercial artists knows that in a given year, everyone you hire is liable to produce certain kinds of lines and compositions: "We want to give this a contemporary look," they tell you. We too readily miss similar tendencies among elite artists, probably because we have been trained through surveys, which select masterworks. Even discussions of schools usually fail to show the characteristics which a school shares, perhaps unconsciously, with contemporary design mannerisms. Caffin's book, because it concentrates so heavily upon his own day, is more satisfying in this respect.

All this is part of a larger problem: can we learn to see through the eyes of the past? Can we, for example, be moved as Caffin was by Thayer's "Virgin Enthroned" (p. 183)? An unwritten hope in American Studies is that immersion in a number of aspects of a period will enable us to do such things. I find that Caffin's prose helps. An unprejudiced friend says of "Virgin Enthroned," "That's nice. The children look natural." She's right, though I never would have thought to say so. For me, the prose is necessary to make the response possible: all of Caffin's chatter about tenderness, unselfishness, the "beautiful qualities of personal character, strong, tender, simple," and, above all, "the spiritual ideal" (p. 182). Trick yourself for a moment into believing in "the spiritual ideal," and the dated painting speaks.

Caffin, as we've noted, will criticize a painter for being literary—it's a quality he dislikes in Ryder, for instance—but when his own imagination is caught up by the result, he will praise it. This is sometimes true even when an artist's work exhibits a number of tendencies which run counter to Caffin's ideals. Thus he admits that Edwin Abbey is a colorist in only a limited sense, did a poor job of decorating a frieze in the Boston Public Library (p. 320), and, far from being forward-looking, is rather "the most important survivor . . . of the vogue of the historical subject" (p. 194). He is, moreover, merely an illustrator who works in oils. Yet Caffin likes to see a scene from Shakespeare visualized, handled with a sense of drama, showing "diverse individualities of character and emotion" (p. 195), so he praises Abbey's "Trial of Queen Katherine." He is telling us, in effect, that he knows that his usual aesthetic, while valid, is not a cosmic truth.

Having noted errors in Caffin's facts and praised him for what he shows us, sometimes unconsciously, about the art world of his day, it is time to add that he knows his business—art shows and contemporary painters—very well, and can be trusted as a source of new information on the works of painters of his own period. He is very good at pinpointing groups, ties, attitudes, and influences. Caffin tells us that in the middle and late 1870's, for example, the first group of Paris-trained painters began working in the United States, and that their influence could be seen almost immediately on the popular level in the improvement of magazine illustration, and in the organization of the Society of American Artists in 1877. He then goes on to discuss in detail the nature of representative work of their hands. What he says about illustration is not in any textbook, and is surprising in terms of the usual assumption that commercial media follow the "elite" arts rather than lead them. The facts and dates he mentions certainly would not be new to any student of American painting; they were not even in Caffin's day. But his familiarity with the whole area is unusual and comfortable. He perceives training and influence with the kind of detail that only a practicing popular reviewer or an *aficionado* could provide. His reaction is less that of a historian than that of an enthusiast.

Quite often, of course, one can extrapolate from Caffin's evidence. Later in his discussion of the impact of the French-trained painters, especially figure painters, he says that their presence on the scene helped popularize French academic figure painting, and that the result, paradoxically, was to discourage the continuation or imitation of French academic art. This was because our French-trained artists had a hard time: collectors preferred that such paintings be by Frenchmen. If he is right, and if the same attitude affected our art historians, he has provided us with excellent context to explain the survival in our texts primarily of those artists who did not paint like Frenchmen.

VII

I am aware that in discussing Caffin's significance for students of American culture I have tended to respond most strongly to topics which interest me personally. I have by no means covered all I see, and certainly a reader with different interests would respond to others. I hope that I have succeeded in suggesting angles of attack, methodologies, if you will: ways to use works of the sort exemplified by the book herein reproduced. *The Story of American Painting* is neither a major contribution to scholarship nor an example of the popular response to the art situation. It is rather what they call in the publishing business a "trade book," designed to sell. Its success alone is significant as an index of the intellectual needs and interests of its audience; it gives us clues to the structure of the art audience and the nature of taste-development.

Books of this sort are too often ignored by the scholars, who tend to look either "higher" (to works of solid intellectual attainment) or "lower" (to examples of mass response). In a culture as complex as ours, in which changes in taste often amount to changes in social status as well, the trade-book market is a valuable source of evidence. If it is true, as I believe and as Caffin laments, that Western culture separates art from the totality of human experience, and understands it as something that is good for you rather than as something which you pretty automatically have and use, then the desire for "enrichment" need not be regarded simply as "phony." It is a healthy response to our rather unique value-system, as valid and "genuine" as any other response, and certainly worthy of study.

Moreover, as I hope I have succeeded in showing, Caffin is no fool, and no simple exploiter of a ready market, either. He knows his trade, has been moved by important intellectual currents in his day, and responds to the combination with conviction, independence, and originality. His inconsistencies are usually the result of his best qualities, and he usually spots them himself. Were he more consistent, he could be used simply as an example of the force of popular ideas of his day, and we could think of his works as evidence to confirm our stock generalizations about turn-of-the-century America. But if we try to use him that way, we find either that our generalizations are faulty—as I'm sure they are—or that he is too good to fit their patterns—which I'm sure is true, too.

Acknowledgment

I would like to acknowledge the contributions to this introduction of the members of my seminar, Studies in the Arts in America, and particularly James Girard and Arthur Townsend.

Stuart Levine

SELECTED BIBLIOGRAPHY

This is in no sense a complete bibliography for the study of painting in America. It is rather a list of some books which seem useful for comparison with Caffin's volume.

I. A good modern survey of the field, with a fine bibliography:
Edgar P. Richardson, *Painting in America: The Story of 450 Years.* New York: Thomas Y. Crowell Company, 1956.

II. A detailed study of Copley, too recent to be in Richardson's bibliography:
Jules David Prown, *John Singleton Copley.* Volume I: *In America 1738–1774.* Volume II: *In England 1774–1815.* Cambridge, Massachusetts: Harvard University Press, 1966. Since Caffin's treatment of Copley is used as a test case in our Introduction, this extensive study is useful as a reliable guide to the facts.

III. Two contemporary works on similar topics:
Samuel Isham, *The History of American Painting.* New York: The Macmillan Company, 1905. A contemporary survey, excellent for comparison. Available in an enlarged edition, with supplemental chapters by Royal Cortissoz, New York: The Macmillan Company, 1927. Reissued again in 1936—cf. reissue dates of the Caffin text.
John C. Van Dyke, *American Painting and its Tradition/ As Represented by Inness, Wyant, Martin, Homer, LaFarge, Whistler, Chase, Alexander, Sargent.* New York: Charles Scribner's Sons, 1919. Excellent for contrast: the "culture bind" binds Van Dyke far more tightly than it does Caffin.

IV. Some Books by Charles H. Caffin
Charles H. Caffin. *American Masters of Painting: Being Brief Appreciations of Some American Painters.* New York: Doubleday, Page and Company, 1902.

FERNALD LIBRARY
COLBY-SAWYER COLLEC
NEW LONDON, N.H. 032

————. *American Masters of Sculpture: Being Brief Appreciations of Some American Sculptors and of Some Phases of Sculpture in America*. New York: Doubleday, Page, and Company, 1913.

————. *The Appreciation of the Drama*. New York: The Baker and Taylor Company, 1908.

————. *Art for Life Sake: An Application of the Principles of Art to the Ideals and Conduct of Individual and Collective Life*. New York: The Prang Company, 1913.

————. *The Declaration of Independence and the Constitution of the United States, Illuminated by Nestore Leoni*. Bound extract from *Everybody's Magazine*, VII, I (July, 1902).

————. *A Guide to Pictures for Beginners and Students*. New York: The Baker and Taylor Company, 1910.

————. *How to Study Pictures By Means of a Series of Comparisons of the Painters' Motives and Methods*. New York: Century Company, 1904. Reissued, with additions by Roberta M. Fansler and edited by Alfred Busselli, Jr., New York: D. Appleton-Century Company, Inc., 1941. The revision contains new material and some chapters by Caffin from his other writings.

————. *How to Study Pictures By Means of a Series of Comparisons of Paintings and Painters from Cimabue to Monet, with Historical and Biographical Summaries and Appreciations of the Painters' Motives and Methods*. New York: The Century Co., 1905.

————. *How to Study the Modern Painters By Means of a Series of Comparisons of Paintings and Painters from Watteau to Matisse, with Historical and Biographical Summaries of the Painters' Motives and Methods*. London, New York, Toronto: Hodder and Stoughton, 1914.

————. *Photography as a Fine Art: The Achievements and Possibilities of Photographic Art in America*. New York: Doubleday, Page and Company, 1901. (Discussed in the Introduction.)

————. *The Story of American Painting: The Evolution of Painting in America from Colonial Times to the Present. New York: Frederick A. Stokes Company, 1907.

————. The Story of Dutch Painting. New York: The Century Co., 1909.

————. The Story of Spanish Painting. New York: The Century Co., 1910.

Caffin is also the author of A Child's Guide to Pictures (1908), The Art of Dwight W. Tryon (1909), The Story of French Painting (1911), Francisco Goya Lucientes (1912), How to Study the Old Masters (1914), The A.B.C. Guide to Pictures (1914), and How to Study Architecture (1917), works I have been unable to examine.

V. Works listed under other authors, with texts substantially by Caffin:

Timothy Cole, Old Spanish Masters, with Historical Notes by Charles Caffin and Comments by the Engraver. New York: The Century Company, 1901. The "notes" comprise most of the book. Reissued in 1902, 1903, 1904, 1905, 1906, and 1907.

Julian B. De Forest, A Short History of Art. Edited, revised, and largely rewritten by Charles H. Caffin. New York: Dodd, Mead and Company, 1913.

THE STORY OF AMERICAN PAINTING

Copyright, 1907, by Frank J. Hecker

THE MUSIC ROOM   JAMES A. McNEILL WHISTLER

*W*HISTLER was experimenting with ideas derived from the Japanese.
There is the obvious suggestion of Outamaro in the color-spotting and
unusual form of the figure in black, and the subtle suggestion of something outside the picture, so characteristic of Japanese art.   Contrary to all academic notions, the lady in the riding habit looks out of the picture, while on the
left is shown a reflection of something again outside the picture. Technically there
was the contrast between the reflection and the actual figure, and again between
the one in black and the one in white; to keep the white in its proper place behind
the black. At the time the picture was painted all these things represented new
technical problems.

In the Collection of Colonel Frank J. Hecker

THE STORY

OF

AMERICAN PAINTING

THE EVOLUTION OF PAINTING IN AMERICA
FROM COLONIAL TIMES TO
THE PRESENT

BY

CHARLES H. CAFFIN

NEW YORK
FREDERICK A. STOKES COMPANY
PUBLISHERS

Copyright, 1907, by
FREDERICK A. STOKES COMPANY
October, 1907
All rights reserved

Printed in the United States of America

AUTHOR'S NOTE

My aim has been to trace the growth of American Painting from its scanty beginnings in Colonial times up to its abundant harvest in the Present. At first the story is necessarily associated with the efforts of a few individuals. Later, however, as students in increasing numbers seek instruction abroad, it becomes concerned less with individuals than with principles of motives and method. The influence, in turn, of England, Düsseldorf, Munich, and Paris, is discussed, and allusion to individuals is introduced mainly in illustration of the general theme. I have tried, in fact, not only to help the reader to a knowledge of some few painters; but, much more, to put him in possession of a basis of appreciation, on which he may form judgments for himself of the work that is being done to-day by American artists.

CHARLES H. CAFFIN.

NEW YORK, *September 23, 1907.*

CONTENTS

ILLUSTRATIONS

[ix]

ILLUSTRATIONS

ILLUSTRATIONS

ILLUSTRATIONS

[xii]

ILLUSTRATIONS

THE STORY OF AMERICAN PAINTING

The Story of American Painting

CHAPTER I

COLONIAL AND REVOLUTIONARY CONDITIONS

IN 1784 the House met in Philadelphia to
ratify the Treaty of Peace. After seven
years of struggle the United States of America had shaken off the foreign yoke and were com-
mencing another struggle of seven years among
themselves before their full birthright as a united
nation should be established. Once more, as during the much longer struggle of the United Prov-
inces against Spain, a new nation had been born,
and a combination of racial energy and local advantages was to produce an extraordinary harvest
of national development. But it was not to include, as in the case of Holland, an immediate
development in the art of painting.

For the latter, something more is needed than
a virgin soil, spotted over, as in pre-Revolutionary
America, with a few isolated growths, struggling
bravely, but at a disadvantage, in an uncongenial
environment. Wherever in the world painting has
flourished, it has done so after a period of development, gradually enriched by the accumulation of

local or borrowed traditions, until at length it has blossomed into independent vigour.

Such scatterings of tradition as existed during the Colonial period had been derived from England, and reflected mostly the poor conditions of English portrait painting which prevailed before the rise of Reynolds and Gainsborough. Even the influence of the latter, when it came to be established, was overshadowed, so far as Americans were concerned, by that of their countryman, West, whose extraordinary reputation among his contemporaries has not been sustained by subsequent judgment.

Nor in the years preceding the Revolution had the scanty traditions of painting been favoured by local environments. Men's minds were turned to other things than art, and the only conception held of painting was as a means of producing portraits. In the language of the times, the "limner" (this title itself a corruption of the old English word "illuminer," namely, of manuscripts) was spoken of as having an accurate "pencil" in the delineation of "counterfeit presentments." The school from which he had graduated was more than seldom that of carriage painting.

❋ ❋ ❋ ❋ ❋ ❋ ❋ ❋ ❋ ❋ ❋

Such had been the start of John Smibert, a native of Edinburgh. He reached this country in 1720, three years after the arrival of Peter Pelham,

MRS. ROBERT WEIR nee LUCRETIA TUCKERMAN, 1770-1797

B<small>Y</small> *an unknown painter, who tried to imitate the manner of the great English portrait school.*

In the Collection of the Worcester Art Museum

PORTRAIT OF MRS. NORTON QUINCEY
née MARTHA SALISBURY, 1727–1747

A "*COUNTERFEIT presentment*" *of a Colonial dame by some unknown "limner," a contemporary of Smibert.*

In the Collection of the Worcester Art Museum

portrait painter and mezzotint engraver, and seven years after that of the Swedish painter, Gustavus Hesselius, who is credited with having been the earliest painter in this country. In England Smibert had had the good fortune to be taken up by Dean, afterwards Bishop, Berkeley, accompanying him to Italy, and later to Rhode Island, when the philosopher-philanthropist came over to found a missionary college in this country for the conversion of the Indians. At what is now Middletown, three miles from Newport, Berkeley bought an estate which he called Whitehall, and for two years and a half officiated at Trinity Church, Newport, visited the Narragansett Indians, and worked upon his book, "The Minute Philosopher," writing the greater part of it in a crevice in the cliffs overlooking the sea. It was at this time that Smibert executed the portrait group of Berkeley surrounded by his family, which picture, together with the Dean's library of a thousand volumes, became the property of Yale College. When, in consequence of the failure of the home government to give financial support to his scheme, Berkeley returned to England, Smibert established himself in Boston, and lived there until his death in 1751.

It is characteristic of the times that his sitters were chiefly the New England divines, those leaders of a stern theocracy that exercised political as well as spiritual authority. Think of the mental and

moral atmosphere which surrounded the beginnings
in this country of an art which we regard to-day as
making an appeal to our æsthetic sensations. Not
even in the sister art of literature, though much
had been written, had any work of the imagination
been produced, nor would be until after 1820.
Upon political pamphlets, or local records of places,
persons, and events, the writers had expended their
activity; their intellectual force upon the subtleties
of religious controversy. Such appeals as had been
made to men's imaginations were of the kind that
may be read in the sermons of Jonathan Edwards,
whose keen mind revelled in analysing the vividly
imagined horrors of hell.

"O sinner," he preached,* "consider the fearful danger
you are in; it is a great furnace of wrath, that you are held
over in the hands of that God, whose wrath is provoked and
incensed, as much against you, as against many of the damned
in hell!—you hang by a slender thread, with the flames of
divine wrath flashing about it, and ready every moment to
singe it and burn it asunder. It is everlasting wrath. You
will know certainly that you will wear out long ages, millions
and millions of ages, in wrestling and conflicting with this
Almighty merciless vengeance; and then, when you have so
done, when so many ages have actually been spent by you in
this manner, you will know that all is but a point of what
remains."

Nor was this awful fate to be avoided by a man's

* "Sinners in the hands of an Angry God."—Jonathan
Edwards.

RTRAIT OF JOHN LOVELL   JOHN SMIBERT

ORN 1710, graduated from Harvard 1728, "Master Lovell" became in 1729 usher of the Boston Latin School, and its principal from 1734 to 1775. Being of loyalist persuasion, he embarked for Halifax, Nova Scotia, in 1776, and died there two years later.

In the Collection of Harvard University, Cambridge.

HAGAR AND ISHMAEL · BENJAMIN WEST

AN example of the grandiose impotence that passed for the "grand style" among the Italian imitators, at the end of the eighteenth century; it is sweetened with West's particular brand of elegant sentimentality.

In the Collection of the Metropolitan Museum of Art, New York

own doing. All humanity—men, women, and little children—all for the sin of one man and one woman, were predestined to this horror for eternity; only the " goodness " of God selected at gracious random a few souls from damnation. These were conscious of being saved, and were correspondingly puffed up with self-satisfied righteousness. All their fellows lay under the thick pall of eternal wrath; by it was darkened the sky of their lives; lives already hardened through long conflict with severe physical conditions and inured to the constant presence of death and danger. What wonder that their hardy and indomitable natures took refuge in a grim and strenuous severity. The theatre in New England was proscribed. Even as late as 1784 Massachusetts re-enacted the earlier sharp laws against the stage; and New York and Philadelphia still frowned upon it.

To this mental and moral rigour, however, the Southern States presented a notable contrast. Baltimore was a warm supporter of the drama, and much addicted to balls and routs, while the open-air promenades of gaily-dressed people, with their scenes of courtship and merriment, were a distinguished feature of her social life. Charleston also was famous for wealth and gaiety and for the elegance of her homes. In these and in the country mansions, thickly sown over the Southern States, were to be found most of the pictures which had been imported from Europe. It would seem as if the conditions of life among these descendants of cavalier settlers should have been favourable to art, yet it is a strange fact that it was not in the rich, luxurious South, but out of the flinty rigour of the North and East that American painting began its thrifty growth. Some of the painters, it is true, made professional tours through the South, and Southerners, attracted to Philadelphia, when it became the capital of Government and fashion, were among the best patrons of the painters then established in that city. Nevertheless the fact remains, that not Charleston or Baltimore, but Philadelphia and Boston are the places chiefly identified with the early beginnings of American painting.

❋ ❋ ❋ ❋ ❋ ❋ ❋ ❋ ❋ ❋ ❋

In pre-Revolutionary times the most notable of the native-born painters were Benjamin West, John Singleton Copley, Charles Wilson Peale, and Gilbert Stuart. By his contemporaries West was regarded as a prodigy. That a child, born in 1738, in a Quaker village, Springfield, near Philadelphia, and reared among conditions of strict and primitive simplicity, should have evolved out of himself a craving to be an artist; that his earliest lessons in colour had been derived from the Indians, in the crude pigments of yellow, red, and blue with which they decorated their own persons; that, after the present of a paint box from a certain Mr. Pennington, the youth was able in time to produce results that secured him commissions for portraits in Philadelphia and later in New York, and eventually, in his twenty-second year, attracted a patron who provided the necessary means for his visit to Rome—all this seemed phenomenal. And so also was his reception when at length he arrived in London.

But from this point he belongs to England rather than to America; so completely that, when Reynolds died, West was elected President of the Royal Academy, and received the order of Knighthood. He died in 1820, and was buried with pomp in St. Paul's Cathedral.

It is true, however, that he had an indirect influence upon his countrymen, for his success fired their imaginations, and his assistance was generously given to American students who had found their way to London. Yet this influence was unfortunate. The English, giving him the privileges of a pampered child, had encouraged him in the direction in which Reynolds, fortunately for himself, had been discouraged. Accordingly, while some of West's portraits, such as that of C. W. Peale, possess considerable vivacity, his works of imagination are pompous and pretentious in conception, in technique tentative and clumsy. They created a taste for grandiloquent subject rather than for painter-like excellence of workmanship. But, as we shall frequently have occasion to notice, the general aim of painting in the nineteenth century, in which American painting will share, will be to get away from excessive preoccupation with subject, and more and more to develop the resources of painting, as an art, independent of literary alliances. So in this way, also, West is cut off from the stream of movement.

❋ ❋ ❋ ❋ ❋ ❋ ❋ ❋ ❋ ❋ ❋

On the other hand, John Singleton Copley, although he subsequently settled down in England, remains a vital factor in the story of American painting. He identified himself very closely with pre-Revolutionary times by the number of his portraits of eminent men and women; and is himself also distinguished even to this day for the life-like vivacity of these portraits and for his skill in painting. Indeed, this Boston painter, practically self-taught, and with no examples of painting to guide him, save the portraits by Smibert and such of West's as had found their way into the homes of the city, developed a facility of craftmanship that, considering the straitness of his opportunity, is most remarkable. And it is to be observed that his powers were fully matured before he settled in England.

Copley's parents had come from Ireland, and settled in Boston to engage in the tobacco business. About the time of his son's birth (1737), the father, Richard Copley, died, and the boy was named after

PORTRAIT OF C. W. PEALE

BENJAMIN WEST

*A*N engaging picture, though the elegantly affected pose of the hand may be more suggestive
of West's mannerisms than of the character of Peale.

In the Collection of the New York Historical Society

PORTRAIT OF LADY WENTWORTH   JOHN SINGLETON COPLE

*N*OTWITHSTANDING *the hardness of the drawing and the metal-like textures, t
portrait is charming in its high-bred elegance.*

In the Lenox Collection of the New York Public Libra

his maternal grandfather, John Singleton, of Quin-
ville Abbey, County Clare. Ten years later the
mother married that Peter Pelham, painter and
mezzotint-engraver and precursor of Smibert, who
has been mentioned above. His assistance to young
Copley, who early showed a gift for drawing, must
have been considerable, especially as the stepfather
taught him his own art of engraving. When Pelham died, in the same year as Smibert, Copley was
fourteen, and for the rest had to be his own master.
He had no lack of commissions, however, and his
progress was rapid.

At this time Boston was a city of some eighteen
thousand inhabitants, confined to three hills, which
gave it its second name of Trimountain. As yet
there was no bridge across the Charles River, and at
high tides the city was cut off from connection with
the mainland. The better class of dwellings were on
the west side; houses of brick, with Corinthian pi-
lasters adorning the façades, and columned porches
covered with roses and honeysuckles, and approached by sandstone steps which led up from
gardens filled with English elms and shrubs. The
fine furniture in these dwellings was from England
or France. Moreover, since Smibert's day the
rigour of life was lessening. Two conditions had
contributed to the change. In the first place, the
domination of the divines had given way before the
rising influence of laymen, such as Otis and Samuel

Adams; men of broad culture who became by force of character and through their zeal in public affairs the natural leaders of the community. In the second place, class distinction had become more defined. The men and women who throng the canvases of Copley are conscious of their worth and importance, perhaps more than a little *self*-conscious. " Pride of birth had not then been superseded by pride of wealth. The distinction of gentle blood was cherished. Equality had begun to assert itself only as a political axiom; as a social principle, it had not dawned upon the ultra-reformers."

The *Portrait of Lady Wentworth,* painted when she was nineteen and the artist twenty-eight, shows him in full possession of his powers. It is true that the draperies are inclined to be metallic in texture, and the flesh parts marble-like in polish and hardness; indeed, that the various textures throughout the picture have a prevailing similarity of shining rigidity, since the suggestion of atmosphere is lacking, as it is more or less in all of Copley's works.

" Yet, the want of ease and nature in his portraits is as authentic as the costumes. They are generally dignified, elaborate, and more or less ostentatious and somewhat mechanical, but we recognise in these very traits the best evidence of their correctness. They illustrate the men and women of the day, when pride, decorum, and an elegance, sometimes ungraceful but always impressive, marked the dress and air of the higher classes. The hardness of the

outlines and the semi-official aspect of the figures
correspond with the spirit of those times." *

Despite, however, some deficiency of painter-like
quality, the portrait of Lady Wentworth bears an
impress of fine authority and is full of personal
character.

This Boston belle, who is represented toying with
the chain of a captive flying squirrel (a detail which
Copley several times introduced into his pictures),
was a daughter of Samuel Wentworth, and had
been engaged to her cousin, John Wentworth, the
last Royal Governor of New Hampshire. But, in
pique at his prolonged absence on some affair of
business, she married Theodore Atkinson, and it is
as his wife that she is here represented. He died,
however, in a few years, and within a fortnight of
his funeral she married her old love. When the
troubles with the Mother Country arose she accompanied her husband to England. He was appointed
Governor of Nova Scotia, holding the position from
1792 to 1808, when he resigned, but continued to
live in Halifax until his death in 1820. He had
been created a baronet in 1795; and three years later
Lady Frances was made a lady-in-waiting to Queen
Charlotte, with permission, however, to live abroad.
For eleven years she lived in Nova Scotia, and then
returned to England, where she died in 1813.

Considered on the one hand solely as a personal
document, this picture has extraordinary interest.

* Tuckerman's " Book of the Artists."

What an air of birth and breeding the lady exhibits, a consciousness of indisputable social rank and beauty; what a complete poise of self-possession, tinctured, however, with just a flavour of prim severity! How the portrait vivifies a certain phase of the past to our imagination! Nor less remarkable is the technical charm of the picture, when one remembers out of what a poverty of artistic opportunity Copley had emerged to this proficiency. Only a few years separate his art from Smibert's, and yet it is as far in advance of the latter's as the freer social conditions of Copley's day surpass in attractiveness the narrow rigidity of Smibert's. And it is precisely these altered social conditions which had much, perhaps most, to do with Copley's achievement. Himself of good family, handsome, brilliant in manner, and early gaining skill and success as a painter, he moved in the best society, and dressed and lived in style. Within the limited range of New England life he played such a part as Van Dyck in his day played in the larger world of Antwerp and London. His art, moreover, has so much of the same kind of distinction as Van Dyck's that one hazards a belief it might have approached it very closely in degree of distinction also, had his early opportunities been as favourable.

In 1769, when he was thirty-two years old, Copley, now a thoroughly successful painter, married the daughter of Mr. Richard Clarke, a wealthy mer-

PORTRAIT OF MR. AND MRS. IZZARD   JOHN S. COPLEY

*T*HIS picture was painted during Copley's visit to Rome (1774–1775). It shows that he was influenced by the prevailing fashion for the "grand style." But while the paraphernalia of the background is absurdly affected, the figures are treated with a charming sincerity.

In the Collection of the Boston Museum of Fine Arts

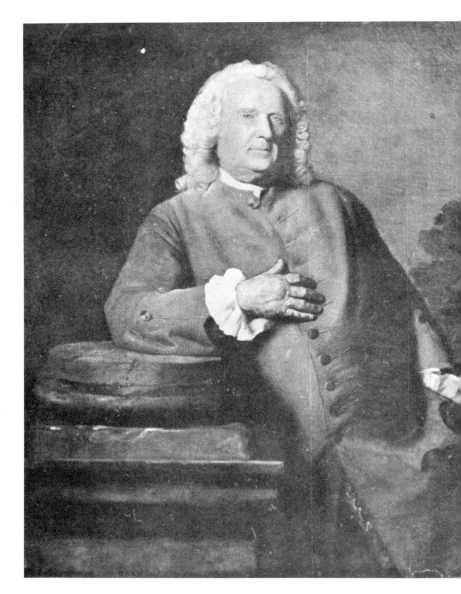

PORTRAIT OF COLONEL EPES SARGENT   JOHN S. COPI

*T*HIS *fine example of Copley's power of characterization, attributed to the period bef*
1760, represents a shipowner of Salem, whose fleet of vessels was destroyed by
French. Some of his descendants are still receiving instalments of the indemn
from the French government.

In the Collection of Mrs. G. M. Cleme

chant and agent of the East India Company, to whom later was consigned that historic cargo of tea which was flung into Boston harbour. Anticipating the trouble with England, Copley went to Rome, where he painted the portrait of Mr. and Mrs. Ralph Izard, the former a wealthy planter of South Carolina, and his wife, before her marriage a Miss Alice DeLancey, of Mamaroneck, New York. Her figure, as she submits a sketch to her husband, is full of charm; but his exhibits Copley's weakest trait of hardness in drawing. Moreover, the elaborate artificiality of the whole composition, in so marked a contrast to the rather severe refinement of the earlier portrait, throws an interesting side-light, both on the influences he had encountered since leaving home and on his own predilections. We see that he had already come under the fascination of that pretentious grandiloquence which was passing for the " grand style " in Europe; and may judge from the rapidity with which he imitated this mannerism, that at heart he was disposed toward it. It is an interesting example of the artistic spirit, curbed by the narrowness of environment, such as Copley experienced in Boston, bursting forth under freer conditions. Unhappily, the latter, in his case, were inclined to be meritricious.

From Rome the painter went to London, where he was kindly received by West, and soon became popular with a public already familiar with his work through the exhibitions of the Royal Academy. His wife joined him, sailing in the last American ship which passed out of Boston harbour under the British ensign, and the rest of his life was spent in England. Here he gained a great reputation for historical pictures, such as *The Death of Chatham*. But they were little more than an aggregation of portraits, and do not compare in actual artistic merit with such a single portrait as that of Lady Wentworth. He died in 1815, at the age of seventy-eight, and was buried in the Church of St. John, at Croydon, near London. His son, under the title of Lord Lyndhurst, was three times Lord Chancellor of England.

West had left this country before there was any suggestion of strained relations with England, and had become so identified with the latter that probably no question of choice of allegiance occurred to him. With Copley, however, it was different. Clearly in his case the instinct of the artist was stronger than that of the patriot. He was the first of a numerous band of American painters who have deliberately chosen to live in Europe, because there they could find an atmosphere more congenial to their art.

We have now to consider a group of men who, after studying abroad, with equal deliberation returned home or settled here, to throw in their lot with the new nation.

CHAPTER II

AT the conclusion of peace, there were among the painters whose work attracts particular notice just four, practising their art in America. Of these, Joseph Wright was at Mount Vernon, painting portraits of General and Mrs. Washington to the order of the Count de Solms. A native of Bordentown, N. J., where he was born in 1756, he had been a pupil of West, and then visited Paris. Returning in 1783, he painted during the autumn of that year at headquarters, Princeton, a portrait of Washington, having first taken a plaster cast of the sitter's head. When the United States mint was established at Philadelphia, he was appointed designer and die-sinker, and there is reason to believe that the first coins and medals executed in this country were his handiwork. He died, a victim of the plague which ravaged Philadelphia, in 1793.

In the latter city were residing at the termination of the war the three others of the four painters alluded to above: Robert Edge Pine, Matthew Pratt, and C. W. Peale.

For Boston's share in the story of American painting is by this time retrospective, and remained so until Stuart settled there ten years later. For the present the attractions of Philadelphia, as the seat of government and fashion, were superior. It was the biggest city in the country. No other could boast of so many streets, arranged with regularity and well paved, but so full of filth and dead cats and dogs that their condition was made the subject of a satire by Francis Hopkinson, better known as the author of the "Battle of the Kegs." No other city could boast so large a population or so much renown. There Franklin had made his discoveries, the Declaration of Independence had been signed, and Congress had deliberated. No other city was so rich, so extravagant, so fashionable. Lee, in his correspondence with Washington, described it as an attractive scene of amusements and debauch; and Lovel, also writing to Washington, had called it a place of crucifying expenses.* Moreover, her citizens had the shrewdness to permit one permanent theatre as a concession to the unregenerate taste of Senators and Congressmen; although there was a strong objection to legalising this new species of luxury and dissipation.

❧ ❧ ❧ ❧ ❧ ❧ ❧ ❧ ❧ ❧ ❧

It was the Honourable Francis Hopkinson, mem-

* J. B. McMaster.

tioned above, one of the signers of the Declaration of Independence, a graduate of Princeton, and an Admiralty Judge of Pennsylvania, who was the first in this country to sit to the Englishman, Pine. The latter, born in London in 1742, a son of John Pine the engraver, arrived in 1784, and settled in Philadelphia, causing no little stir by exhibiting privately to the select few—"the manners and morals of the Quaker City forbidding its exposure to the common eye"—the first cast of the "Venus de Medici" brought to this country.

It was his ambition, in which he anticipated Trumbull, to paint a series of historical pictures, commemorating the events of the Revolution and including portraits of the principal participants. For this purpose, in the intervals of his labours as a teacher of drawing and a painter of occasional portraits, he executed a number of "distinguished heads." Among the latter were studies of Washington, General Gates, Charles Carroll, and Baron Steuben. However, before he could realise his ambition, he died in 1790, at Philadelphia.

❧ ❧ ❧ ❧ ❧ ❧ ❧ ❧ ❧ ❧ ❧

"At the corner of Spruce Street, in Philadelphia, a few years since," wrote Tuckerman in 1867, "hung a shop-sign, representing a cock in a barnyard, which attracted much attention by its manifest superiority to such insignia in general." It was from the brush of Matthew Pratt (born at Philadelphia in 1734), who also executed a famous signboard, containing portraits of leaders of the Convention of 1788, which used to hang at the corner of Chestnut and Fourth Streets.

For in those days (I quote from J. B. McMaster) the numbering of shops and houses had not yet come into fashion, and every business street presented an endless succession of golden balls, of blue gloves, of crowns and sceptres, dogs and rainbows, elephants and horseshoes. They served sometimes as advertisements of the business, sometimes merely as designation of the shops, which were indicated popularly in the newspapers by their signs. The custom still lingers, but now we are accustomed to regard the sign as bearing a direct relation to the character of the business it advertises. One hundred years ago, however, no such relation was understood to exist, and it was not thought remarkable that Philip Freeman should keep his famous bookstore at Boston at the "Blue Glove" on Union Street.

Through the exigencies of the times in which he lived, Pratt painted many such signs, and seems to have gained among his contemporaries more reputation for them than for his portraits. Perhaps not unjustly, since the latter, as may be seen in the portrait of Cadwallader Colden, Lieutenant-Governor of the Province of New York, 1761-1775, which

PORTRAIT OF MRS. REID IN THE
CHARACTER OF A SULTANA

ROBERT EDGE PINE

*THIS canvas recalls the fad in society during the latter part of the eighteenth century for
ladies to pose for their portraits in classic or romantic costumes. It was encouraged by
the painters because it offered extra opportunity for picturesque arrangement.*

In the Collection of the Metropolitan Museum of Art, New York

THE AMERICAN SCHOOL
MATTHEW PRATT

*T*HE scene represented is the painting-room of West in London. On the extreme left stands the master, looking at a
drawing that is being shown him by Pratt. It was exhibited at the Old Spring Gardens. London, in 1766.

now hangs in the Chamber of Commerce, New York, are heavy in colour and laboriously dignified. They reproduce the worst features of West, with whom Pratt studied for two years and a half, being, indeed, his first American pupil. The occasion of his visit to London was to escort thither his relative, Miss Shewell, the long-affianced bride of West, to whom he " gave her away " at St. Martin's in the Strand. The sojourn in his master's studio is commemorated in *The American School* of the Metropolitan Museum, his most important work. The figure to the left, with the hat on, is West's, who is represented in the act of criticising one of Pratt's drawings, while the other students listen. With the exception of this visit to London, one to Ireland in 1770, and another to New York in 1772, Pratt's life was spent in Philadelphia, and there he died in 1805.

But, by all odds, the most famous resident American painter of the period, and the one most interesting to ourselves, is Charles Willson (or Wilson) Peale; for his life was remarkably characteristic of the time, and so intimately related to some of its most important events. Born at Chesterton, Maryland, in 1741, he displayed from his youth mechanical ability and remarkable versatility. In early life he proved himself a clever worker in leather, wood, and metal. He could make a harness, a clock, or silver moulding; he stuffed birds, extracted, repaired, and manufactured teeth, and delivered popular lectures. By degrees, discovering some skill in drawing, he first took lessons in Annapolis from the Swedish painter, Gustavus Hesselius, then studied under Copley in Boston, and finally with West in London. Upon his return to this country he lived for two years in Annapolis, and in 1772 painted the first life-size portrait of Washington, showing him in his aspect before the Revolution. Washington was at the time forty years old, and is represented as a Virginia colonel, in blue coat, scarlet facings, scarlet waistcoat and breeches, and a purple scarf over the left shoulder. It was the uniform in which he had served eighteen years before against the French and Indians near the headwaters of the Ohio, and in which a year later he had taken part in Braddock's disastrous expedition, where his coolness and bravery saved a remnant of the force.

At the outbreak of the Revolution, Peale joined the army and commanded a company at the battles of Trenton and Germantown. In the intervals of fighting he worked upon his second portrait of Washington, which had been commissioned by Congress. The picture was begun during the gloomy winter of 1777-1778 at Valley Forge, and continued at Monmouth. Here Washington suggested introducing as a background the view from the window of the farmhouse in which he was at the time sitting for his portrait, and Peale painted in the Monmouth Courthouse with a body of Hessians issuing from it under guard. Later, when he finished the picture at Princeton, he added a view of Nassau Hall. In all he painted fourteen portraits of Washington, and it is upon these, although his work includes the portraits of many other famous men, that his reputation is chiefly based.

It is customary to speak of these portraits as being more interesting in the way of memorials than as works of art. Yet it may be doubted if this estimate is just, for Peale's portraits have an actuality as vivid as Copley's. He lacked, it is true, the latter's versatility, his elegance of suggestion, and facility in rendering sumptuous fabrics, because he was more concerned with virility of character in men than with the graces of femininity. He had even less feeling than Copley for the æsthetic qualities of painting, as in itself a source of emotional expression; for with him it was purely a means to an end. Yet within this narrow conception of art he was so single-minded and sincere that his pictures are extraordinarily convincing, and, if you view them for what they aimed to be, faithful records of objective facts, most stimulating and conclusive. They are the work of a man who in many respects was less than a painter, but in others very much more.

He was active in the service of his country as in that of art. In addition to his military career, he had been a member of the Philadelphia Convention of 1777. Having discovered some mammoth bones, he commenced a collection of objects relating to the sciences and arts, which was the first step in the direction of a museum in this country. He also attempted to establish in Philadelphia a school of fine arts, and was successful in organising the first exhibition of paintings. Finally, in 1805, he co-operated in the foundation of the Pennsylvania Academy, the oldest of all our existing art institutions. For the New York Academy of Fine Arts, though founded four years earlier, had succumbed to straitened circumstances, and it was not until 1828 that the present National Academy of Design was launched upon its career. It is an interesting characteristic of the Pennsylvania Academy that, while its promoters included some painters, its management has always been in the hands of laymen. Its original object, as set forth in its parchment of incorporation, was:

" To promote the cultivation of the Fine Arts in the United States of America by introducing correct and elegant copies from works of the first masters in Sculpture and Painting, and by thus facilitating the access to such standards, and also by conferring moderate but honourable premiums, and otherwise assisting studies and exciting the efforts of artists, gradually to unfold, enlighten and invigorate the talents of our countrymen."

PORTRAIT OF WASHINGTON   C. W. PEALE

*H*ARD *in drawing and suggestive of a scrupulous imitation of the subject, bit by
bit — the very opposite of the modern synthetic method of suggestion of the whole as
a whole — yet full of force by reason of its sincerity of purpose.*

In the Lenox Collection of the New York Public Library

THE ARTIST IN HIS MUSEUM   C. W. PEALE

A PICTURE *of extraordinary interest, illustrating in the first place the beginning of our museums, and in the second a portrait of Peale by himself at the age of eighty-three.*

In the Collection of the Pennsylvania Academy of Fine Arts, Philadelphia

AFTER THE CONCLUSION OF PEACE

This quaintly expresses the high and stalwart purpose of the times; a consciousness of the limited conditions of the start, a conviction of the harvest of the future; and among the contemporary painters none was so representative of his time as Charles Wilson Peale.

✻ ✻ ✻ ✻ ✻ ✻ ✻ ✻ ✻ ✻ ✻

On the other hand, the great exception to the otherwise limited conditions of the period was Gilbert Stuart; for his qualifications as a painter were not to be rivalled by any other American for nearly half a century. He was born in 1755, at Narragansett, where his father, a Scotch refugee, who had been mixed up in the troubles of the Pretender, owned a snuff-grinding mill on the Petaquamscott Pond. He had married a Welsh lady, from whom the son inherited a taste for music and skill in playing the organ. The boy, when quite young, had shown an inclination for drawing, in which he was encouraged by a local physician, Dr. William Hunter. In course of time a Scotch painter, Cosmo Alexander, paid a visit to Newport. He was attracted by the promise of talent in the youth, who was now eighteen, gave him some lessons, and invited his companionship in a journey back to Scotland, where he placed him in Glasgow University. Very shortly afterwards, however, Alexander died, and Stuart, friendless and homesick, found passage back to Newport on a collier. He continued to progress in his art, and was practising at Boston, when the first shots were fired at Lexington; whereupon, his family being of the Tory party, he made his way to New York and thence sailed for London. Not until all his funds were spent did he make application to West, who with characteristic kindness immediately befriended him, and, recognising his ability, took him into his own house and at length engaged him as an assistant. But, although he worked for eight years in West's studio, he was uninfluenced by the latter's point of view or method of painting.

Perhaps it was because of the Scotch and Welsh blood in his veins that he remained independent of all the tendencies around him and saw exclusively with his own eyes. In an age of considerable affectation, when public taste was largely moulded by the drama and the histrionic feeling was reflected in painting, his portraits were singularly devoid of any display. His aim was to get his sitters to reveal their natural selves, and to put them at their ease he exercised his remarkable gift as a *raconteur,* drawing freely from his store of anecdote and experience. It was the actual humanity of his subject, the individual character of the men or women before his easel, that enlisted his shrewd and sympathetic interest, and in defence of his frequent slurring over of the drapery parts of the picture he would say: "I copy the works of God, and leave clothes to the tailor and mantua-maker." Yet, if he felt the clothes to be characteristic of the personality and contributory to its expression, he would bestow upon them the most exact and loving care.

No better example of this could be desired than the *Portrait of Dr. Fothergill* in his drab quaker costume. This famous London physician, who had been born in Yorkshire and educated in Edinburgh, warmly sympathised with the American Colonies and had espoused their cause in a pamphlet entitled " Considerations Relative to the North American Colonies." He had associated himself very closely with Franklin, and the latter's comment on hearing of his death was, " I can hardly conceive that a better man ever existed." In full accord with the elevated refinement of the doctor's personality are the exquisite modelling of the face and hands and the delicate craftsmanship exhibited in the rendering of the wig and coat and accessories. This early example of Stuart is all the more precious because of the dissimilarity which it presents to his usual, more vigorous, and suggestive method. For what distinguishes him from the famous English portrait painters of his day is the entire absence of a *parti pris* in his work; he does not set out to make a picture, but to seize with certainty and directness the actuality of the person in front of him. In doing so, he was accustomed to concentrate the emphasis on some salient feature. This is particularly illustrated in his famous portrait of Washington, known as the *Athenæum Portrait*.

Stuart's admiration for Washington had grown into a passion. He was upon the flood tide of success; "tasked himself with six sitters a day," had painted portraits of George III., and of the Prince of Wales; his position in the fashionable world of London—and he himself was a *bon vivant*—was assured; yet he gave up all to return to America, impelled by his admiration of Washington and his desire to paint this man among men. He reached New York in 1792, and two years later arrived in Philadelphia, during the session of Congress, to present to Washington a letter of introduction from John Jay. Those were stirring times. The "Whisky Boys" were rioting against the tax on liquors; the nation was in commotion over the stoppage on the high seas of American merchantmen by British privateers, and everywhere clanged the opposing arguments of Federalists and anti-Federalists, of Republicans and Democrats. Amidst the tumult of passion and prejudice reared the strong, calm personality of Washington. In his presence Stuart, who had seen all manner of men from high to low without blinking, confesses that he lost his self-possession. The first attempt at a portrait was a failure; the artist rubbed it out; the anecdotes with which he had beguiled other

THE "ATHENAEUM PORTRAIT" OF WASHINGTON   GILBERT STUART

*S*TUART *painted only three portraits of Washington from life. The first*
he was dissatisfied with and destroyed; the second is in England. This
one came nearest to Stuart's conception of the original, and in order that
he might not have to part with it, he kept it purposely unfinished.

In the Collection of the Museum of Fine Arts, Boston

PORTRAIT OF DR. FOTHERGILL

*A*N *unusual example of the artist, since in representing this Quaker gentleman*
has painted the head and the hands and the accessories of the wig and cloth
with a minute regard for texture and expression.

In the Collection of the Pennsylvania Academy of Fine Arts, Philadelp

men into revealing their inner selves were of no avail to unmask the impassive calm of Washington. A second picture was begun; Stuart had discovered that upon the experiences of the late war Washington would expand. He painted the portrait, which was presented to Lord Landsdown and is now in England. It is known as the *Lansdown Portrait,* a full length, with left hand on the sword-hilt and the other extended. Still later, at Mrs. Washington's request, the President gave another sitting, and in 1796 the *Athenæum Portrait* was produced. It came nearest to Stuart's conception of his subject, and he delayed to finish it, that he might not have to part with it. After his death it was sold by his widow, and presented to the Athenæum, Boston. It now hangs in the Museum of Fine Arts in that city. These three, the first of which was destroyed by the artist, were the only portraits of Washington that Stuart made from life. The numerous others are either replicas of these or imaginary portraits, such as the *Washington on Dorchester Heights.*

While Peale's first portrait of Washington represents him in his prime, the *Athenæum* shows him in the evening of life, when the stress of day had been succeeded by ample calm. It illustrates also Stuart's faculty for seizing on the vital, salient features of the subject. " There were," he himself said, " features in Washington's face totally different from what I have observed in any other human being; the sockets of the eyes, for instance, were larger than I ever met with before, and the upper part of the nose broader. All his features were indicative of strong passion, yet, like Socrates, his judgment and great self-command made him appear a man of different class in the eyes of the world."

The colour of Washington's eyes was a light, greyish blue, but, according to Mr. Custis, Stuart painted them of a deeper blue, saying: "In a hundred years they will have faded to the right colour." The immobility of the mouth is due to the loss of teeth and to the ill-fitting substitutes constructed by Wilson Peale.

In 1794 Stuart settled in Boston, where he continued to reside until his death in 1828. His career stands out in the early chapter of American painting as a single unrelated episode. He was the only American of his day who was in the true sense a painter. Beside him Peale and even Copley are still limners, enclosing figures in hard outlines and laying on the colours with tight and rigid primness, so that, as we have remarked, there is little or no difference in texture between the flesh parts and the fabrics, no suggestion of the figures being enveloped in atmosphere or illumined with natural light, very little also of living movement in gestures and poses. Their work, as compared with Stuart's, betrays the feeling of the draughts-man, who secures first the exact form of his objects and then increases their semblance to reality by overlaying colour. Stuart's, on the other hand, has its origin in brushwork, guided by a painter's way of seeing his subject as an arrangement of coloured masses, variously affected by light and atmosphere. Consequently his outlines are varied —defined, indefinite, firm, or fluent, as they appear in life; the flesh, solid and yet supple, glows with light, its texture clearly differentiated from the other textures in the picture; the expression of the faces is animated with life, and the figures are easy and elastic in their poses. Moreover, while Peale and Copley elaborately recorded as far as they could all that was presented to the eye, Stuart summarised his impressions in a forceful general-isation.

He was unrelated to the conditions that preceded and clustered round 1784, and differed in the char-acter of his achievement from any contemporaries either in America or England. For, when Stuart arrived in London he was only twenty years old, too young to have been permanently affected by the lack of opportunity in his native country, and, perhaps because of that blend of Scotch and Welsh blood in his veins, too independent to be directly influenced by West or anybody else. He looked upon life with his own eyes, and discovered for himself a way of seeing and representing what he saw. The sum of his work is uneven in quality, but at its best it anticipated the brilliant suggestiveness of modern brushwork.

For this very reason one may possibly feel that his portraits have less of the flavour of the period than those of Peale and Copley and his other American contemporaries. In the light of our present study, which is not to drag the beginnings of American painting into remorseless comparison with the finer achievements of our modern painters, but to put them back in imagination into the scenes and conditions of which they were a part, Stuart's share in the story may seem an anachronism. It was admiration of Washington personally that drew him back to this country, not a zeal for republican ideas, in the furtherance of which he had borne no part. He did not share in the life-spirit of the nation, and it may be suspected that his portraits are more than a little tinctured with an elegant cosmopolitanism. On the other hand, before the grimly intellectual or austerely visionary faces of Smibert's New England divines, the precise elegance and proud self-sufficiency of Copley's men and women of the world, or Peale's bald masculine records of the man upon whom devolved the leadership of a new nation, we can recognise a series of types and in our imagination reconstruct their environment. The very limitations of the painters possess a value of human and historical interest. We may transport ourselves beyond the then present, as the founders of the nation did, "and feel the future in the instant."

CHAPTER III

WHILE the struggle for independence was proceeding it had little or no effect upon the story of American painting. Its influence became apparent later in the resultant growth of national consciousness, and it is this phase of the story that occupies our present study. Again we will select a date as a vantage point from which to obtain a survey; and, as in the previous chapters we adopted that of 1783, when the first peace with Great Britain was confirmed, so now it shall be the conclusion of peace in 1815, after the second War of Independence.

There are two good reasons for the choice. In the thirty-one years which had elapsed, the idea of Independence had been fully realised, especially during the three years of the later struggle, when the succession of victories by sea and land reinforced the patriotism of the people with a new sense of national confidence. Moreover, out of the latter developed two new phases of independence: the one industrial, which was born immediately; the other, to appear some twenty years later, in its character spiritual or intellectual.

GROWTH OF THE NATIONAL SPIRIT

The second war was scarcely over before the need of industrial independence was felt. Already, while hostilities were proceeding and the cotton of the South was debarred from exportation to Liverpool, and the cotton and woollen goods of England from importation to this country, mills for the manufacture of cotton and woollen goods had been started in New England. These, upon the conclusion of peace, when the markets were glutted with foreign importations, found themselves threatened with extinction. The manufacturers immediately demanded protection, and in the following year obtained from Congress an act establishing a tariff. It was the beginning of a new idea, that political independence involved the need of industrial independence. Nor was it long before the idea of economic independence, originating in the necessities of the moment, discovered its relation to the spiritual and intellectual aspirations of the new nation. In 1837, before the Phi Beta Kappa Society of Cambridge, Emerson delivered that address entitled, " The American Scholar," which was hailed by Oliver Wendell Holmes as " Our Intellectual Declaration of Independence." In it Emerson sounded a new note. " Our day of dependence," he said, " our long apprenticeship to the learning of other lands, draws to a close. The millions that around us are rushing into life cannot always be fed on the sere remains of foreign harvests. Events, actions arise, that must be sung, that will sing themselves."

The utterance represents a singular combination of fallacy and truth. For in the kingdom of thought, wherein Emerson himself dwells and of which painting is a province, there are no boundaries of oceans or continents, no disabilities of dependence or alienship, but a community of free intercourse. Before another generation had passed away Americans would realise the need of this and begin to take full advantage of it. Meanwhile, in their pertinence to the conditions of the time in which they were spoken, those were true words.

For, by the wars with England and the restoration of the monarchy in France, this country was isolated. Moreover, the problems before it, political, industrial, and educational, were peculiar to itself and to be wrought out only by self-reliance. So this utterance had all the power of an exhortation and all the encouragement of a prophecy. For the time being, too, its application to painting rang true; for the feet of the painters of this period were turned toward Rome, and the decadent art of Italy, whence certainly was to be derived no source of strength for our infant art.

This new spirit of intellectual and spiritual independence and that other of economic independence, accompanied by so marvellous a territorial expansion, were reflected, as we shall see, in the growth of an American school of landscape painting. Meanwhile, before considering it, we must look back from our vantage point and attach the new phase of our story to the preceding one. The connecting link is John Trumbull.

❊ ❊ ❊ ❊ ❊ ❊ ❊ ❊ ❊ ❊ ❊

Born in 1756, in Lebanon, Connecticut, a son of the Colonial Governor of that State, he was twenty years old when the Declaration of Independence was signed. A graduate of Harvard University, he had been influenced by the portraits of Smibert and Copley, and was already learning to become a painter when the War of the Revolution began. Immediately he joined the army, and, his skill in drawing being noted by Washington, he was set to making plans of the enemy's works. From this he was promoted to a position upon the general staff, with the rank of brigadier-major, and subsequently served as colonel under Gates. But aggrieved at the date which Congress assigned to his commission, he resigned from the army, made his way to France, whence he proceeded to England, and under West recommenced the study of painting. The execution of Major André, however, had aroused in England a spirit of retaliation, and Trumbull was arrested and imprisoned as a spy. The intercession of West saved his life, and after eight months' imprisonment secured his release, on condition that he leave the country. When peace was established, however, he went again to England and continued his studies with West, not returning to the United States until 1789.

It must be admitted that his qualifications as a painter were not commensurate with the scope of his ideals. Moreover, he approached his subject from the patriot's rather than the painter's point of view. He was filled with the seriousness of his time, with the sense of responsibility to the grave issues through which the young nation was progressing, moreover, with that self-consciousness of the part which it behooved a patriot to play. His nearness to the great events made it impossible for him to view them apart from their political significance and to regard them, as a painter should, principally as an opportunity for a painter-like presentation. Further, the very temper of the time was antagonistic to any other view than the immense importance of the facts as facts, and nothing he could have learned from West tended to modify this unpainter-like point of view. For upon the point of view from which a painter approaches the subject of a historical painting, hinges the whole matter.

It may appear to some a hard saying that painting is a vehicle of doubtful suitability for the commemoration of great historical events, such as the

PORTRAIT OF ALEXANDER HAMILTON   JOHN TRUMBULL

*CONSIDERED one of the painter's best portraits.   It was painted not from life, but from
a bust by Ceracchi.*

In the Collection of the Metropolitan Museum of Art, New York

BATTLE OF BUNKER HILL

JOHN TRUMBULL

THE moment chosen is when General Warren has fallen, mortally wounded, and the English Colonel Small, seeing a grenadier about to bayonet him, springs forward to stop the act. Behind him appears the dying form of Colonel Pitcairn, of the British Marines, in the arms of his son. On the right a young American, wounded in the breast and sword-hand, hesitates whether to retire or go to the relief of General Warren. In the distance lies the Somerset ship of war...

Battles of Bunker Hill and Trenton, which among others Trumbull essayed to picture; still more hard, that patriotism, so far from being a stimulus to the painter in his art, may be a cause of weakness. But look at the illustration here reproduced of Trumbull's picture of *the Battle of Bunker Hill,* and ask yourself if the effect it produces upon your imagination is in any way comparable to, say, that of Longfellow's poem, " Paul Revere's Ride." If it is not, what is the reason?

We have already noted one reason, in the painter's preoccupation with accuracy of facts, so that the spirit of the occasion is ungrasped. There is another; that the poet had the advantage because his medium was words, by the sound and rhythm of which, as well as by their meaning, he could present picture after picture to our imagination, kindling it more and more by each successive appeal to our emotions, until we seem to hear the very clang of the horse's hoof, its laboured panting, and the heavy breathing of its rider; see the startled faces appearing at the windows, as each quiet village is awoke, and feel the torrent of patriotic ardour that swept through the country-side on that fateful night. It is conceivable that a painter might paint a picture of this incident which should move us as much as the poem does. But recognise at the outset the odds against him. Instead of the impetuous variety of words and tramp and rhythm of the lines, he must fix on some one action of horse and rider; instead of villages flying past, some one set scene for a background; instead of a gradual working up of fervour to a point of culmination, some one fixed, first and final, display. If he does, after all, succeed in awakening our emotions, it will not be through his restricted array of facts so much as through some suggestion to the imagination, by means of the impressiveness of the picture's composition and of its colour and light and shade. In a word, not by accuracy of detail or emulating the artifices of the stage manager, but because of the painter's reliance upon those qualities which are peculiar to his own craft.

That the first requisite of a picture should be to have pictorial qualities, that is to say, that it should embody a subject which can be more vitally expressed in paint than in any other medium, and should be so treated as to bring out to its full possibilities the craft of the painter, would never have occurred to Trumbull, any more than it did to West, or, for that matter, to Reynolds. The latter, fortunately for his subsequent reputation, was held by his public almost exclusively to portraits, otherwise he would have squandered his talent, as more than once he did, over ambitious canvases based on mythological, historical, or religious themes. For the eighteenth century in England was characterised by the growth of English prose, culminating in enthusiasm for oratory and stage representations. It was a period of triumph for the written and spoken word, especially for the latter, and the ambition of the painter was to emulate this triumph in his pictures. Similar conditions prevailed in this country, and even in a heightened form, owing to the stimulus of national events. Consider the hold which the phraseology of the Declaration of Independence still has upon the imagination, and how much more powerfully it must have possessed those who had witnessed the realisation of its principles. Its phrases, familiar and oft repeated, gave an impetus to the worship of the written and spoken word that has continued to our own day, and it is a fact to be noted that the first genuine art expression of the new nation was not in the form of painting or sculpture, but of literature and oratory.

That Trumbull recognised the power of the word is illustrated amusingly in one of his letters. It was addressed to his agent in Washington, through whom he was expecting to make sales of the engravings of his pictures. Apparently, the results were not satisfactory, for he urges his correspondent to go about among the Senators and Congressmen, and talk, talk, talk. "You must remember," he adds, "that we are living under a *logocracy*." *

* Word-government, or government of the word.

His attitude toward painting may be gathered from another of his letters:

"I am fully sensible," he wrote, "that the profession [of painting], as it is generally practised, is frivolous, little useful to society, and unworthy a man who has talents for more serious pursuits. But to preserve and diffuse the memory of the noblest series of actions which have ever presented themselves in the history of man, is sufficient warrant for it."

Thus, his highest conception of a painter was to be a historian in paint; and his pictures illustrate it.

❧ ❧ ❧ ❧ ❧ ❧ ❧ ❧ ❧ ❧ ❧

Very different from this practical man of affairs who practised painting, was his contemporary, Washington Allston. The latter in one of his letters describes his sensations in presence of the works of the Venetian colourists, Titian, Paul Veronese, and Tintoretto. He tells how the magic of the colouring affected him irrespective of the subjects; that he recognised in it an abstract language, comparable to that of music. In a word, he acknowledged the independence of painting as a medium of expression; and, idealist, dreamer, romanticist, that he was by nature, had most of the qualifications that distinguished the great romantic painter, Delacroix. But he lacked the capacity of the latter to keep himself detached from the

A SPANISH GIRL

Washington Allston

THE artist was never in Spain. The picture in its sentimental aloofness from any reality of life is characteristic of the period in which it was painted.

In the Collection of the Metropolitan Museum of Art, New York

THE DEAD MAN RESTORED TO LIFE   WASHINGTON ALLSTON

*A CLEVER composition, elaborated on artistic-scientific lines, therefore lacking
in spontaneity and in the suggestion of being the record of an actual scene.*
In the Collection of the Pennsylvania Academy of Fine Arts, Philadelphia

literary alliance, while yet drawing from literature his inspiration. It was the tragedy of Allston's life that he was subservient to the dominion of the word; moreover, he was a man of frail physique, whose ideas outstripped his strength.

An exception to the rule that the South, while patronising art, did not produce artists, he was of good Southern family, born at Waccamaw, South Carolina, in 1779. At seven years old, in consequence of the frailty of his constitution, he was sent to the more bracing climate of Newport, Rhode Island, where his school days were passed in the companionship of Edward S. Malbone. The latter, a native of Newport, two years his senior, had early displayed that skill in drawing which resulted in his becoming an excellent miniature painter, and his example confirmed the young Allston's own taste for drawing. Also there was much in the latter's gentle nature, with its love for the marvellous and the poetic, that fitted in with the refined abstraction of Malbone's disposition. The result was an ardent friendship between them, that continued while Allston was studying at Harvard and the older youth was working as a portrait painter in Boston. His college days over, Allston returned to South Carolina and found Malbone successfully engaged in Charleston, and the two planned a visit to England; Allston, with characteristic imprudence. disposing of his share in the family estate for a small sum of ready cash. They were together in London for a few months, and there Malbone painted *The Hours,* three girl figures representing the Past, Present, and Future, circling in a dance, which is regarded as his most important work. Then the companionship ended, for Malbone returned home, and six years later, after a vain attempt to restore his shattered health by a voyage to Jamaica, died at Savannah in 1807.

During four years' sojourn in Rome, where, in companionship with Vanderlyn, Allston enjoyed the intimacy of many famous men, among others of Keats, Shelley, Byron, Hans Anderson, Washington Irving, and Turner, he came under the spell of Raphael, "the greatest master," as he put it, "of the affections in our art," and of Michelangelo, "of whom I know not how to speak in adequate terms of reverence—even Raphael bows before him." The grace of the one may well have been dangerously seductive; the terrific power of the other, engulfing to a young man whose instruction in the actual rudiments of his art had been so limited, and whose mind was already apt to be overoccupied with reverie and contemplation. One result of his Italian experience, therefore, was to direct his thoughts to conceptions beyond his ability and strength to body forth, many of them more adapted to poetic than to pictorial expression. He left numerous drawings of studies for

RTRAIT OF THE ARTIST   JOHN VANDERLYN

In the Collection of the Metropolitan Museum of Art, New York

ARIADNE OF NAXOS

JOHN VANDERLYN

his pictures, in which the æsthetic intention shines forth spontaneously and clearly, whereas in the finished work it became laboured over and obscured. Thus in the *Dead Man Restored to Life* (by touching Elisha's bones as he was being buried), notwithstanding the general handsomeness of the composition, there is evidence of a laboured piecing together of its several parts, so that the total effect is rather one of pose and artifice, reminiscent of the mechanics of the Italian "grand style," but without that comprehending grasp which welds all into an appearance of having grown into being, spontaneously and inevitably.

Allston married a sister of the celebrated divine, Dr. Channing, and settled in Cambridge, Massachusetts, where he lived a life of very beautiful seclusion in the society of a few choice friends. Twenty-six years before his death he had made what he called " a highly finished sketch " of a very large picture, *Belshazzar's Feast*. He had been still working over the unfinished canvas on the day that he died, in 1843. It remained a pathetic memorial to the magnitude of his ideals and the insufficiency of his personal accomplishment.

✳ ✳ ✳ ✳ ✳ ✳ ✳ ✳ ✳ ✳ ✳

To this early period of the Republic belongs another notable name, associated also with promise only partially realised, that of John Vanderlyn. Though he painted many excellent portraits, his

[63]

fame rests chiefly on two pictures, *Marius Among the Ruins of Carthage,* and the nude figure of *Ariadne.* Born in Kingston, New York, in 1776, he worked as a boy with a local blacksmith. His brother was established in New York as a physician, and through his influence and that of Aaron Burr Vanderlyn studied under Stuart, and then, with his patron's help, paid a visit to Paris. He revisited that city in 1803, when he became intimate with Allston, the two friends later, as we have seen, living together in Rome. It was there that he painted the two pictures mentioned above. The *Marius* was shown at the Paris Salon of 1808, where it attracted the notice of Napoleon, who personally selected it for one of his gold medals. The *Ariadne* is in the old-fashioned style of painting of that period, being neither a study of life such as we are accustomed to to-day nor invested with that quality of abstract beauty that characterises the work of the Italian masters, on which it was modelled. It is, however, a picture of considerable distinction, both in drawing and colour.

Though an early work, it was nevertheless the last of Vanderlyn's notable achievements. Whether it were a fact that he was an instance, and there are many in painting, of quickly reached maturity as quickly exhausted, or that the times in America were not yet ripe for works of imagination, or that the slowness with which he painted interfered with his popularity as a portrait painter, certain it is that Vanderlyn became an unsuccessful and disappointed man. One day, in 1852, he reappeared at Kingston and borrowed a shilling of a friend to pay for the transportation of his baggage to the hotel. Arrived there, he retired to his room, and the following morning was found dead. The brief vitalising influence of his career, as of Allston's, had been the " grand style " of Italian art. In Vanderlyn's unfulfilled promise, in Allston's later years as he sat in front of his never-to-be-finished picture, impotently trying to re-enact the miracle of the dead restored to life, and to make the present live by contact with the dead bones of the past, there is a deep pathos. Both looked backward, while all the energy of their countrymen and of their time was bent in a direction forward. They were also by instinct cosmopolitan and aloof from the spirit of independent nationalism, which had became the guiding influence of their contemporaries. Meanwhile this spirit, encouraged by Emerson, had inspired a group of painters, who are remembered as the " Hudson River School."

CHAPTER IV

THE most direct outcome of the development of a national spirit was the appearance of the so-called "Hudson River School." It was a title given to a group of landscape painters who began by working in the neighbourhood of the Hudson. It is customary to speak of these men disparagingly because they did not paint as well as the majority of modern painters. They should, however, be honoured, despite their technical deficiencies, for the motive and manner of their inspiration.

In the first place, they went to nature for their motive, and, secondly, they studied it in that love and pride of American conditions which, outside of painting, characterised their age. They were the first of American painters to give expression to the prevailing spirit of nationalism.

✻ ✻ ✻ ✻ ✻ ✻ ✻ ✻ ✻ ✻ ✻

While the earliest of these landscape painters was Thomas Doughty, the one who gave the impetus to the new movement and helped most to make it popular was Thomas Cole. In a sense also

[66]

DESTRUCTION   THOMAS COLE

ONE of a series of allegorical pictures, entitled "The Course of Empire." The mixture of exaggeration and impotence in the colossal statue is characteristic of the whole canvas.

In the Collection of the New York Historical Society

THE EXPULSION FROM PARADISE   THOMAS COLE

*F*ROM the unaffected study of nature, pure and simple, Cole passed to extravagant conceits such as
this. The reproduction betters the original, since it does not betray the latter's faded color and tame,

he was a link between the new enthusiasm for
nature-study and the older predilection for historical and " grand style " subjects, since in those
pictures which his contemporaries particularly
applauded—*Expulsion from Paradise,* and the two
series respectively called *The Course of Empire*
and *The Voyage of Life*—he was not satisfied to
depict nature for its own sake, but made it the
vehicle for moral allegories. The public recognised
in them what it had already appreciated in Bryant's " Thanatopsis "—the introduction of nature
as a setting for elevated sentiments. But Cole's
more enduring claim to be remembered consists in
his having aroused an appreciation of the pictorial possibilities of the Catskills, and of American
landscape in general.

He was born in England in 1801, and when
nineteen years old accompanied his family to this
country, his father, a wallpaper-maker, settling in
Steubenville, Ohio. But the son was of a wander-
ing disposition, and his roamings led him farther and farther afield, until at length he reached
Philadelphia, and in the Academy had the first
chance of studying pictures. Meanwhile it was
nature that prompted his own desire to paint, and
when he finally arrived in New York it was with
a number of studies made in the Catskills and along
the Hudson. These came to the notice of Trumbull and Durand, who saw in them the beginnings

of a new development of native art. They were exhibited; Bryant among others praised them; some found purchasers, and Cole's successful career was started. He made visits to England, France, and Italy, and his pictures appeared in the Royal Academy. But, though he made his permanent home near the village of Catskill, close to some of the most beautiful scenery of what he called his " dear Catskills," his love of nature, pure and simple, became confused with other motives. Possessing a religious and romantic temperament, a student of Bunyan and Sir Walter Scott, he yielded to the stronger influences of the time, which, as we have seen, were literary, didactic, and oratorical, rather than pictorial. In *The Expulsion from Paradise,* for example, we miss the note of nature-study; the landscape has been compiled; while in *Destruction,* number four of his *Course of Empire,* he has emulated the artifices by which Claude built up his imaginary scenes of classic grandeur; only, unlike the Frenchman, whose artistic instinct kept him to the sole motive of a beautiful picture in which the figures count simply as spots of animation, Cole, with no skill of figure-drawing, has made these puppets the main actors in the great spectacle. The total effect is in consequence bombastic and the details pitifully weak.

❧ ❧ ❧ ❧ ❧ ❧ ❧ ❧ ❧ ❧ ❧

Yet, as we have seen, he was not the first American landscape painter. This title belongs to Thomas Doughty (1793-1856), who had been painting from nature for five years before Cole's appearance in New York. His work, like that of Asher B. Durand (1796-1886) and J. F. Kensett (1818-1872), breathes the true spirit of what the French call the *paysage intime,* that love of the simple country-side, of nature for its own sake, which characterises the pictures of the Barbizon School and of their forerunner, Constable. These paintings of the Hudson Valley had in them the true stuff that has made landscape painting the sincerest form of modern expression; what they lacked was skill in the craftsmanship of painting and the painter's point of view. These men looked on nature with an eye at once too niggling and too comprehensive.

In the first place, for example, the landscape by Durand, reproduced here, is too big in size and too extensive in subject to be embraced by a single vision. The eye wanders over it, as it would in presence of the original scene, receiving a number of enjoyable impressions, but no impression of unity and completeness. Lacking these qualities, which are the result of selection, simplification, and organic arrangement, the subject is not so much pictorial as panoramic and topographical. It represents the ordinary way of looking at a landscape rather than the artist's way. In the second place, there is an absence of synthesis, that is to say, of a summarising of essentials, in the actual representation of the details. A uniformly patient and conscientious putting together of little effects is spread like a network over the whole; the painter has not grasped the salient characteristics of the whole or its parts, has not enforced these and subordinated the rest. The result is, that his trees and mountains do not assert themselves as masses, but invite attention to the infinite, niggling strokes of which they are composed,* and this is partly the cause and partly the effect of the way in which the brush was handled.

In some parts it has spread a thin tint over the canvas, in others worked like a pencil point; nowhere with the breadth and fulness and firmness that distinguish the methods of the real painter. We recall the fact that Durand, until his thirty-ninth year, was only an engraver, a very skilful one, and it is the engraver's rather than the painter's feeling which is evident throughout the canvas. Kensett also began life as an engraver, and his landscapes equally betray the fact. But the previous occupation of these men was not the only

* This lack of synthesis is much less apparent in the small reproduction than in the larger original, because the photograph and the subsequent half-tone process of reproducing it have tended to compress the details into masses of tone, and have, in a way, effected a synthesis.

LANDSCAPE   ASHER B. DURAND

A BEAUTIFUL example of the "Hudson River School." The work of a man who was self-taught and had
few opportunities of seeing pictures, it exhibits a genuine love of nature and no mean technical skill.
But the latter is concerned with an infinity of details, and the attitude toward nature is objective,
wherein the landscapes of this "school" differ from the synthesis of modern work and its expression of a
mood.

In the Lenox Collection of the New York Public Library.

ON THE HUDSON

THOMAS DOUGHTY

A LANDSCAPE of the "Hudson River School," showing in the distance the hills of West Point. Notwithstanding that the trees in the

reason for this lack of painter-like quality in their work. With the sole exception of Stuart, no painter in the true sense of the term had appeared in America. It was not until later, when Americans came in touch with the Barbizon men and learned from them how to look at nature, how to select from it and compose the essentials into a picture, and how to paint with a full, firm brush in masses, that landscape painting, as distinct from mere representation of landscape, commenced in this country.

Meanwhile it is very cheap criticism to decry these men of the Hudson River School for their lack of technical ability. Rather should they be remembered as the leaders among us in that return to nature which, unknown to them, had also led Rousseau and his followers to Barbizon, and was to become in literature and painting the strong, distinctive characteristic of the nineteenth century. Nor should it be overlooked how closely in our own country the movement was related to the general trend of thought and action. While Cole with his palette and brushes retraversed the ground that Washington Irving had made famous with his pen, and his landscapes embodied the elevated senti-ment of Bryant's poetry and the mystery and vast-ness of Cooper's descriptions of nature, the work of all these painters reflected and contributed to the love and pride of their own country which was filling high with hope and certainty the heart of the nation.

It should be noted that the careers of these men of the Hudson River School lasted far on into the century. Accordingly, we may as well shake ourselves free from the shackles of chronology for a little while, and complete this portion of our story.

The simple study of nature, begun by Doughty, Durand, and Kensett, was carried on by the two brothers, William and James McDougal Hart. Both were born in Scotland, the former in 1823, the latter in 1828, and were brought to this country in 1831, their family settling in Albany. Here, as they grew up, they were apprenticed to a coachmaker, and gained their first experience as painters in decorating carriages. William Hart by self-instruction graduated from carriage panels to canvases, working first on portraits, later on landscapes. He passed on his experience to his younger brother, who also studied under Schirmer at Düsseldorf.

This was in 1851, the year in which Leutze returned to America, after studying in the same school; and Hart may have been influenced by him to go thither, as certainly other students were. Indeed, for a short time during the middle of the century Düsseldorf represented to American students the goal of their desires, just as Paris does to-day; and the fact was not without influence upon our painting. For Schirmer himself was a tame and sentimental painter, and the whole tendency of the school was toward a trivial exactitude of method and a banality of motive; both seen most characteristically in the sentimental *genre* pictures of lovely and virtuous peasantry. A great many such pictures found their way to America, and, of course, because of their representing a little anecdote or story, were popular with a public that was still very much under the dominion of the Word and not yet trained to an appreciation of a painting as a painting. So, indirectly on public taste, and directly on a considerable number of painters, the influence of the Düsseldorf school was unfortunate.

Hart, however, lived it down, gaining with experience more freedom of brushwork and developing a charming resourcefulness in colour. Nor was he touched by the sentimentality of the school. His landscapes, like his brother's and those of the other painters of the Hudson River School, represent as frank and sincere a delight in the lovable aspects of nature as one can imagine. It is, however, a purely objective one; and this fact, I think, is very interesting. It is not until later, when our painters shall have come under the influence of the Barbizon group, that they will begin to concern themselves with the moods of nature, the reflection in the latter of their own moods. This consciousness of self and need of self-expression represent an older, if not necessarily a maturer, habit of mind— a product of the effort everywhere to realise and emphasise the individual. But, as yet, our early painters had not begun to think of themselves as individuals; like the rest of the community, they were engaged for the present in building up a nation; it was the spirit of nationality that fired them and found its natural expression in love of country and in love of nature as its embodiment. So their attitude toward it was that of the child, frankly delighting in the beauty of the thing spread out before their eyes.

By degrees, as the country was opened up and the wonders of the Rocky Mountains were unfolded, the painter's imagination, like that of his fellows, became stimulated and his ideal expanded. He turned from the simple surroundings of the homestead to the miracles of nature, and began to be affected by the prevailing enthusiasm for "the biggest thing on earth." It was the grandest and most tremendously impressive manifestations of nature, demanding large canvases, which now attracted such men as F. E. Church, Thomas Moran, and Albert Bierstadt; and, a thing to be noted, this preoccupation with the grandiose, which had begun in an awakened pride of country, led to the pursuit of bigness for its own sake. Church sought his subjects from South America to Lab-

SCENE AT NAPONACH

WILLIAM HART

*T*HE work of a carriage-painter, who taught himself to paint pictures and then studied for three years in Scotland, this landscape
is a good example of the "Hudson River School." It exhibits on the painter's part a genuine love of nature and a determination
to imitate nature as closely as possible. But the imitation is of details, put together bit by bit. This lack of synthesis, itself
resulting from the lack of a large, embracing comprehension of the whole, produces an effect of pettiness, notwithstanding the handsomeness of the composition. This impression is enforced if one compare the picture with Inness's landscape "Midsummer."

In the Collection of the Metropolitan Museum of Art, New York

YOSEMITE VALLEY

ALBERT BIERSTADT

WHILE Bierstadt was the first to introduce into this country the influence of Düsseldorf, he followed Church in his fondness for the grandiose in nature. His better examples, such as the present one, very cleverly represent the facts of the scene, but with a uniform precision of detail that becomes monotonous

rador; Bierstadt and Thomas Moran in the Rocky Mountains. But how thoroughly these men belonged to their age is proved by the enthusiasm which their work aroused in the public.

Bierstadt, of German origin and with a German's passion for the romantic, had the faculty of possessing himself with the spirit of the scene. Moreover, although his method of painting was hard and sleek—owing to his Düsseldorf training— his draughtsmanship was excellent. One may see in the accompanying illustration of *Yosemite Valley* what a power he had of representing the constructive force of mountain masses, and of suggesting perspective. A thing, however, to be observed, as affecting the dignity of the picture, is that its size is comparatively small. The painter concentrated his effort, and concentration on the part of the spectator is also possible, whereas over a very large landscape-canvas there is a corresponding lessening, by dispersion, both of effort and effect.

Yet even this picture, though unquestionably it may give us a sense of nature's impressiveness, does not conclusively impress us. We are not made to realise the emotions which the painter must have felt and we ourselves should feel in presence of the actual scene. We are conscious of no condition of feeling but one of purely intellectual comprehension; we are pretty well assured what the scene

[81]

looks like, but not what it feels like. It is almost exclusively a view.

Apart from questions of technical skill, this is the sharp line of difference between the earlier landscapes and those of the present day, in which we shall find the expression of a mood in nature to be the painter's aim. It is a difference of point of view and motive. The mental attitude of Bierstadt, Church, and Moran still remained like that of Trumbull, and their landscapes might be styled, without straining the word, "historical."

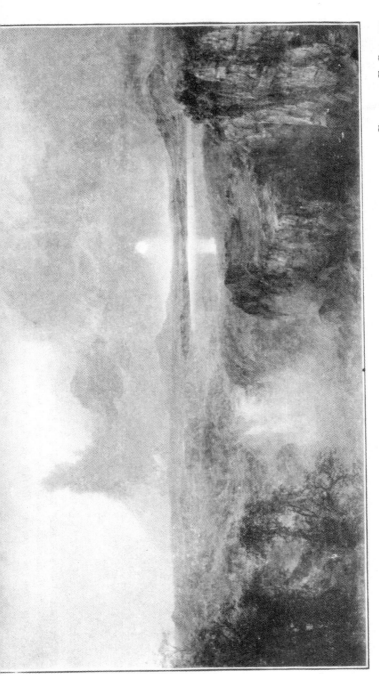

COTOPAXI

FREDERICK E. CHURCH

*I*N the sky effects, even more in the composition of the middle distance and foreground, there are instances of the influence of Turner. But the big feeling of the latter is wanting. The eye has comprehended a big subject, but scarcely in a big way.

In the Lenox Collection of the New York Public Library

SHOSHONE FALLS, SNAKE RIVER, IDAHO

Copyright, 1901, by Detroit Photographic Co.

THOMAS MORAN

THE best of our painters of the grandiose in nature, Thomas Moran studied Turner to some purpose. The strength of the rampart-like rocks and the impetuous rush of water are admirably depicted. It is in the rather inert and heavy treatment of the misty part of the picture that the latter especially falls short of the technique of modern work, with its closer observation of phenomena under the effect of light.

CHAPTER V

IN the previous chapter we saw how the development of national consciousness found expression in a native growth of landscape painting. We noted that, while the beginnings of the " Hudson River School " were inspired by a simple love of nature, its followers gradually developed an enthusiasm for the grandiose and spectacular; and, moreover, that from first to last the work of these painters was technically insufficient. It will be the topic of the following chapters to show how the technical resources of American painting were fertilised by foreign influence.

For Emerson's doctrine, that " our long apprenticeship to the learning of other lands draws to a close," had been put to the test and found wanting. It could arouse a motive, and a good one; but not provide the means to realise it adequately. The fallacy of the doctrine consists in this—that it took account only of the subject matter of an artist's work. He felt, and rightly, too, that there should be enough in the accomplishments and aspirations of the American nation to supply all the needed

STORY OF AMERICAN PAINTING

suggestion of ideas. But for a work of art something more is necessary than ideas; of even more importance is the form in which they are expressed. For it is the form in which the poetic idea, or the musical harmony, or the pictorial representation is embodied, that gives each its particular qualification to be reckoned as a work of art. The building must be erected before it can be used for the purpose for which it is intended. Similarly, technique is the necessary structural antecedent to the expression of an idea through a work of art.

Of technical knowledge all that survived in America in the middle of the century was a remnant of the English tradition. It was insufficient for real progress, as the few men who went abroad at the middle of the century discovered. They found new forces in fermentation, and straightway began to assimilate them. Indeed, a convenient way to study the modern development of the story of American painting is to recognise the fermentation which occurred in European art during the past century and to trace how American painting gradually alligned itself with the foreign movement. So far from its being a story of self-sufficient isolation, it has come to be one of complete identification with the strivings of other countries. For, to-day, so far as concerns technical considerations, painting is an international art with a free trade in methods, the clearing-house of which has been Paris.

Before, however, the latter became generally recognised as the metropolitan centre of art instruction, a few Americans travelled to Düsseldorf and Munich. Therefore the telling of the story demands an allusion to the remnant of the English tradition and to the influence of these other schools, as preparation for the concluding and decisive influence of Paris.

The English influence had never been completely dissolved, notwithstanding the tension of political feeling, which perhaps had somewhat abated, though it was to be tightened again during the period of the Civil War. Our painters were welcomed in England; and English painters, coming over here, were well received. Thus, until the middle of the century, the English tradition still lingered on, especially affecting portraiture and genre painting.

But even in England the great day of portrait painting was past. It had reached its meridian in Gainsborough and Reynolds and in the Scotchman, Raeburn, who in the pure force of painting was often their superior. It had declined through the tender sweetness of Romney and Hoppner, until it reached a sunset of superficial splendour in Lawrence. The latter's facile skill and exuberant inventiveness delayed the catastrophe, while at the same time it helped to make it inevitable and complete. The study of nature had yielded to sentimentality, that of men and women to an extravagant interest in their clothes, the original vigour of the motive was undermined, and it needed only less skilful practitioners to reduce the art to a mere representation of insipid prettiness or of middle-class banality.

During the second quarter of the nineteenth century portraiture in America, as in England, exhibited hard polished surfaces of colour, a dry regard for details, and little discernment between the textures of flesh and fabrics. Still, to so sweeping a summary there are some exceptions, among which, for our present purpose of studying conditions rather than men, we may mention four—Thomas Sully, Henry Inman, Chester Harding, and Charles Loring Elliott.

✻ ✻ ✻ ✻ ✻ ✻ ✻ ✻ ✻ ✻ ✻

The life of Sully covers the extended period of eighty-nine years, and would be memorable if only for its enormous productivity. He was born at Horncastle, Lincolnshire, England, in 1783, his father and mother being popular figures on the English stage. When the son was nine years old they accepted an engagement to settle in Charleston, South Carolina, where in time the boy received instruction from his brother-in-law, M. Belzons, a miniature painter. After painting in Richmond and Norfolk he moved to New York, and thence to Boston, where for a few months he studied under Gilbert Stuart. In 1809 he went to London and painted for a little while with West; but from the evidence of his work it is probable that the painter in London who chiefly interested him was Lawrence.

His style, indeed, represents a mixture, considerably diluted with himself, of Lawrence and Stuart. It exhibits the latter's purity of fresh tones and the other's tricks of giving the sitter an expression of pleasant prettiness; but misses alike the virility of Stuart's and Lawrence's decorative elegance. From 1810 to his death in 1872 he lived in Philadelphia.

❦ ❦ ❦ ❦ ❦ ❦ ❦ ❦ ❦ ❦

Henry Inman was a far stronger painter than Sully, and one whose work hardly receives to-day the recognition that it deserves. No doubt, it was uneven in quality; but some of his portraits of men are remarkably strong in characterisation. That, for example, of Chief Justice Marshall, owned by the Law Association of Philadelphia, is one of those sterling achievements in the presence of which one loses the idea of paint and is conscious only of the living, forceful personality. Yet, if one examines the method of painting, there is no disappointment. It is painstaking without being laboured or fumbling; very solid and conscientious.

It lacks Stuart's free-handed happiness of touch that hits off expression as if by improvisation, yet Stuart never painted anything more alive than this.

Inman was born at Utica, New York, in 1803. He became in time a pupil of that eccentric painter, John Wesley Jarvis, an Englishman by birth, who was as much a glutton for work as he was for the delights and weaknesses of the flesh. Inman was elected the first vice-president of the National Academy, and enjoyed unusual success both in Philadelphia and New York. But he was a victim of asthma, and frailty of health reduced his capacity for productiveness. Some friends, among whom was James Lenox, the founder of the Lenox Library and its collection of pictures, arranged for him to visit England to paint the portrait of Wordsworth and other famous men. His visit was altogether a happy episode; the asthma for the time being ceased to trouble him; he made many friends; his portraits were appreciated, and he was urged to settle in England. He returned, however, to America; but a few months later, in 1846, died of heart disease.

❧ ❧ ❧ ❧ ❧ ❧ ❧ ❧ ❧ ❧ ❧

The vicissitudes of Chester Harding's early life present an interesting reflection of the state of the times. He was born at Conway, Massachusetts, in 1792; but when he was fourteen years old the family moved into Western New York. He was

PORTRAIT OF ELIZA LESLIE   THOMAS SULLY

*A*N American authoress, sister of the painter, Charles Robert Leslie, R. A.
In the Collection of the Pennsylvania Academy of Fine Arts, Philadelphia

PORTRAIT OF DANIEL WEBSTER   CHESTER HARDING

*A*N *example of what has been called the "competent but commonplace" style,
that characterizes so many portraits of the first half of the nineteenth
century. The modelling is secured by forcing the high lights and shadows,
until the head looks as solid as wood. The result is a recognizable likeness, but as
lacking in vitality as the canvas is in charm.*

In the Collection of the Cincinnati Museum Association

a young giant, over six feet in height and of great strength, expending the latter until his twenty-first year in the rough hardships of pioneer work. Then he supported a roving existence by peddling and chair-making, settling down for a little while as a tavern-keeper, and then moving afield again until he reached Pittsburgh. Here, while engaged as a house-painter, he made the acquaintance of a travelling portrait-painter, who kindled his imagination but refused him any technical instruction. Undeterred, however, by this early symptom of trades unionism, he went to work with brushes and paint and produced what was at least a resemblance of his wife. The rest is a story of steady endeavour. Having gained some facility, he migrated to Kentucky, thence to Cincinnati and St. Louis, everywhere securing customers and increasing alike in his skill and prices. Finally he reached Boston, and, meeting with a success that seems to have impaired even the popularity of Gilbert Stuart, established himself in that city, which, except during a visit paid to England, continued to be his home until his death in 1866. Like Inman, he enjoyed in England a very considerable vogue. But, so far as I am acquainted with his work, it never equalled Inman's at its best, and is rather on a par with that painter's average work; creditably lifelike, but lacking in distinction either of character or style.

It is in the latter respect that Charles Loring

Elliott proved himself in advance of his time. The son of an architect in Auburn, New York, where he was born in 1812, his father wished him to follow his own profession. But, set on being a painter, he was allowed to go to New York, where Trumbull gave him some instruction, which was afterward supplemented by an indifferent painter named Quidor. But it had involved a good deal of drawing from the cast, and resulted in Elliott becoming a sure and ready draughtsman. His skill in paint, however, must have been the product of a natural gift, for he developed a facility in using the brush, fully charged with paint, that had a character of its own and was expressive also of character in the sitter. He could not have learned this from his contemporaries, and it is not recorded that he ever went abroad, so that this individuality and meaningfulness of brushwork are the more remarkable. He anticipated by some instinct the qualities of painting that, during the generation after his death in 1868, were acquired by others from abroad.

❅ ❅ ❅ ❅ ❅ ❅ ❅ ❅ ❅ ❅ ❅

The genre painting of the middle of the century is interesting to-day chiefly as an illustration of the kind of picture that amused our forebears and still amuses those of us who care more about some little anecdotal subject-matter than the method of the painting. Because of the perennial nature of this

PORTRAIT OF THE ARTIST   CHARLES LORING ELLIOTT

*E*LLIOTT *appears at his best in bust portraits, such as this one, which fully sustains his reputation of being the foremost American portrait-painter of the middle of the nineteenth century.*

In the Collection of the Metropolitan Museum of Art, New York

HEELS OVER HEAD   J. G. Brown

Copyright, 1894, by J. G. Brown

U SUALLY this painter's pictures include from one to three figures. This one, therefore, is an exceptional opportunity of illustrating his tendency to transform the various characteristics of the street gamin into a uniform type
of well-fed, well-mannered, jolly little good boy. It is full of clever drawing, rendering naturally the varieties of

preference and the fact that John G. Brown's long career bridges the past with the present, we may select him as typical of the many genre painters that might be mentioned.

We shall again have occasion to notice genre painting when we consider the influence of Düsseldorf; for the present let us summarise the English phases of it. It originated with Hogarth in the first half of the eighteenth century; firstly, in his little domestic groups or " conversation pictures," as he called them; secondly, in the scenes from fashionable life or vulgar life, which, as he explains, he composed " on canvas similar to representations on the stage." " My picture is my stage, and men and women my players, who by means of certain actions or gestures are to exhibit a dumb show."

This was a motive very different from that of the Dutch genre. While the latter was occasionally preoccupied with the rendering of incidents, its best and most usual characteristic was the prime intention of making a picture, in which the incident was assigned to a secondary function of supplying an excuse for a beautiful arrangement of colour and light and shade. The Dutchmen were painters first, illustrators of manners second, but seldom moralists, as Hogarth was. Such picture-dramas, as the series of *Marriage à la Mode,* proceed from act to act with a logic as relentless, a satire as pungent, a moral force as compelling, as the dramas of

Ibsen. On the other hand, like the latter's, they are saved by their art from being didactic. Hogarth, besides being a moralist, was an excellent painter. Yet the latter quality is the one that was overlooked by the public on whom the didactic, story-telling, literary-dramatic features of his pictures made a deep impression. They helped to confirm the English preference, not, however, exclusively English, for what is intelligible to the understanding rather than suggestive to the imagination, for intellectual concreteness rather than abstract sensations. They established the vogue of the picture which enacts a scene.

Fifty years after Hogarth, Moreland approached nearer to the Dutch genre. He, too, was an excellent painter, and his pictures of rural scenes are thoroughly pictorial in their charm of colour and light. But he lived at a time when the highest thing in art was held to be the painting of the historical or mythological subject in the " grand manner " of the Italians, and a public, intent on subject matter rather than on qualities of painting, considered his work vulgar. The same charge was brought still fifty years later against the genre pictures of Wilkie; but by this time the reputation of the bombastic picture was a little stale, the middle class was coming to its own, and popularity with the public meant success to the painter. Wilkie, accordingly, followed by Landseer and Mulready, all three of them clever practitioners with the brush, so far as representing the actual appearances of things, held their own in the popular estimation, and followers of them, less skilful with the brush, confirmed the public in their appetite for the story-telling pictures. The latter were no longer trenchant with satire, but amiably humorous or sentimental: little literary pleasantries in paint. It was this sort of influence that John G. Brown inherited and has continued to transmit.

He was born at Durham, England, in 1831. He attended the schools of the Edinburgh Academy, and also painted in London until 1856, when he transferred his life and work to New York. With the quick eye of a stranger for what is novel to him, he began to paint the types of people around him, and then the street boys of New York. His pictures of the boy upon the sidewalk, selling papers, shining shoes, or larking with his fellows, won admirers, and he has continued to paint them ever since. Such consistency to one subject was no doubt the result, partly of choice, partly of the taste of his public. His genial nature has always gone out to his boy-subjects; he has discovered the best that is in them and represented it with sympathy, though, it must be admitted, with some sacrifice of reality. For his boys have a mildness and ingenuousness that, to the casual observer, at least, is not characteristic of the class. But this very softening of the type pleased a sentimental public, and they insisted on having Brown's street boys as they had learned through him to know them. In this way not a few painters are compelled, whether they wish it or not, to go on repeating their motives. The public, demanding an example of what it calls one of their " characteristic " pictures, will not let them change.

So there are few collectors in this country who have not at some time or other owned a " Brown "; still fewer who have not in the course of their artistic development disposed of it. The reason of the public taste is not difficult to trace. In the early stage of our appreciation we are attracted, as I have already said, by the subject matter of the picture. The first consideration is—" What is it about? " Then, if it is about something with which we are familiar, we take a curious delight in identifying all the little details of resemblance to reality —the bristles in the blacking-brush, the label on the bottle, the seam of the breeches, and the stitches of the patch. It all looks " so natural," and we think it a wonderful piece of painting; because in our infancy of appreciation, just as in our infancy of age, we place a high value on the faculty of imitation. To mew like a cat is quite an accomplishment, so also to make a painted boy look like a real boy.

At least we think it looks " real," but this is a

begging of the whole question. We shall come to this topic of realism later on, when we describe how our painters came in contact with the teachings and study of realism abroad, but meanwhile may briefly anticipate the inquiry, Are these boys of Brown's regarded as character studies, really like the boys of the streets? Have not their crude mixture of good and bad, of ugliness and attractiveness, their queer, intensely human, if distorted, individuality been scoured to a characterless propriety, and polished into a meek amiability by an application of moral sapolio, until they may be fit for the parlour but are no longer suggestive of the streets? Compare, for example, the studies of street boys which Murillo made, as they lay basking in the sunshine of the market place of Seville. These, indeed, are the real thing, even to the suncaked dirt on their feet, which so disturbed Ruskin. And the pictures of them have a further pictorial reality. The warm air envelopes their lazy bodies, the sunshine burnishes their limbs. There is no suggestion of air in Brown's pictures, no light of nature, no burnish save that of varnished paint. Actual boys in actual daylight could not look like his; the latter have neither realism of character nor realism of representation. Still less have these pictures the capacity to arouse an abstract enjoyment through the qualities of colour, light and shade, and tonality.

In brief, then, it was to learn to look at nature naturally, and to represent it as it is, and yet with such creative artifice of technical charm as shall affect the imagination independently of the subject, that our painters had to seek inspiration from abroad. England had failed them; Düsseldorf and Munich will be tried and found wanting; the lesson, at last, will be acquired in France.

CHAPTER VI

IT was in the beginning of the 'fifties that American painting came under the influence of Düsseldorf. We have noted already that the landscape painters, James M. Hart and Albert Bierstadt, were students of its Academy, and shall now allude to the two figure-painters, Emanuel Leutze, who was a distinct product of its teaching, and Eastman Johnson, who outlived its influence. Further, we shall note how greatly the importation of Düsseldorf pictures affected the taste of the American public.

The reputation of Düsseldorf as an artistic centre had been the growth of some twenty-five years, since Schadow had been appointed director of its Academy and had gathered around him a body of students who remained faithful to the spot and bound themselves into a community, as interesting as it was unique. Let it be said at once that Schadow's influence rested upon the fact that he was a real painter; and that, while others were draughtsmen who tinted their drawings with paint, he revived in Germany the art of actually constructing the picture in paint—the art, in fact, of

[103]

painting. But the characteristic distinction of Düsseldorf, at first, was a psychological one. This quaint little town upon the Rhine had become, as early as 1830, the nucleus of German Romanticism. Bound together by sympathy with this spirit, the painters spent their days in painting, their evenings and occasions of recreation in reinforcing their imaginations with the reading and discussing of Romantic poetry and legends. The world of the present did not exist for them, their preoccupation was solely with the past. Mendelssohn, the musician, for a while was a member of the little community; but the one person, not a painter, who exerted the greatest influence on the movement was a certain Judge Immerman, the reformer of the stage at Düsseldorf. Under his direction two performances a week were given, and the younger painters engaged in amateur performances. The stage became a mirror of the past. In it the painters found suggestions for representing the themes derived from literature and legendary tradition.

Such was the inspiration at Düsseldorf. It was not a product of the present that had in it the capacity of further growth. Moreover, its dependence upon literature and the drama had in it the germ of sterility. For, by the time that the original fervour of a Schadow and a Lessing had dwindled to the poetic sentimentality of a Schirmer, what had been an alliance with the written and spoken word sank into a bondage to it. And even when the precise and petty style of brushwork, which since Schadow's time had characterised the methods of Düsseldorf, was later broadened and enriched by some of its followers who, like Knaus and Vautier, studied subsequently in Paris, their pictures could not escape altogether the taint of their literary inspiration.

Lessing, the strongest of all the school, became the teacher of Emanuel Leutze. Though the latter was a native of Germany, having been born at Gmund, in Württemberg, in 1816, he is reckoned an American painter, since he was brought to Philadelphia as a child, and received his first instruction there, and, in after years, when his course at Düsseldorf had been supplemented by study at Vienna, Munich, and Rome, settled permanently in this country, dividing his time between New York and Washington.

His best-known picture, and, by general assent, his strongest, is *Washington Crossing the Delaware,* now in the Metropolitan Museum. It has one virtue: it is simple and sincere, without heroics. It almost illustrates the incident as it may have been conducted by men far too absorbed in the peril and possible failure of the enterprise to have any thought of arranging themselves in a striking theatrical group. On the other hand, it represents a plodding and constrained method of brushwork, tame even in a small canvas, spread here over one that measures twenty-one feet by twelve. It is worthy of note that with Leutze the attempt of American painters to execute large historical subjects ceased, not to be revived until nearly fifty years later, when it reappeared in Abbey.

While Leutze worked upon this picture in Düsseldorf, Eastman Johnson was one of his pupils. When still a youth in his home at Lovell, Maine, where he was born in 1824, Johnson had begun to make portraits in crayon, and with so much success that at twenty-one he moved to Washington, and later to Cambridge and Boston, securing patrons in all these cities. He was now in a position to go abroad, and at Düsseldorf improved his drawing and acquired a knowledge of painting. Fortunately he supplemented his study with a four years' sojourn in Holland, during which he familiarised himself with the Dutch paintings of the seventeenth century. Their influence was twofold. It led him to prefer genre subjects to historical, and developed his own natural gift of colour. At a time when the prime consideration both with painters and the public was that a picture should represent an incident, a poem, or a story, he, following the example of the Dutch artists, learned, while choosing a subject of popular appeal, to treat it as an opportunity of inventing a scheme of harmonious colouring. In a word, he merged the narrator

in the artist. After his return to America he painted many pictures of country-life in New York State and Kentucky, and during the war many subjects of patriotic significance. They are small in size, but broad in handling, having little of the tightness and dry smoothness of surface characteristic of Düsseldorf. They are also very charming in colour, the work of a man who could enrich the mere subject matter with artistic suggestion.

In the portraits also that occupied his later life he exhibited the Dutch faculty of seizing the external character of his sitter, and of depicting it in a forcible and straightforward way. Although they lack the dash and bravura of some modern portraits, they hold their own by their disciplined methods of virility and decision.

At Düsseldorf, as we have hinted, the flames of Romanticism dwindled to the candle light of domestic genre; the drama was superseded by light opera, and a virtuous and picturesque peasantry, seen across the mild effulgence of rose-coloured footlights, thronged the stage. Until Millet pricked the pretty bubble of misrepresentation, and taught men to study human life as it really is, these fancy idylls of peasant genre, turned out from Düsseldorf or under its influence, flooded our American market. Anyone who is conversant with the operations of the picture salesrooms knows how large a part they have played in the greater number of collections. Their popular appeal may have done much to interest people in pictures, but it certainly postponed for a considerable time a just appreciation of the true nature of pictorial art.

✳ ✳ ✳ ✳ ✳ ✳ ✳ ✳ ✳ ✳ ✳

By the middle of the century the fame of Düsseldorf, as a school, had passed to Munich. The latter's relation to American art, in point of time, began after the topic which is to be treated in the next chapter; but it will be convenient to dispose of it here, particularly as it represented only a brief phase of foreign study and had no abiding influence. The ideal of Munich was the historical picture: its greatest pride, Piloty. The latter's training had been enforced by foreign study, especially in Paris, and when he returned home in 1855 he produced a sensation, for among the Munich painters of the day, who had almost lost the sense of colour, he suddenly appeared as a master of what he called " colouristic realism." He had, that is to say, a faculty of representing vigorously with broad strokes and juicy brushwork the colour properties and appearances of objects. If he painted a boot, for example, there was no mistaking its bootlike quality; it was leather, sure enough, black and hard and polished, and gleaming with high lights—unmistakably a boot.

TWO MEN

T HIS double portrait is distinguished by the dignity and character of the heads, by ease of gesture and firmness of drawing in the figures, and by a rich and fairly luminous color-scheme. It was painted in 1881.

EASTMAN JOHNSON

In the Collection of the Metropolitan Museum of Art, New York

WELL AND WATER TANK, ITALIAN VILLA

FRANK DUVENECK

INTERESTING as an illustration of any early effort by a Munich-trained painter to get away from the studio tradi-
tion of dark old-masterish canvases and elaborately corraled compositions to the natural effects of open-air paintina

Moreover, Piloty was a man of mental vigour, with the German exuberance of temperament, that entered heartily into the grandeur of the historical ideal, and attacked the intricacies of a crowded canvas with the assurance and facility of a man pulling on his gloves. By him the dramatic motive was introduced upon a larger stage with a fuller company of principals and supers, a more magnificent *mise-en-scène,* and a more grandiloquent libretto. For, though he taught men how to paint, he tightened for a time the bondage of painting to literature. It was not yoked, as at Düsseldorf, to a peasant's ox cart, but followed behind a triumphal car, on which History sat enthroned. Nor was he a great painter in the modern sense of the term. His realism was of the mannered kind. It did not take account of the appearance of things in real light and atmosphere, but imitated with a plentiful use of the brown pigment, bitumen, the heavy shadows of the old pictures in the galleries, discoloured by time and dirt and varnish. Among the pupils whom his magnetism attracted and who subsequently became professors at Munich were Wagner and Diez, the latter a robust painter of old German scenes in small pictures of delicate tonality, modelled on the genre of the Dutchmen. It was under these three men that a few of our painters received instruction: Frederick Dielman studying with Diez, William M. Chase with

Piloty and Wagner, while the latter was one of the teachers of Walter Shirlaw during his six years' stay in Munich.

The interest of this Munich episode in its relation to the story of American painting centres around Duveneck and Chase because of the influence they have exerted upon others. The former spent ten years in Munich, and during that time himself became a teacher. Among those who studied with him there, and in the little village of Polling in the Bavarian Alps, and in Venice, were John W. Alexander, Frederick P. Vinton, Joseph R. De Camp, and Julian Story. For many years he has been instructor in painting at the Cincinnati Art School.

Indeed, it is as a teacher, rather than as a producer of pictures, that his position is notable. He was the first of American instructors to make the brushwork instead of the crayon-drawing the foundation of the picture; to impart a painter's rather than a draughtsman's point of view. Instead of completing an elaborately shaded drawing and then painting over it with a careful observance of the lines and details and more or less finishing up of each part as one proceeded, he taught the student to cover his canvas with paint, boldly blocking in the large masses of the subject; afterwards superimposing the various succeeding planes to produce the modelling, and, in order to secure an

ELIZABETH BOOTT DUVENECK FRANK DUVENECK

*T*HE *costume throughout is in shades of brown. The brushwork, while inclined to be a little sleek, is broad and
direct. It reflects the influence of Munich training before the artist had learned for himself to study the effects of
nature's lighting.*

In the Collection of the Cincinnati Museum Association

LADY WITH THE WHITE SHAWL   WILLIAM M. CHASE

 PORTRAIT of the artist's wife, as choice in feeling as in the delicate breadth of its technique.

In the Collection of the Pennsylvania Academy
of Fine Arts, Philadelphia

ensemble of effect, gradually advancing the whole canvas through the separate stages to a finish.

Whether Chase learned this process from Duveneck, or acquired it subsequently from the example of the famous French teacher, Carolus-Duran, whose somewhat similar method we shall discuss in another chapter, it has been the one that he also has imparted to innumerable students. But his influence has not been confined to the public; he has taken a leading part in most of the artistic movements of the last twenty-five years, and has been prominent at exhibitions with his own pictures. In oils, water-colours, pastels, and even etchings he has proved his versatility, revealing an extraordinary dexterity in the use of each medium, and a refined sense for the pictorial qualities of colour, tone, and lighting. Portraits, genre subjects, landscape, and still life have occupied him by turns. A few of his portraits, notably *The Woman in a White Shawl*, exhibit genuine insight and feeling; but these are qualities one does not generally associate with his work, any more than one looks for evidence of imagination. It is with the external appearances that he is preoccupied; he is primarily and almost exclusively a painter, pure and simple.

It was not until about 1875 that the older of these Munich students made their mark in the exhibitions at home; so that we have anticipated by many years the place which the school occupies chronologically in our story. But as I have said before, it seemed convenient to dispose of this phase of it, that the French influence, which is now to occupy our attention, may be considered without interruption.

SUMMER IDYLL

WALTER SHIRLAW

A N example of the Munich influence at its best. Landscape and figures are well drawn and solidly painted. But the feeling is of the studio, not of nature. The coloring is not of nature seen in outdoor light, while the grouping of the figures with the obvious repetitions and contrasts of line is distinctly academic.

MOTHER AND CHILD · · · · · · · · · · WILLIAM MORRIS HUNT

A GOOD *example of Hunt's preference for strong and simple lines
and large, handsome masses of form, distinguished also by a noble
sincerity of feeling.*

In the Collection of Mrs. Richard Morris Hunt

CHAPTER VII

FROM the middle of the century onward
France has been the main source of influence, as well for American painting as
for that of other countries. In a word, painting
has been affected like other departments of thought
and culture by the centripetal tendencies of modern
times. The ease and rapidity of modern com-
munication has drawn the world into closer and
more intimate consciousness of what is being
thought and accomplished elsewhere, so that a free
trade in ideas, resulting in a kind of cosmopolitanism, is the characteristic of the day. And for
painting, the clearing house of the world has been
Paris.

This, however, is not to be understood as imply-
ing that American painting is to-day merely an
offshoot of French art, having no character or
quality of its own. Later on in our story we may
be able to discover some traits sufficiently marked
and widespread to constitute an American characteristic, and without doubt we shall find plenty of
evidence of individuality on the part of separate

painters; yet it is no less true that the foundations of our progress have been derived from Paris. They consist in motive and method.

It is from the conflict of opinions upon these topics, which has occupied Paris for the past fifty years, that our painters, like those of other nations, have derived, on the one hand, their point of view, their way of looking at their subject; and, on the other, their manner of representing it. The particular use which they have made of both is the measure in each case of the painter's individuality.

Nor is the conflict of which Paris has been the centre founded upon entirely novel principles; it has been largely concerned with the readjustment to its own times of old ones. Briefly, it has been the modern phase of the old perpetual struggle between conservatism and progress; and to appreciate it properly we must recognise the advantage alike of the one and of the other: of conservatism as the expression of something fundamentally and perennially desirable, of progress as the adaptation of this to the forward spirit of the age. Painting, no more than any other art, can afford to detach itself from the past, still less stand still in the face of the present. If it is to be vital, it cannot be a stagnant pool; its tributary streams and tidal movements must be related to the ocean of great waters.

The conservative element in modern art has been supplied by the Academic system, notably in Paris by that of the French Academy and its official school, the *École des Beaux Arts;* while the progressive involves the various efforts which individuals or groups have made to combat it. At the middle of the century, when the three pioneers of Paris-seeking students—Hunt, Inness, and La Farge—went abroad, the issue was between the *École* on the one hand and the Barbizon movement on the other. A generation later, individualism having adopted a number of cries, was exhibiting itself under various aspects of realism, impressionism, " art for art's sake," and *plein air;* all of which, like the earlier Barbizon movement, were but attempts to render nature naturally, rather than in accordance with certain principles, adhered to arbitrarily, as it was thought, by the Academy.

The latter, with its *École des Beaux Arts,* has been officially maintained in order to preserve a standard of excellence and a system of teaching. Both are based upon the pre-eminence of line over colour, of drawing over painting. Such an out-and-out doctrinaire as Ingres asserted that " Form is everything, colour nothing." Whether the doctrine be applied to landscape or figure painting, it implies the superiority of art over nature, and the need of modifying the forms of nature that they may be made to emulate the perfection of classic models. Thus the so-called classic landscape is an elaborate piecing together of natural and architectural features, selected from various sources, including the imagination, and assembled on the canvas to produce an ideal composition, that shall affect us in a purely abstract way by the dignity of line and massing.

It was this attitude towards nature that the painters of the Barbizon group opposed, both in their lives and in their art. They set out, not to improve upon nature, but to learn from it. Anticipating the spirit of scientific research which became the leading characteristic of the age, they substituted for abstract and typal generalisations an intimate study of individual appearances. In studying the individuality of nature they became themselves intensely individual—thus embodying another leading characteristic of the age. They discovered also a new conception of the ideal.

It was founded, not, as in the case of the Academicians, upon fancied perfection, but upon truth. It was the result of a new principle of selection. Instead of borrowing from many sources or of modifying the forms to produce an arbitrary perfection, it selected from the scene itself its salient features, eliminating the unessentials and compressing the whole into a vivid synthesis. And the latter included not merely the external appearance, but the inward spirit of the scene.

Through communing with nature, these men acquired so strong a sympathy with their subject that the mood of their own spirit became reflected in nature; their works interpreted their own souls in terms of nature; they were nature-poets. It was in this respect that their idealism was of a new kind, based, not upon a material perfection, but on spiritual expression. This again was a very wonderful anticipation of what came to be the need of the nineteenth century. In the rapid advance of materialism, the claims of spirit were being overlooked; and not the least of the benefits conferred on painting by the men of Barbizon, was this restoration of spirit to its proper relation to matter. They became, one might almost say, the religious painters of the century. Add to this loftiness of motive the fact that they were in a technical sense excellent craftsmen, and the importance of the influence which they exerted upon the first of our France-seeking students may be realised. It was fortunate also that these students —William Morris Hunt, George Inness, and John La Farge—were men of commanding ability. The impressions gleaned at Barbizon were transmitted by them to other painters in this country, and to the general public, with a degree of authority and persuasiveness that have given the principles involved a firm and lasting hold upon the American imagination.

❀ ❀ ❀ ❀ ❀ ❀ ❀ ❀ ❀ ❀ ❀

Hunt, the oldest of the trio and the first to go

abroad, was born at Brattleboro, Vermont, in 1824. He entered Harvard, but was compelled by poor health to seek the benefit of a change of climate, and accordingly went to Düsseldorf and joined the Art Academy, with the intention of becoming a sculptor. This was in 1846. Nine months later he moved to Paris, suddenly altered his plans for the future, and determined to be a painter. Perhaps the fame of a certain picture, *Romans of the Decadence,* and the extraordinary interest which its appearance at the Salon of 1847 aroused, had something to do with stimulating his imagination in a new direction; at any rate it was the painter of this picture whom he sought as a teacher. He joined the studio of Couture. The latter, a pupil of Delaroche, had been trained in the " classic " manner of drawing the figure, which may be summed up in Tennyson's description of Maud:

"Faultily faultless, icily regular, splendidly null,
   Dead perfection, no more."

But in Couture's case the frigid and sculptor-like character of the so-called " ideal " figure was warmed with a romantic ardour and enriched with colour. It was this combination of qualities that had created a sensation; for it seemed to reconcile the conservatism of the older men with the eager throb of younger life. Yet as a matter of fact, the picture, like its subject, belonged to an older order of things and had no relation to the spirit of the age. The latter, in scientific and mechanical affairs, was directed to an exact study of the cause and effect of natural phenomena; in literature, likewise, to a realistic examination of present life. This picture, with its elaborate classic setting, composed of fragments of Roman architecture cemented together by the painter's imagination, with its crowd of voluptuaries, men and women, under the influence of liquor, in shameless abandonment, contained an element of perennial truth. By inference men could draw from it a moral for the present, but it was hidden under a masquerading of the past. Zola, presenting the same moral, clothed in the actual forms of the rich and poor of his own time, thereby made it sting the conscience of the public. That was shocking, for people do not like the naked truth. In this picture there was no such violation of propriety; the truth was, as it were, only nude; nakedness diffused through a prism of make-believe perfection—art not life.

But there was a contemporary of Couture's whose ideal was art and life; life in art, art vitalised by the expression of life. As yet, however, he was only that " wild man of the woods," Jean François Millet, unheeded. He, too, in his early struggle for bread had painted " ideal nudes "; now his subjects were the peasants of Barbizon, rough-hewn types of men and women, coarsened and twisted out of shape by toil, as far removed as possible from Couture's.

Yet Hunt, and it is a strange fact, became, during the latter part of his sojourn in France, as strongly influenced by Millet as he had been by Couture. Perhaps it may be explained in this way: Starting out with the intention of being a sculptor, he had evidently a prior sensitiveness to form; then, as he came to know pictures, the feeling for colour was aroused; he found both satisfied in Couture's work. Moreover, he had come out to learn, and the student's first craving is for definite formularies. Couture, well equipped with set methods and maxims, could show his pupils exactly "how to do it," and in his studio Hunt remained for several years, an enthusiastic follower of the master's technique.

But gradually the eagerness of the mere student abated. The influence of Millet, coming later, touched a maturer need. Firstly, it gave him the inspiration of a motive. Millet's uncouth simplicity of truth struck a vein of sincerity in himself. It taught him a notion of the "ideal" very different from the one aimed at and inculcated in Couture's studio—an idealisation, not of unnatural perfection, but of human nature as it is, not of high-wrought passion and romance, but of the fulfilment of the daily routine of duty. It was a motive at once artistic and moral, based on Truth. And secondly, it was presented with a correspondingly simple sincerity of technique. Millet's strong, broad generalisation was as far removed from the exquisite refinement of Couture's method as from the niggling exactness of the Düsseldorfians; its grand sweep of line and dignity of masses were not obviously enforced, but to be discovered under the guise of clumsy forms; it was a method in which nothing is sacrificed to truth of nature, and yet commonplace is always overcome by art.

It was a technique so peculiarly the product of Millet's own conscience that it was not to be learned by anyone else; and the principle which it involved, of beginning with nature and ending in art, was so different from Couture's, which was art only, first, last, and all the time, that Hunt never wholly emerged from the conflict of these two influences. He attempted to affect a compromise, but with only partial success, and remained to the end a painter of whom more might have been expected than he actually achieved, since he never gained the assurance of belief in himself which is possessed by many a smaller man.

Returning home, he settled in Newport, Rhode Island, and then moved to Boston, where the remainder of his life was spent. Around him gathered a number of pupils, impressed by the charm of his personality and the dignity of his artistic ideals. This in itself helped to impede his own technical advancement, since it kept him over-occupied with theories and limited his opportunities for the actual practice of painting.

Yet this sacrifice of himself certainly redounded to the benefit of others, for he sowed the seed which has since grown and multiplied. The gist of his teaching was that it is not the subject but the way in which the subject is rendered, that determines the artistic merit of a picture; that in the hands of an artist, any subject, no matter how simple and insignificant, can be made artistic, and that this artistic quality, a product and expression of himself, is what the painter should aim chiefly to embody in his pictures. Furthermore, that the ideal of good brushwork is not to concern one's self with niggling precision of detail for detail's sake, but to obtain truth of character and expression.

A writer in the 'sixties describes his work as "naïve," which, from our present point of view, it certainly was not. There is nothing in it of the child-spirit; on the contrary, very much of the virile and intellectual. But it displayed, what was an unfamiliar quality to his contemporaries, a capacity for seeing artistic possibilities in the simplest subjects.

Turn to the accompanying reproduction of *The Bathers*. There is here involved no elevated conception, as in Cole's *Course of Empire,* nor grandeur of visible appearance, as in Church's *Coto-*

THE BOY AND THE BUTTERFLY   WILLIAM MORRIS HUNT

*H*UNT'S *influence and teaching were directed against the popular interest
in the subject-matter of a picture, and on behalf of the claims of painting as a form of expression. Here the child's figure is but an excuse for
the broad and simple rendering of the tones and texture of the flesh and the
movement of the figure.*

In the Collection of Mrs. Richard Morris Hunt

From a Copley Print, Copyright, 1898, by Curtis and Cameron.

THE BATHERS

WILLIAM MORRIS HUNT

THE strong, elastic poise of the young body, and the flesh tones, golden in the sunlight, afforded the artistic motives of this beautiful picture.

paxi, yet, as a picture, it is vastly superior to either. The reason is that in the making of it the artist's motive was a joy in the possibilities of beautiful expression that the subject offered. First, the poise of the figure, the elastic force of the body and limbs, suspended rather than resting in perfect ease of balance; secondly, the charm of colour as the sunlight plays over the nude form, glistening upon the ripples of flesh, illuminating the shadowed parts and kindling all the tones into a healthy, vigourous glow. Everything else in the picture is made contributory to these two possibilities of beautiful expression—poise and sunlit flesh-colour—so that, if you had the good fortune to see the original at the recent Comparative Exhibition, I think you will agree that it communicated a heightened sense of joy in life.

If this is so, then, you will observe this picture after all has an idea involved in its subject that appeals to the imagination. We perhaps reach the heart of the matter when we realise that an idea may be an abstract one, not connected with any definite individual or incident, about which a great deal can be said in words, or which can be described in the form of a story. But the trouble is that so many people are lacking in imagination, or, even if they have imagination, it is not stirred by feeling, it needs to have the idea conveyed to it through a tale of words. I wonder how many people cared about Millet's *Man With a Hoe* before Mr. Markham versified its appeal, and, on the other hand, how many of those who had appreciated it already found the appreciation increased by the verbal exposition?

Hunt's pictures included portraits, figure-subjects, and landscapes, some of the last named containing sheep, which are painted with a truth of character that recalls the work of Jacque. At a time when precision of detail was apt to be considered the highest requisite in a picture, Hunt substituted for it truth of character and expression. Some of his portraits are said to have been indifferent likenesses, but the representation, as it appears in the picture, is invested with distinction and seeming individuality. His last important works were two decorative paintings for the Capitol at Albany, which, owing to a threatened collapse of the dome, have been hidden by a ceiling, and have perished. They were executed under a very severe pressure of having to be finished by a certain date, and the strain proved too much for the artist. He died the following year (1879), at the Isle of Shoals.

＊ ＊ ＊ ＊ ＊ ＊ ＊ ＊ ＊ ＊ ＊

George Inness was a pathfinder whose originality and fiery zeal for nature blazed a new trail that has led on to the present notable expansion of American landscape painting. Born at Newburg,

BEGINNING OF FRENCH INFLUENCE

New York, in 1825, the son of a retired grocer, he
was apprenticed as a youth to an engraver. This,
as we have seen, was the profession in which those
landscape painters of the Hudson River School,
Kensett, Durand, and Casilear, began by achieving
success.   In fact, at that time it was the one branch
of art most likely to yield a comfortable livelihood,
but it was of too exacting a nature for the frail
health of George Inness. His father would have
set him up in business, but the son's heart was resolutely fixed on things artistic, and he sought instruction from a French painter residing in New
York.   For the rest, Inness was his own teacher,
though the tenor of his career was changed into a
new direction by the influence of the Barbizon
artists.

He went abroad in 1850, and again for a longer
period in 1870.   We will attempt to summarise the
impressions derived from the two visits.

Hitherto he had been chiefly engaged in studying
form, in learning to draw the appearance of trees
and rocks and ground, of water and sky.   It may
have been his short experience in engraving or the
example of Durand and Kensett that set his study
in this direction, but the thoroughness with which
he pursued it was from within himself, an instinct
for analysis, derived perhaps from his Scotch an-
cestry.

He learned, first of all, that principle of synthesis, of selection and arrangement, to which I have already alluded, that the best art does not consist in representing everything in sight, but in discovering what are the salient and essential characteristics, and in setting these down in a masterly summary. He learned, in effect, the value of omitting details so as to secure additional force for the *ensemble;* and his previous rigour of minute study now helped him, for it is recognised among artists that only he who has learned to put in, can be successful in leaving out.

He learned, in the second place, a new motive: no longer to look for "views" in nature, but to study fragments of it intimately; to render portraits of nature, in which the local facts should be of importance, not as facts, but as vehicles of expression. It was a mood of nature, or a mood aroused in himself, that he strove to embody; and, by thus becoming a subjective painter, he cut himself off entirely from the objectivity of contemporary American landscape. And the peculiar quality of his subjective motive is interesting.

In his temperament the logical was combined with the spiritual. He was given to reasoning upon the eternities, and for many years was a professed Swedenborgian. Thus he was particularly drawn toward Corot, in whose work he recognised the spirituality. In fact, Corot and Inness both approximated to what we shall later find to be one

DSUMMER   GEORGE INNESS

*THE suggestion of a mood of nature, or, if you will, of the artist's own mood, induced by the
    appearance of nature.   In the massy foliage, piled-up clouds, and spread of landscape there is
        a sense of opulence and vigor, but all activity is suspended in the drowsy warmth, as if the earth
e taking a siesta.   The picture, painted in 1875, illustrates the artist's middle style, wherein details
e become absorbed into a synthesis of effect, full of suggestion both of the scene as a whole and of the
ression it makes upon the imagination.*

In the Collection of James W. Ellsworth, Esq.

EARLY MOONRISE—FLORIDA   GEORGE INNESS

THE forms of the trees have melted into drowsy shapes, massed against the
luminosity of the sky.   The moonlight, creeping over the shadowed
meadow, touches into soft prominence an object here and there.   The
picture is a fine example of the expressional value of synthesis.

of the underlying principles of motive in Japanese art. It is, in effect, to distinguish between " appearance " and " reality "; to regard the material visibilities of nature, subject as they are to change, as being mere appearance, while the reality is the inward spirit, a portion of the Universal, Eternal Spirit, that is embodied in the impermanent appearances of matter. Both Corot and Inness came in time, like the Japanese painter, Hashimoto Gaho, to discover for themselves a method of painting in which they carried the principle of synthesis as far as possible, so as to subordinate the assertion of form to a suggestion of its essence or spirit. And lest some reader have no sympathy with this transcendental attitude toward nature, I would remind him that, if he is fond of nature, he must have experienced some occasion when to lie upon the ground and let the beauty of the scene, irrespective of this or that feature of the landscape, soak into him, was pleasure enough. If so, it was the result of physical contentment, leading to a satisfaction of the emotions; and from the latter to a consciousness of spiritual refreshment or elation is but a step, to many temperaments a natural and inevitable one.

This progression of Inness's motive and manner of painting, however, was a gradual one. Not all at once could he free himself from the habit of minute representation. His earliest pictures are liney, filled with details carefully drawn in with the brush.   Later, his style, of which *Peace and Plenty* at the Metropolitan Museum is a good example, becomes broader; he no longer draws, but paints, with the brush; the objects begin to count as masses. Notwithstanding the large size of the canvas and the multiplying of features, which prevent us grasping the scene as a whole, the impression which it produces on the imagination is a tolerably single one, very well summed up in the title.   It is a notable step in the direction of rendering the expression of the landscape.   But compare the other example illustrated here, *Midsummer,* and note the progress which has been made in the way of synthesis.   How masterful is the characterisation of the great oak tree!   We recognise at once its lusty vigour and the luxuriant opulence of its massy green foliage.   Yet note how little detail or even modelling it presents; it is painted flatly in broad, simple masses of tones of green, differing from one another in the amount of light which they reflect.

Later his pictures have still less solidity of painting; the pigment has been spread thinly with a large brush, and at close range the broad flat spaces of colour may seem to be perfunctory and careless. In reality, they are a mingling of subtly differentiated tones, pricked here and there with an accent of detail; and, when viewed from the proper stand-

PEACE AND PLENTY   GEORGE INNESS

*P*AINTED *as early as 1865, this picture, 77 inches high and 112 wide, still shows a fondness for extended views and
an analytical regard for details, characteristic of the "Hudson River School." But it also exhibits a mastery over
the rendering of the forms of nature, which, when the artist had learned the value of synthesis, enabled him to suggest the forms with so pregnant an economy of means. In the evening glow that pervades the picture there is already a
foretaste of the spirituality of the artist's later work.*   In the Collection of the Metropolitan Museum of Art, New York

THE GOLDEN AGE   JOHN LA FARGE

A *RARE and lovely instance of this artist's rendering of the nude.*

In the Collection of Otto Heinigke, Esq.

point, a short distance from the frame, are full of meaning and suggestion.   These landscapes are the product of a mind that, in the matter of painting, had freed itself from the necessity of conscious intellectual processes and entered into liberty of spirit, and of a hand become so facile by practice that it moved in immediate and faithful response to the suggestion of the mind.   They are the expressions, not of what is palpable and material, but of an emotional or spiritual mood.

The artist died suddenly, during a visit to Scot= land, in 1894.

CHAPTER VIII

JOHN LA FARGE was born in New York in 1835, and grew up under conditions very favourable to the acquisition of superior knowledge and taste. For his father's house in Washington Square, well stocked with books and pictures and prints, was a rendezvous of cultivated people, many of them belonging to families who had escaped the revolutions in France and San Domingo. Thus his classical studies at school, which were of the old-fashioned, extensive, and thoughtful kind, were supplemented by the literary, artistic, and critical atmosphere of the home life.

In 1856 he visited Paris, residing with his cousin, Paul de St. Victor, a writer and critic, in whose house he came into direct touch with the best thought of Paris of that day. During his "wander-year" in Europe he visited Munich, Dresden, and London, but returned home at length with the conviction that the most important developments of the day were represented by the Barbizon artists, Rousseau, Corot, and Millet, and by Delacroix. He now entered a lawyer's office in New York, for, as he says, "No one has struggled more against his destiny than I; nor did I for many years acquiesce in being a painter. Though I learned the methods and studied the problems of my art, I had hoped to find some other mode of life, some other way of satisfying the desire for a contemplation of truth, unbiased, free, and undetached."

To my mind there is something very interesting in this slow, gradual growth of La Farge toward the vocation in which he has since become so distinguished, that he may be reckoned the most profoundly learned artist that America has yet produced. His love of art antedated his professional practice of it; he pursued it, first of all, as a branch of the wider culture in which he was training himself; and, at an age when most students are trying to adapt some little particular phase of art to their own purpose, he was seeking to discover its relation to the large field of human thought and life. In his case, for a time, the particular and the personal aspect of art was lost sight of in the universal aspect.

What I have in mind is the difference between thinking and working outward from a centre, and thinking and working inward toward the centre from the horizon of a large circumference. For example, the average student starts with learning to draw and paint the human figure. This is his tiny centre, and from it he begins to broaden out a little, arranging his figures into compositions, and by degrees, perhaps, making them the source of some kind of expressional appeal. But as a general rule, the start made in this way does not lead very far; the circle around the centre is circumscribed; the picture has little capacity to stir the emotions or the imagination, and shows a tendency to be mostly a manipulation, more or less dexterous, of the thing it started with—the drawing and painting of the human figure. On the other hand, suppose a man whose mind has been habitually directed toward the larger aspects of human life and its relations to its seen and unseen environment, who has learned to regard the scheme of men and things as parts of a vastness of design, the limits of which melt into infinity of time and space. He analyses the relations of these parts to one another and to the whole Universe, discovers principles of agreement and antagonism, and works, not by rule of thumb or at the uncertain beck of temperament, but along the lines of a plan that, for him at least, affords the basis of a sound hypothesis for motive and method. When a man, possessed of this habit of seeing things in relation to the Universal, draws inward to the particular that lies under his hand to be done, he brings to the doing of it qualities of mind and principles of practice that make the particular no longer a little

JOHN LA FARGE

DESIGN for the stairway in the house of the late Mr. William H. Vanderbilt.
In the Collection of Otto Heinigke, Esq.

CHRIST AND NICODEMUS   JOHN LA FARGE

*T*HIS *composition has also been used by the artist in one of his windows in the*
Church of the Ascension, New York. Very rich and subtle is the coloring
under the varying effects of lamplight in conjunction with the faint light
from the moon.

In the Collection of William T. Evans, Esq.

centre from which to spread out tentatively, but the white-hot core into which are fused the forces that he has gathered from outside.

It has been so with La Farge. Just as art is to him only one of the phases of material and spiritual being, so an individual work of art, while suggesting to him that it is all sufficient in itself, a complete harmonious unity, will yet be the greater in its power to move and hold the imagination if it suggests also that it is but a fragment of a universal harmony and unity. He conceives of a "Universal Geometry," with which man's separate, fragmentary "plans" of arranged beauty—his works of art—can be and should be co-ordinated. Space will not allow me to pursue this idea, except to suggest an analogy to it in the laying out of Central Park, New York, by the late Mr. Frederick Law Olmsted. As you traverse it you are confronted with a great number of separate vistas; they appear one after the other, very different in character, yet each seems complete in itself. A fuller knowledge reveals that each is harmoniously related to the others, and that all are correlated to what, for the purpose of illustration, straining the words, we may call the "Universal Geometry" of the whole plan. And although this ultimate harmonising of all the different ingredients can nowhere or at any one time be seen with the eye, yet, when it has been once realised, it persuades the imagination to find a greater beauty than before in each part.

When La Farge at length determined to follow the practice of art as a profession, he studied for a time under Hunt, at Newport, which place, since 1860, along with New York, has been identified with his work. The latter, apart from decoration, which will stand as the most striking manifestation of his genius, has consisted of oil paintings of landscape and flowers, of drawings for illustration, and of water-colours of scenes in Samoa and Japan. The last named are studies of the luxuriant colouring of vegetation, sky, water, and rock, rapidly brushed in under the spontaneous enthusiasm of the moment, and, to some extent, as notes or records of colour, to be elaborated later in some window or wall painting. His drawings, some of which were made to illustrate poems by Tennyson or Browning, are of unusual interest, powerful and subtle in characterisation, and beautiful also as a decoration of the page.

It is as a colourist that he has gained distinction and influenced others. Not that a man can learn to be a colourist; but the natural gift for it has to be cultivated, and in discovering new secrets for himself he has been a guide to others. During his early travel abroad he was naturally drawn toward the work of the old Venetian colourists; but, being an original genius, he could look outside of tradition, and was greatly interested in the colour experiments of Holman Hunt and John Everett Millais, two members of the Pre-Raphaelite brotherhood, and of Ford Madox Brown.

It was one of the tenets of these young painters to represent everything exactly as they saw it, and accordingly to give each object its "local" colour. Other painters of the day imitated the prevailing tone of old pictures, that was partly the result of original use of glazes, partly of the fading out of colour, of the accumulation of dirt, and of successive varnishings. These men, however, put their bright colours in a vivid and harsh juxtaposition that, while it might be true to the local tints of nature, was artistically false. Could the natural and artistic truths be reconciled? If so, then the limited range of colours used in the convention of Venetian painting could be enlarged, reinforced, and intensified by the brilliance of nature's colouring.

Briefly, La Farge solved the problem. By degrees he discovered what we shall have occasion to refer to later, that the imitating of the local colours is only a part of truth to nature. To confine one's self to this is like taking fish out of the water in which they belong. The local colours must be represented in their own medium of lighted atmosphere, which surrounds all things and draws them together into a natural appearance of tone. Light, in a word, became the study of La Farge; light in its operation upon local colour; in the infinite diversity of its way of striking objects, directly or by reflection or refraction; and the diminution of light on objects, as things recede from the eye, owing to the layers of intervening atmosphere. He noted also that under the influence of light, a local colour is made more or less brilliant by the juxtaposition of other local colours, which in turn are similarly affected. This briefly summarises the principles gradually reached by La Farge, as the result partly of his own observations and partly of the research of scientists. Working thus independently, he anticipated, as we shall see later, the French artist, Manet, and the Impressionists, in applying their principles to painting.

He began by working on subjects of still-life and flowers, turning later to landscape. Of the last he painted but a few examples, yet they are very remarkable. Like the Barbizon men, he depicted only a fragment of nature, comprehending it with intimacy of feeling, while, like a Pre-Raphaelite, he attempted an actual portrayal of the local colours of the scene; but he went further than either, in what he himself has called " the rendering of the gradations of light and air through which we see form "; and a step even beyond this, in that he was not satisfied with a generalised appearance of light, but sought to represent it under special aspects of time and season. Thus he not only had assimilated the foremost movements of that time, but also anticipated the later studies of Manet and Monet. The explanation of this fact, I believe, is that the advance made by Manet and Monet was based on scientific principles, upon the application to painting of that exact scrutiny of phenomena which was the predominate feature of thought in other phases of life, and that La Farge is himself a scientist as well as an artist. He has given an incidental corroboration of this in the following words: " There is in each competent artist a sort of unconscious automatic mathematician, who, like the harmonist in music, the colourist in painting, resolves in his way the problem of sight and sound which the scientist puts into an equation."

A nature so compounded of the scientific and the artistic presents the kind of soil in which symbolism flourishes. In La Farge's case it produced some remarkable drawings, such as *The Wolf Charmer,* and attracted him toward the painting of religious subjects. But this phase of his work we will consider later in connection with mural painting. For the present let us notice how this combination of the scientific and artistic has served him in another branch of decoration, that of coloured windows.

It was a happy coincidence that to an artist, thus occupied with the problems of light, should have come an opportunity of working in the most translucent of all mediums—glass. It resulted in the practical invention of a new kind of material, and the production in the window of a richness and subtlety of colours impossible in the older form of glass.

To put it as briefly as possible: the makers of so-called " stained glass " windows had used what is called in the trade " pot-metal," that is to say, glass which is coloured in the mass, while it is molten in the crucible or pot. Such glass, which was imported from England, was necessarily limited in its range of colour, and there was also a limit to the amount of richness and subtlety that could be obtained by what is technically known as " plating," that is, placing one tone or tint of glass behind another. Accordingly, the English window-makers, even such as Burne-Jones, relied chiefly upon the patterns of the forms, the drawing of the designs. But this would not satisfy La Farge, who saw his design from its inception, not in outline, but in full-fleshed form of colour.

He happened to be sick in bed, and, observing some toilet articles made of what is called " opal glass " in imitation of china, noticed that in the imperfect specimens the material, like an opal, exhibited, as well as the local colour, its complementary one.* He noticed also that when the opal

* White light being regarded as a combination of blue, red, and yellow, the complementaries to each is the union of the

glass was placed alongside a piece of pot-metal
the opalescent quality brought out a certain harmony. He felt he had discovered a means of increasing subtlety of colour effects, and of extra
richness, too, for it is a known fact that the bril-
liancy of a colour is intensified by the juxtaposition
of its complementary. Moreover, his mind, travelling quickly on, foresaw other possibilities in the
use of this material, owing to the variety of modu-
lations of thickness, surface, and colour to which it
can be treated in the making.

He began to experiment with pieces cut from
objects made in opal glass, and then found a glass-
maker who was willing to make him sheets of the
material. He used it at first in conjunction with
pot-metal, and gradually elaborated his methods,
until, in the *Battle Window* in Memorial Hall,
Harvard University, he combined a variety of effects. " In this window," he says, " I used almost
every variety of glass that would serve, and even
precious stones, such as amethysts and the like.
And I began to represent effects of light and mod-
ulation of shadow by using streaked glass, glass
of several colours blended, and glass wrinkled into
forms, as well as glass cut into shapes, or blown
into forms; even glass into which other glass had

two others; thus red and yellow—orange, is the complementary
of blue; blue and red—purple, that of yellow; blue and yellow—green, that of red.

been deposited in patterns. I also painted the glass very much and carefully in certain places; so that in a rough way this window is an epitome of all the varieties of glass that I have seen used before or since."

This quotation gives some idea of the variations possible in the actual making of the material; and since the date of the *Battle Window* (1870) they have been multiplied. What is now called " American glass " is capable of unlimited effects; and in the hands of a master-colourist, like La Farge, it is an instrument which produces the richest harmonies and extraordinarily subtle orchestration. So far, no other artist has approached him in the variety and originality of his use of the material. It was the child of this artist-scientist's genius, and has yielded to him its choicest service.

❀ ❀ ❀ ❀ ❀ ❀ ❀ ❀ ❀ ❀ ❀

The reader will remember that it was in the early 'fifties that Hunt, Inness, and La Farge sought their first impressions in France, and that, since that date, the movement of students had been to Düsseldorf and Munich. Indeed, it was not until the close of the third quarter of the century that Paris became the regular goal of American students.

AUTUMN   JOHN LA FARGE

THIS figure, notwithstanding its classical drapery, has no flavor of the academic. The type of the head is not what is popularly considered "ideal." But the main difference, as it is the chief beauty, lies in the subtlety of the color, particularly in the various reflected and refracted lights of the drapery.

In the Collection of John Gellatly, Esq.

THE PORTRAIT   WILL H. LOW

*A N example of an "ideal" subject, according to the academic point
  of view; sweetened, however, with a little tinge of sentiment.*

CHAPTER IX

THE year 1876 is a memorable landmark in our industrial and artistic development. Then it was that the Centennial Exposition at Philadelphia revealed for the first time to numbers of our people the artistic resources of the Old World. They were displayed not only in pictures and sculpture, but in the products of factories and workshops, and the lesson of the occasion was the commercial value as well as the desirableness of beauty. To the superior attractiveness of the foreign articles, in which the skill of the maker had been supplemented by artistic design and treatment, neither merchants nor public could be blind; and when, upon the close of the Exposition, a large number of these objects were presented to the City of Philadelphia, they were installed as a permanent exhibition of arts and crafts in one of the buildings at Fairmount Park. Then it was recognised that some practical step should be taken to give technical and artistic training to our own craftsmen. Accordingly, as the result of a citizen's movement, was founded the Philadelphia

School of Industrial Art, the first of its kind in this country.

The Centennial, however, only quickened and broadened forces that were already at work in the community. Gradually at first, and later with leaps and bounds, the little America of the Fathers had grown into a vast continent, already too small to confine the impetuous energies of its people. The increase and diffusion of wealth, and the growing facilities of oceanic transportation, prompted foreign travel, and made it easy; the barricades of national isolation were being broken down, and already the tide of travel toward Europe was in flood.

The familiarity with the art of the Old World, thus made possible to many, had already produced concrete results. In 1870 the Museum of Fine Arts, Boston, was incorporated, and the Metropolitan Museum of Art, New York, was granted a charter by the Legislature, which in the following year, at the request of the municipal authorities, passed an Act making an appropriation for a building in Central Park. These new museums, like the earlier Pennsylvania Academy, were organised by business and professional men. They were the product of the layman's interest in art. And, whereas, in the case of the older institution in Philadelphia, the motive had been the modest one of introducing " correct and elegant copies of works of the first masters in sculpture and painting," now the enterprise of the promoters was more ambitious, and their wealth made it possible to supplement the necessary copies of antique sculpture with original works of painting. The American amateur had begun to invade the foreign picture-market and offer alluring inducements to private owners to part with their treasures. When, therefore, the Centennial Exposition stirred the public imagination, there was already an active nucleus of organised and private appreciation of art around which the extended interest could gather. It served to give immense impetus to a movement already under way. But one thing more was needed—a stirring among painters themselves; and this, by a happy chance, coincided in point of time with the Exposition.

During 1875 and 1876 the first harvest of Parisian teaching reached our country. A group of young painters arrived, trained in the newest methods of the French School, proclaiming its superiority, and equipped to prove it. They appeared at a moment when they could do much to draw attention to the Exposition, and also receive from it an indorsement of what they themselves stood for.

All along the line of artistic production it was realised that some approximation must be made to foreign methods and standards of taste, and here, at least in the department of painting, was a body of enthusiasts, eager and able to show the way.

If you study the magazines of the period, you will find the evidence of an immediate and continuing improvement in the quality of the illustrations. It was primarily due to the quick apprehension of new talent on the part of the editors, and then, later, to the additional opportunity given to the artist by the gradual development of the photo-engraving process. But this exceedingly interesting chapter in our native art is outside the scope of our present story. More to the point is it that many of these younger men became teachers in our art schools, and thus effectually spread the knowledge of the new technique among students, until the French method of teaching has become the basis of instruction in this country.

But the way of these enthusiasts was not altogether smooth. By the older men of the National Academy of Design they were regarded somewhat as revolutionaries; troublesome disturbers of almost sacred traditions; dangerous, and not to be encouraged. Thus a cleavage in the ranks of painters ensued. Some of the older men, pre-eminently John La Farge, gave the new arrivals the support of their encouragement, and, as a consequence, a new organisation was effected. The Society of American Artists was founded in 1877, and incorporated the following year. John La Farge was elected president, and among its early members were Robert Swain Gifford, William Sartain, Louis C. Tiffany, J. Alden Weir, Will H. Low, William M. Chase, J. H. Twachtman, Abbott H. Thayer, Francis Lathrop, and D. Maitland Armstrong. These names belong to the years 1877-1879, and were supplemented a little later by those of Frederick Arthur Bridgman, Edwin H. Blashfield, George de Forest Brush, Thomas Allen, J. Carroll Beckwith, Robert F. Blum, Kenyon Cox, Bruce Crane, Frank Duveneck, Birge Harrison, Frank Fowler, George Inness, Jr., H. Bolton Jones, Francis C. Jones, George W. Maynard, Frank D. Millet, John H. Niemeyer, Eastman Johnson, Walter L. Palmer, William T. Smedley, Dwight W. Tryon, Elihu Vedder, Frederick P. Vinton, Douglas Volk, Sarah C. Whitman, George Fuller, Thomas Hovenden, William L. Picknell, Arthur Quartley, Charles S. Reinhart, Alexander H. Wyant, and Theodore Robinson.

With very few exceptions these painters received their training abroad, and for the most part in Paris. Indeed, in those early years admission to the Society was in the nature of a final graduation of the studentship abroad. It is interesting to recall this roll of names, for, although William Morris Hunt and George Inness are absent, it includes practically all the men of the advance guard in that progress which has put American painting in line with the art of other countries. Nearly two-thirds of them are figure-painters, and the product of Academic training. It is this that we have now to consider.

✵ ✵ ✵ ✵ ✵ ✵ ✵ ✵ ✵ ✵ ✵

As we have already seen, the three pioneers in the movement to France—Hunt, La Farge, and Inness—came under influences that existed in antagonism to the Academic teaching. But it was under the latter that the figure-painters of the next generation came. It was natural enough that the great teachers in the official schools should attract them. As Duveneck and Chase at Munich put themselves, respectively, under the famous Diez and Piloty, and Maynard and Millet under Van Lerius at the Academy at Antwerp, so the French students clustered around such eminent masters as Gérôme, Cabanel, Bouguereau, Boulanger, Lefebvre, Bonnat, and Carolus Duran.

The last named stands apart from the others in that he made the actual brushwork rather than the charcoal drawing the foundation of his method. Bonnat also was distinct, because in consequence of his close study of old Spanish painting he had modified his Academic training with a strongly naturalistic tendency. He painted, for example, wonderful portraits in which every inequality of the surface and texture of the flesh was faithfully rendered—marvels of characteristic physiognomy.

FRENCH INFLUENCE

On the other hand, the rest of the masters we have mentioned were neither naturalistic in their motives nor skilful painters in their methods. Their aim was beauty of individual forms and elegance of line in composition; the basis of their method was perfectly finished drawing, to be subsequently coloured. They were not colourists, nor had their brushwork any character of distinction, while matters of light and atmosphere concerned them little. Yet they had not escaped entirely the influence of outside tendencies; for example, they frequently popularised their pictures by giving them a sentimental or anecdotal appeal.

It is no part of our purpose to attempt to show how American students were influenced individually by one or another of these masters, but rather to summarise results. What they acquired, briefly stated, was a precise and scholarly knowledge of the human form in its relation to painting. The crux that confronted them, on returning home to America, was the use to which this knowledge could be put. Those, who at this period or later remained in Paris after the conclusion of their student days, in a measure evaded the issue by devoting themselves to the kind of subjects that were interesting the Frenchmen, and their work became French in feeling and character. But to those figure-painters who returned to America the problem was far more difficult.

They had returned because their sympathies were with their own country, but the latter offered them little encouragement. Abroad the figure-painters devoted themselves primarily to the representation of the nude; then to classic and historic subjects, or to costume or peasant genre. But in none of these directions was there much opening for the painter in America.

To the American public the nude was scarcely distinguishable from the naked. It had not the familiarity with culture that discovers in the human form the highest symbol of abstract beauty; and two centuries of Puritanical tradition and prejudice had engendered a prudishness that even to-day, while not quite so virulent, is still prevalent and hide-bound. The classics, as a mine of poetic thought and concrete ideals, were equally unfamiliar, while the scope of history had become narrowed down to episodes of the Revolution and the Civil War. Costume subjects smacked of an "effete" aristocracy, while the people over here who correspond to the *ouvrier* and peasant abroad lacked the latter's individuality. The painter in search of the picturesque found himself confronted with the monotonous uniformity of store clothes, of a public-school average of manners, and of organised labour, regulated by union conventions.

This is how the home conditions appeared to the

returning students, and it was not much exaggerated by their imaginations.

Meanwhile the influx of foreign pictures was increasing, and collectors who would have hesitated to buy a nude, a classical or historical subject, a costume or peasant genre, by an American, invested in the foreign article. For, an investment they considered it, and a safe one, since the foreign painters had received the official indorsement of their own country, in the shape of medals and honours. Such pictures, it was presumed, though in many cases erroneously, would always bring their money back with interest. Moreover, foreign things were the fashion. The Exposition and the return of American students, while they were to be of ultimate benefit to native art, were for the time being a source of impoverishment to the individual artist. He found it difficult to sell his pictures, for the investor-collector was swayed by the argument of the dealers—that, granted the superiority of the foreign article, it was a shrewder speculation to invest in the real thing. And this had a further advantage. It saved the collector's face. The nudes might seem to be shamelessly indecent, the classical subjects completely unintelligible, but they were French, and that covered a multitude of embarrassments. Is it not a fact that one does a lot of things in Paris, that one would not so much as speak of in New York or Phila-

STORY OF AMERICAN PAINTING

delphia or Boston? These pictures were French, which at once explained, even if it did not condone, them, and, most important, gave them a *caché*.

Now, these conditions, distressing enough at the time to individual painters, were on the whole to the advantage of American art. It is true they drove many men to the necessity of seeking a living in illustration rather than in painting, and of forsaking the precariousness of imaginative work for the surer returns of portraiture. They even postponed for nearly twenty years an active demand for figure-subjects; until, in fact, the vogue of mural painting was established. On the other hand, these conditions had their compensations. They headed off any general tendency that might have existed to imitate the motives as well as the methods of the foreigner; brought to the surface such individuality as existed in American figure-painters, and set the current of our art in the direction of expressing what is distinctly American. They helped to bring the painting of the figure in line with that of landscape. For the latter, though gaining reinforcement from abroad, has throughout its course of steady progression been a product and expression of native sentiment. By comparison, the progression of figure-painting has been fitful and uncertain.

✻ ✻ ✻ ✻ ✧ ✻ ✻ ✻ ✦ ✻ ✻

Among the few painters who in the 'seventies

ARIADNE   WYATT EATON

*B EAUTIFUL in drawing and modelling.   A product of Munich painting that has not yet felt the effect of open-air
light in an open-air scene.*

In the Collection of William T. Evans, Esq.

THE REFLECTION   BENJAMIN R. FIT

*T*HIS *artist died young. He was of Munich training, and, although this figure in it*
purity of drawing and feeling comes near to being the loveliest nude yet painted i
America, it misses what a later knowledge might have given. The figure, notwithstandin
that it is represented naturalistically in the open air, is not enveloped with lighted atmosphere.

In the Collection of William T. Evans, Esq

and early 'eighties ventured to render the nude in easel pictures, the most notable were B. R. Fitz and Walter Shirlaw, of Munich training, Wyatt Eaton, a pupil of Gérôme, and Elihu Vedder, who studied under Picot in Paris, but derived his real instruction from living in Rome.

The best example by Fitz, *The Reflection,* represents a girl standing on the edge of a pool, looking down into the water. It has the charm of absolutely unconscious loveliness, and the technical merit of being well drawn and painted. On the other hand, though the figure is shown in the open air, no attempt has been made to render the effects of light and atmosphere. In this it betrays its academic origin, as also do the easel pictures of nudes by Wyatt Eaton and Walter Shirlaw. These represent a riper type of beauty than the girl by Fitz, but the same words of commendation can be given them. Less skilful as a painter, Vedder has far more facility of drawing and a richer imagination than either of the others possessed. His illustrations to the poems of Omar Kháyyám, as well as his easel-pictures and mural paintings, reveal an unusual gift for decorative treatment of line and mass, and a still more unusual gift of original and creative thought. The latter is a rarer quality in painting than in some other branches of art, such as poetry and music, and there have been painters who have tried to cover up their own lack of it by belittling Vedder. They would say that in the strict sense of the term he is not a painter. It is true; but the same might be said of Gérôme, Bouguereau, and Cabanel, and of many of their pupils. The academic method, as we have already observed, is based upon form; the colouring is rather in the nature of a tinting that only approximates to the realities of flesh colour, since it takes little or no account of the action of light upon the surfaces. Vedder takes none whatever, and goes even further in not attempting even an approximation to the local flesh tones. The reason is that painting, as the representation of real appearances, does not interest him; it is for him a symbol of expression; from his point of view the human figure is but a concrete symbol, and his colouring of the figure like his use of it is not realistic but symbolical. His imagination, these critics have insisted, is too "literary." We shall have more to say about this when we discuss a little later the catch-cry of "art for art's sake," which began to be heard in the following decade. At present we will observe that the charge amounts to this—that Vedder has ideas embracing the mysteries of life and death; a store of conceptions formed by experience and reflection and by intimacy with the thoughts of great minds, and has used his art to give expression to them. If his art were weak and overweighted with the thought, there might be some ground for the criticism; but it is not. In fact, the main point of the criticism is that intellectual and imaginative originality is rare among painters, as in other professions, and the man who possesses it is apt to be an offence to some who do not.

And here a word may be said upon the subject of what many arbitrarily call the "ideal" picture. It involves the use of the nude or of figures wrapped in draperies, for the most part, supposed to be "classical." This class of motive is based upon the assumption that the painter's duty and privilege is to improve upon the imperfections of the human form and to give the figure an ideal perfection. Therefore the world of real men and women will not do; the painter must invent some fancy of his own. As a rule, he does not so much invent as follow along some well-worn ruts that have led for centuries to the same goal. Here some nymph of antiquity for the thousandth time disposes of her maiden beauty to invite the approach of her divine or human lover; or steps into her bath or emerges therefrom; or beautiful youths and maidens pose themselves in self-admiring groups, or weave their bare limbs and nicely calculated draperies into a rhythmic maze. The innumerable changes rung on these and such like themes have produced some of the most beautiful pictures in the world, but by artists who were nearer to the sources of Classic culture than we are to-day, especially in America. Regarded as a product of ourselves, such modern pictures are at best a graceful affectation; and, as a consequence, reach only a pretty mediocrity. Their influence is even detrimental, so far as they help to foster a wrong cenception of the "ideal." In appropriating this attribute exclusively to an aim at material perfection and losing sight of that higher ideal of spiritual and imaginative expression, the modern Academic painter has reduced his art to a condition of inferiority, as compared with music and poetry and even the finer kinds of prose. It is but a more or less elegant make-believe, in a world that is very real. It takes no account of man's higher aspirations and needs, and in its impersonal, unindividual treatment of form runs counter to the individualism and exact study of phenomena, which have become the characteristic of the age. Whereas, in this respect the Academic painter divorces art from life, the trend of the time has been to discover a union of the two.

❦ ❦ ❦ ❦ ❦ ❦ ❦ ❦ ❦ ❦ ❦

With many of our painters, however, the Academic training has been but the prelude to very independent and personal development. Three examples may be quoted. Two of these, George de Forest Brush and Abbott H. Thayer, were pupils of Gérôme, himself a man of intellectuality

Copyright by Elihu Vedder

E KEEPER OF THE THRESHOLD   ᴇʟɪʜᴜ Vᴇᴅᴅᴇʀ

A STRIKING example of this artist's decorative and expressional control of line and mass in composition, and of the character and quality of his imagination; also, in the original, of his symbolic use of color. The meaning of the symbolism, while in eneral way directly grasped, is too abstract to justify any one man in attempting to cur- its significance by confining it within a form of words. It appeals, as symbolism should, ersely to diverse minds and experiences.

In the Collection of the Carnegie Institute, Pittsburg

ARCADIA

H. SIDDONS MOWBRAY

but devoid of imagination. What we may believe they derived from him was a mental discipline and faculty of thought which enabled them to put to entirely independent uses the principles that they learned from him, and ultimately to give free rein to their own imagination.

In Brush's early pictures after his return home the brushwork is trim and sleek and hard, like his master's, and he reflects also the latter's partiality for embodying some story and archæology in his pictures. But as a basis for these qualities Brush did not, like Gérôme, search the Classics or the strange life of the East. His thoughts were toward his own country and what it might yield in the way of motive. He found material for story, archæology, and strangeness in the North American Indians; and food for his imagination by discovering in their present condition a clue to their past. He attempted to recreate the spacious, empty world in which they lived a life that was truly primitive, unmixed with any alloy of the white man's bringing; and to interpret not only the externals of their life, but its inwardness, as with mingled stolidity and naïveté these men-children looked out upon the phenomena of nature, fronted the mystery of death, and peered into the stirrings of their own souls.

In these Indian pictures, far too few in number, Brush still betrayed the tentative technique of the student, for their drawing is tame and the painting constrained and timorous. But the imagination, revealed, is deep and elevated, and no one has approached him in the completeness with which he has suggested the solemn romance of those primitive conditions. In *Silence Broken,* for example, a goose has burst from a bank of foliage immediately above the head of an Indian in a canoe. One is conscious of the rush of sound, vibrating through the vast isolation. The Indian looks up, but does not cease his paddling; he kneels in the boat, a figure of monumental composure. And here, in *Mourning Her Brave,* a squaw, muffled in a blanket, stands in the snow on the mountain side chanting a dirge, as she stares dully at the leaden, unrelenting sky. The suggestion is elemental; a note or world-old wailing and protest out of the void of time. Or again, in the *Sculptor and the King,* the one has wrought upon a block of sandstone, drawing from it some expression of the thought within himself, and now he waits in trembling eagerness for the word of the King. The latter holds himself erect and rigid, with the habit of superiority, but in his mind is embarrassment. This man, his inferior in social standing, has reached out beyond the King's experience and done something that makes royalty itself seem powerless; a strange new thing, a creation. The King is oppressed with wonder.

THE SCULPTOR AND THE KING

GEORGE DE FOREST BRUSH

A WISE man of his tribe or, as his tribe may think, a fool in his generation, seeking after vain things, has for the first time fashioned a thought in stone. The king, fountain of authority and strength, comes in judgment and stands in amazed awe.

In the Collection of Miss Henrietta E. Failing

PORTRAIT GROUP   George de Forest Brush

ONE of the series of this artist's renderings of his wife and children.
    In the Collection of the Pennsylvania Academy of Fine Arts, Philadelphia

FRENCH INFLUENCE

One can only touch upon the thought of these pictures. If you have seen them, you will recall the grip which they exert on the imagination, and join in the regret that Brush did not persevere in this line of work until his technical ability had become equivalent to his conceptions. But he abandoned it, anxious, I believe, to paint ideas more close to the experience of everybody, and not uninfluenced, we may suspect, by the claims of family life upon his sympathy. For his theme now became, and has continued to be, his wife and children, painted in the spirit of reverent devotion that characterised the Madonnas of the Old Masters. But with a difference—the interpolation of a modern note of painful seriousness. It is not the happiness of Motherhood that he represents, but the burthen and responsibility of Maternity, a remnant of the rigid strenuousness of Puritanic tendencies. Even in the sweet faces of the children is a foreshadowing of care. Meanwhile the influence of the Madonna motive threw his study back to the old paintings, and his own technique, recalling that of the early Flemish masters, obtained a fulness and dignity that befit the theme. Whenever his pictures appear, they create for themselves an atmosphere of grave distinction.

❧ ❧ ❧ ❧ ❧ ❧ ❧ ❧ ❧ ❧

The same quality, with a superadded note of tenderness, is to be found in the work of Abbott

Thayer. He, too, has left behind the manner of
his master, and acquired one of his own, characterised rather by sincerity than style, for his colour
is confused, the brushwork laboured. Nevertheless
his pictures move and hold one by the force of their
spirituality. They are the expression of very
beautiful qualities of personal character, strong,
tender, simple.

The girl-figure that haunts his convases, nobly
formed, but free of any cloy of flesh, fronts the
world with starlike eyes, serenely fixed beyond the
range of common things. She is a vestal virgin,
that has in her keeping the spiritual ideal of which
she herself is the creation.

Thayer, in fact, has. done for the spiritual ideal
of American womanhood what Charles Dana
Gibson has done for the physical and mundane—
created a type. Gibson's, through multiplication
of copies and because of its aggressive attractiveness, caught the popular fancy; Thayer's, for exactly opposite reasons, has captivated the imagination only of the few. Gibson's type is sexless, and
self-engrossed; Thayer's unconscious of her mod-
esty, self-contained, but tender and unselfish. She
is typical of the pure, frank outlook upon life,
prepared to accept its responsibilities and renuncia-
tions, to lighten its grossness, and uphold a high
ideal.

In an age and environment, not overgiven to

From a Copley Print.   Copyright, 1905, by Curtis and Cameron

VIRGIN ENTHRONED   ABBOTT H. THAYER

A BEAUTIFUL example of the artist's idealized type of girlhood.

CARITAS   Abbot H. Thayer

"CHARITY," which in its purest form is "Love," represented as a maiden
of noble figure and passionless serenity, standing guardian over the lives
of the little ones. In no other picture has Thayer so completely reconciled
the Greek abstraction of perfection with the practical sentiment of the modern spirit.

In the Collection of the Museum of Fine Arts, Boston

spirituality and imagination, these pictures are a notable embodiment of both.

❧ ❧ ❧ ❧ ❧ ❧ ❧ ❧ ❧ ❧ ❧

From them we may pass very naturally to a study of Thomas W. Dewing's conceptions of woman, as embodied in his pictures. In it also we may find a note distinctly American. For it should be remembered that there are two ways in which a painter may reflect the particularity of his environment. There is, first, the comparatively obvious one of representing the externals; and, secondly, the more subtle one of interpreting the inner nature of the men and women around him.

From an attempt to record the first, as we have already remarked, the earlier home-comers were discouraged, and it cannot yet be said that they or their successors have made considerable contribution to a record of the appearances of American life. Such genre subjects as those of Eastman Johnson, that depict incidents relating to the Civil War, or Thomas Hovenden's *Last Moments of John Brown,* or Winslow Homer's early pictures of rural scenes in the South, were the product of an earlier influence, that at the period we are discussing was losing its force, even if it had not actually expired. It had been undermined by the influence from abroad; for while the latter had done much to put the student on sure ground as regards technique, it had unsettled his motives. It had held up to him certain motives congenial to the conditions abroad, which, however, he could not find at home, and as a consequence he was embarrassed and at a loss.

We do not forget that some turned resolutely to the theme of Colonial times. But these pictures of Puritan maidens and the life of the early settlers, by men like C. Y. Turner, George H. Boughton, and Douglas Volk, though charming in many respects, particularly in that of sentiment, are after all the product of fancy; they are not interpretations of American life, as known and studied by the painter. It was the contemporary conditions that this new generation of painters avoided, and that their successors have infrequently and inadequately attempted. Indeed, it is scarcely an exaggeration to say that the only great interpretation of any phase of American conditions is to be found in Winslow Homer's pictures of the fisherfolk of Maine.

On the other hand, in the subtler domain of the spirit the American environment has made itself felt. Its action has been twofold: subjectively affecting the mental attitude of the painter, and objectively offering to his scrutiny certain distinct qualities in the object of his study. We have seen how these results are exhibited in the attitude of Brush and Thayer, respectively, toward maternity

THE LOOK-OUT — ALL 'S WELL WINSLOW HOMER

*O*NE *may find the texture of the bell, sou'wester, and the man's face pretty much
the same. But such technicalities, that would be detriments to a picture of smaller
import, disappear in the prodigious force of this one. It is a chunk out of the
rude heroism of the lives of the fishermen that ply their calling off the iron coast of Maine.*

In the Collection of the Museum of Fine Arts, Boston

THE SPINET　　　　　　　　　　　　　　　　　　THOMAS W. DEWING

A N example of the artist's rendering of expression. It is not the incident of a woman playing a spinet
that interested him, but the possibilities it involved of emotional expression. The lines and masses of
the chair and gown, the subtle movement of the lady's elbow and shoulders, the exquisite placing of
her head against the drapery of the wall. The lady's bold harmony are the

and maidenhood, and may now study another phase of them in Dewing's rendering of women.

His also betray the inherited trait of seriousness, and are all still the daughters of Puritanism, though many times removed from the original strain. Generations of repressed emotion have made them incapable of passion; strenuousness survives only in supersensitive nerves; their sole religion is the worship of self. From narrow conditions they have emerged into a vision of the Kingdoms of the World and the Glory of them, but have already tasted of satiety. They are motionless in an atmosphere from which all human warmth has been sucked, in a vacuum drained of intellectual and emotional nourishment. These bodily shapes are not of flesh and blood; they are the essence distilled from the withering of what is womanly, the mere fragrance of dead rose-leaves.

It was only by degrees that Dewing evolved this conception. His earlier examples, such as the *Lady at the Spinet,* and some of his small portraits, still have a charm that is physical as well as spiritual. The change may have come about through a change in his technical motive, as he became more and more enamoured of the subtleties of colour and lighting, qualities that, we shall see, began to occupy the attention of students during the 'eighties. It is a phase of our story that belongs to a later chapter. We can only say of it here, that to an artist of Dewing's sensibility both of feeling and hand, it offered a possibility of exquisite refinement of style, such as his has become; and that in the refining of his method his typical conception grew to be more and more rarified; less and less concerned with form as form, increasingly occupied with its suggestion of abstract expression.

In this evolution of motive and method he owed as little to his masters, Lefebvre and Boulanger, as Brush and Thayer did to Gérôme. In each case the individuality of the man gradually declared itself. It took some colour from its native environment and gave back in return an interpretation of something distinctively American in spirit. In the latter respect they are alone among their contemporaries; nor do I know where to look among their successors for any who has done a similar thing. These three men have not exhausted the subject of American womanhood; but, as some of the Florentine sculptors and painters did in the case of the women of the Renaissance, they have represented certain distinct types of contemporary femininity.

We started the chapter with a consideration of the Academic motive, but in following the development of Dewing, especially, have been compelled to wander from it. We may recover our ground by a reference to Edwin A. Abbey, who, though not Paris-trained, is a conspicuous example, almost

LE JASEUR   Thomas W. Dewing

*W*HILE *the coloring presents a web of subtle and subdued harmony, the figures vibrate with a thrill of piquancy. It is interesting to note with what unerring ease the artist has made the movement of the figures and their several kinds of engrossed attention concentrate toward "the chatterbox" on the table.*

In the Collection of John Gellatly, Esq

LA PÊCHE   THOMAS W. DEWING

THE faint radiance of twilight blended with early moonrise, that pervades the quiet spot, is caught in a maze of luminosity in the spray of foliage of the slender trees above the brook where one of the figures is fishing. All the figures are motionless as spirit-forms; in nature also there seems to be a suspension of breathing; the whole

the only one we have in modern times, of the Academic principle applied to historic painting.

✻ ✻ ✻ ✻ ✻ ✻ ✻ ✻ ✻ ✻ ✻

Born in Philadelphia, in 1852, a pupil of the Pennsylvania Academy, he became a draughtsman in the publishing house of Harper & Brothers. Those were the days of reproduction by wood engraving, and his duty was to draw the picture on the block. Gradually this method was superseded by the mechanical process of photo-engraving, and with this transition, Abbey's career as an illustrator is closely identified. The newer methods offered increased opportunity of originality and skill on the part of the draughtsman, and soon Abbey became known as one of the most original and skilful, especially in the use of pen and ink. His illustrations to " Herrick's Poems " had so much charm of invention and such a sympathy with and insight into the old-time feeling and environment, that he was commissioned by his publishers to go to England and gather material for a series of illustrations of *She Stoops to Conquer.* This visit proved the turning point of his career. He found in England, not only material for his drawings, but also the mental suggestion and atmosphere that his artistic development craved. He settled in England, married a New York lady, and has since made his home at Morgan Hall, an old manor house at Fairford in Oxfordshire. The success which his

work achieved enabled him, without abandoning
illustration, to devote a constantly increasing attention to oil painting. In the latter medium he
continued the same purposes and characteristics
that he had adopted in his illustrations. The basis
of the picture is still the subject; an old world one,
frequently taken from some scene in Shakespeare's
plays.

Like his series of decorations in the Boston Public Library, embodying the story of the "Holy
Grail," they are presented with an archæological
exactness of costume and accessories, and with
much dramatic action and regard for individual
characterisation. They are rich in colour, showing
a preference for blacks, whites, and scarlet; though
it is to be noted that Abbey is only in a limited
sense a colourist. To borrow a musical simile, he
does not compose the colours in a harmony, but
introduces separate melodies of colour, and spots
his pictures with these, as a draughtsman with pen
and ink spots the blacks and whites in his composition. Indeed, in this respect, as well as because of
the importance given to subject and his method of
building up his effects for the main purpose of
telling the story of the scene, Abbey, while working in oil, still remains an illustrator; upon that
larger scale which is distinguished as "historical
painting." He is the most important survivor, in
fact, of the vogue of the historical subject; and in

TRIAL OF QUEEN KATHERINE

Edwin A. Abbey

SHAKESPEARE'S "HENRY VIII," Act II, Scene iv ; a Hall in Blackfriar's. The moment chosen is when the queen sinks to her knees with the entreaty, "Sir, I desire you, do me right and justice." The canvas illustrates Abbey's dramatic handling of a situation, with its crowd of figures and diverse individualities of character and emotion, as well as his fidelity to archæological accuracy of costumes and accompaniments. In the original the richness of the coloring adds to the impressiveness of the scene.

In the Collection of the Honorable William A. Clark

THE CONNECTICUT VALLEY

ALEXANDER H. WYANT

A VERY fine example of what may be called the artist's middle style, when his great skill in rendering detail began
to be regulated by an approach to broader generalization. At this time, too, the sentiment represented a more

consequence was selected to paint the official picture of King Edward's Coronation. That vogue has given way before the increased attention paid to the manner of representation, rather than to the subject; to the aim of the modern painter to study his subject at close and intimate range, for which purpose he chooses a simple one, and makes the expression of his picture grow out of the technical expression. These principles, originally learned from the Barbizon painters, have been perpetuated in the steady development of American landscape painting. We will resume, in the next chapter, the thread of these influences during the 'seventies and early 'eighties, noting at the same time some interesting examples of independent growth.

CHAPTER X

IN resuming the story of American landscape,
we meet with two men who are usually associated in our mind with George Inness: Alexander H. Wyant and Homer Martin. These three
may be reckoned the fathers of modern American
landscape.   Martin, like Inness, was directly influenced by the Barbizon painters; Wyant indirectly
through the example of Inness and of the Barbizon
pictures that had reached this country. His artistic
career resembled that of Inness, so far as it developed from analysis to synthesis and from the
representation of landscape to the rendering of a
mood of nature.   Otherwise the two men were very
different.   Inness was versatile, eager, and impul-
sive, a transcendentalist; Wyant, a lyric poet-
painter, in whose mind, as in a still pool, a restricted
range of emotions was mirrored, with a suggestion
of poignant tenderness and depth.

Wyant was born, in 1836, at Defiance, Ohio.
Although as a boy he had the observing eye and
the desire to translate into line the forms of things,
and, as he grew older, trained himself in drawing,

he was twenty years old before he saw any pictures. This opportunity came to him when he visited Cincinnati, and, among the pictures there, one especially attracted him. It was by Inness. It seemed to the young man that one who could paint like that would be able and willing to advise him as to whether he might dare to hope to be an artist. He found means to visit New York, sought out Inness, was most kindly received, and spread out his studies and sketches to await judgment. The verdict was favourable, and Wyant resolved to be an artist.

He went abroad and studied for a time under the Norwegian painter, Hans Gude, who had graduated from Düsseldorf and was teaching at Carlsruhe. There seems to have been a mutual attachment between master and pupil; but, when the former urged an imitation of his own method of painting, Wyant rebelled.

He returned to America, and being in need of funds, joined a Government expedition to explore the West. Hardships overtook the party; his physical strength was unequal to the strain, and, partially paralysed, he was put on board an eastward train. The train passed through his native town; but he reasoned that, if he succumbed to his condition, he might never again be able to emerge and push forward to his goal of being an artist. So he lay still and reached New York. In time he recovered the use of his body, but his right arm remained affected, and henceforth he painted with the left. Moreover, during the rest of his life he was subject always to bodily discomfort, not infrequently to pain, and there hung over him the realisation that his days were numbered. He worked under the intense concentration of feeling that he had so much he wished to do, so little time in which to do it. The remainder of his life, which he shared with a devoted wife and a few friends, Inness pre-eminently among them, he gave to the study of nature, finding companionship all along in the nature-poet, Wordsworth. He worked first in the Adirondacks; then, fearing that he might fall into a mannerism by continuing to represent scenes of similar character, moved to the Catskills. His development, influenced by the Barbizon paintings, that were being imported in increasing numbers, and by the example of Inness, was from analysis to synthesis, from the representation of external nature to the interpretation of a mood. His earlier pictures are marvels of precise mastery of characterisation. By degees they become broader, simpler, more single-minded, or shall I call it single-hearted? For their emotional quality increased until they become the intense expression of a mood —the artist's own feeling, interpreted through nature. And the mood grows to be one of absorbing love and lovableness, frequent with sadness, musical lyrics in a minor key.

ADIRONDACK VISTA   Alexander H. Wyant

*T*HE *original, like most of Wyant's, very difficult to reproduce, is character-
    ized by a complete comprehension of the natural forms and exceedingly
    delicate quality of spiritual suggestion.*

                              In the Collection of William T. Evans, Esq.

OLD CHURCH IN NORMANDY   HOMER D. MARTIN

IN the quiet evening glow the old church with ivied tower and mossy roof dominates the scene, standing, as it has stood for centuries, a symbol of hope and faith to countless generations of simple country folk.

EXAMPLES OF INDEPENDENCE

Throughout his life he was a student, and when he was conscious that the end was drawing near (it came in 1892), he would exclaim: " Had I but five years more in which to paint, even one year, I think I could do the thing I long to."

This is the cry of a true artist, one whose soul was set upon that most evanescent, intangible quality—expression, while his hands were hampered by a medium comparatively clumsy and hard to manage. To others it will seem that he reached achievement; to himself, conscious of what he longed to do, there remained to the end a royal discontent.

❧ ❧ ❧ ❧ ❧ ❧ ❧ ❧ ❧ ❧ ❧

In great contrast to Wyant's tender, poignant lyricism, and to the brilliant improvisation of Inness, is the profound seriousness of Homer Martin's work. To his club-mates he was a " fellow of infinite jest," big-natured in his weakness as in his strength; in the seclusion of his art, a painter of grave purposes and serious imaginings.

He was born at Albany, New York, in 1836, the year also of Wyant's birth. Except for a few weeks' instruction from William Hart he was self-taught, and his early work represents a groping of mind and hand, a searching after the thing that was worth doing and some way of doing it. Already, however, it was distinguished by a feeling for colour and expression. He had always been subject to a weakness of the eyes, which debarred him from admission into the army at the opening of the Civil War, and had a marked influence upon the tenor of his art.

There is no doubt that what we recognise in an artist as a mental idiosyncrasy has frequently originated in some defect or peculiarity of ocular vision; for it is how the artist sees the visible world that will determine how the impression, filtered through his mind, will appear in the picture. Now Martin's imperfection caused him to see nature in mass, not enclosed in sharp outlines; and since crispness and definiteness were a characteristic of such landscape pictures as he had at first the opportunity of seeing, he distrusted himself. Had he known that Corot, after a long apprenticeship to certainties of form, had deliberately brought himself to see nature as a pattern of masses, softened against the spaces of the sky; that this was a phase of the process which other artists were going through in their passage from the analytical to the synthetical method of representing nature, he would have been saved much distress and delay. He might have realised the fact, so frequently illustrated in art, and to be exhibited later in his own, that it is out of a man's weakness that his peculiar strength is evolved. But it was not until after he had been abroad that impressions which he had hesitated to accept became convictions, upon which he could effectually base his self-development.

His first visit was in 1876, to Holland, England, and France, with a short stay at Barbizon. Again in 1881 he went to England, renewing a friendship with Whistler that had been commenced five years before; and thence moved across the Channel to Villerville, a little village near Harfleur in Normandy, where nineteen months were spent. It was during this time that he gathered the impressions which later resulted in some of his finest works— *Low Tide at Villerville, Honfleur Lights, Cinqueboeuf Church,* known now as *Old Church in Normandy; Normandy Trees, Normandy Farm,* the *Sun Worshippers,* and the landscape in the Metropolitan Museum called, erroneously, a *View on the Seine. The Mussel Gatherers* was completed a little later at Harfleur.

It is characteristic of Martin's habit of work that his stay at Villerville, the happiest incident of his career, was a period not of productivity, of giving out, but of taking in impressions, to be realised later. It may have been an instinct for saving his eyes that deterred him from making the colour studies or drawings in the open air with which painters usually equip themselves for subsequent work in the studio. One picture, *Westchester Hills,* which many people consider his masterpiece, was painted from start to finish in the open air; but this was a single exception to his rule of work. His numerous sketches are little more than summary indications of the anatomy of a scene—its lines and masses, jotted down with a pencil or water-colour brush. His real studies of nature were made through half-closed eyes, as he lay or sat smoking, apparently doing nothing. But all the time he was absorbing facts and receiving impressions. These gradually took shape and arrangement in his brain, until he obtained a mental vision of his subject; and it was the memory of the latter that occupied his attention when subsequently he came to paint the picture.

In " A Reminiscence " of her husband Mrs. Martin testifies to this, which is of extreme interest in helping one to understand his work. Incidentally I may remind the reader that it was in this way that many of Corot's most beautiful pictures had their beginning. They were painted in Paris from impressions stored up by the artist during the summer time in Ville d'Avray, as he watched the rising of the sun, or saw it to its setting. As with Corot, it was not the landscape but the impression of a mood experienced in himself at nature's suggestion, that Martin painted. And we have it on Mrs. Martin's authority, and may find corroboration in the titles of two of his pictures, that the mood was not only an abstract sensation, but that the concrete image of the mood was present to his

WESTCHESTER HILLS

HOMER D. MARTIN

IT is twilight; the sky quivering with milky whiteness, the greens and yellows of the hill and foreground already browned over with the dusk. Nature is gathering herself to rest; she breathes slowly and placidly; in a few moments she will be asleep. This picture, by many regarded as the artist's finest work, is said to be the only one that he began and finished in the open air.

In the Collection of Daniel Guggenheim, Esq.

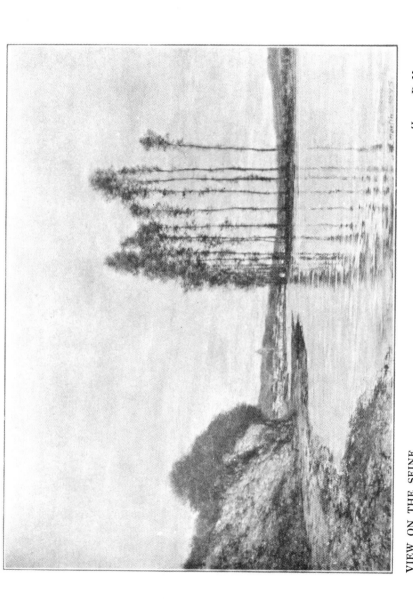

VIEW ON THE SEINE

HOMER D. MARTIN

*O*RIGINALLY named by the artist "The Harp of the Winds," the picture illustrates his extraordinary sensibility to the subtler qualities of nature. For, to a degree that the reproduction fails to show, he has succeeded in rendering

imagination. Thus, the *View on the Seine* was called by himself *The Harp of the Winds*. The scene had suggested music to him, and the tall poplar stems and their reflections seemed like strings vibrating with the quiver of the foliage. But Martin feared that the title might seem to be sentimental, and, abandoning it, changed also the appearance of the trees, in order, I suppose, that the resemblance to a harp might not be too obvious. For he had a great horror of painting anything that might be suspected of a literary motive, and in the titles of his pictures avoided giving any verbal clue to the mood embodied. The only other exception is *The Fire Worshippers;* but I believe it is the exception that proves the rule.

For the appearance of these trees, stunted and bent over by the rigour of the wind, extending their lean and withered arms toward the glory of the setting sun, gives a certain obviousness to the title, when once the humour of the artist's imagination has started the suggestion. But under the obviousness of the title he may have desired to conceal his deeper mood. In the contrast between the splendour of the sky and the cramped, thwarted conditions upon earth, he may well have felt a symbol of the artist's dream of what he longs to do and of the impotence with which he frequently knows himself to be possessed.

For Martin could only work when the impulse

was upon him. " I do not know where the impulse comes from," he once said, "nor why it stays away. All I know is that when it comes I can do nothing but paint; and when it goes away I can do nothing but dawdle." "That was absolutely true; and," his wife adds, "it was also very inconvenient." She gives another hint to the understanding both of the man and the artist when she says that Martin was himself a bit of nature.

Without early education, and despite a desultory appreciation of good literature and a taste for music, unregulated by any sort of intellectual discipline, he remained in a very special and unusual way a child of nature; subject to variableness of mood, reckless of consequences. This was the man—a child. It was only the artist in him that grew up and matured; knit by bonds of serious tenderness to the mother earth, from whose loins he had come, and at whose breast he fed, understanding her voice by instinct, while her heart throbbed to the movement of his own. In a word, he did not absorb nature and then pass it through the prism of his own consciousness, as Inness and Wyant did, and most poetic landscape painters do, but himself passed into nature, and became once more conceived in her, afterwards employing the strength of his intellect to express, as it were, the secrets of the womb. Through this rather fantastical process of thinking, I believe, we can gain

THE FIRE WORSHIPPERS

HOMER MARTIN

*T*HE reproduction fails to suggest adequately the golden glory of the evening sky and the softness of the silhouette of the brownish trees. Hence it misses somewhat the suggestion of the original, as of time-tired creatures, warped by fate, bending in adoration and supplication before the majesty of the universal.

In the Collection of Louis Marshall, Esq.

LANDSCAPE

HENRY W. RANGER

◀ *GOOD example of the tendency which this artist shares with many others to make his pictures decorative in*

a perception of what it is in Homer's finest pictures that moves one so largely and so profoundly. It is the completeness with which he was able to surrender himself to nature that made him able to recover from her the elemental feeling, and to render it in a manner at once so large, simple, and profound.

His work is characterised by the qualities of the colourist. In the earliest pictures there is more than a little gaudiness of colour; but this passes with the work of his maturity into a sober harmony of low-toned hues, grave, sonorous, and musically subtle; the earth-parts kneaded into solidity, the skies thrilling with vibration. The sky, however, in the *Fire Worshippers* is aflame with colour; and again, in the last of all his pictures, *Adirondack Scenery,* he indulged in a profusion of bright tints. Though blind of one eye and threatened with cataract in the other, irreparably shattered in health, he nevertheless asserted once more the unfaltering jollity of the man in an artist's colour scheme of gaiety. He died in St. Paul, Minnesota, in 1896.

❧ ❧ ❧ ❧ ❧ ❧ ❧ ❧ ❧ ❧ ❧

While the three men we have been discussing were influenced more or less directly by the Barbizon painters, their pictures bear no resemblance to the latters'. Henry W. Ranger, however, painted for a while in a manner that is visibly reminiscent, now of Rousseau, now of Diaz; Robert

C. Minor, a pupil of the latter, was noticeably representative of Barbizon choice and treatment of subjects. He is dead, and Ranger has discovered a style personal to himself. In fact, this early Barbizon influence has run its course, and been replaced, as we shall see, by another, in which, through the example of Manet and the other " Impressionists," a closer and more scientific study of light is the main motive. Meanwhile, the salient features of the influence are perpetuated. Our landscape painters still select a fragment of nature, study it intimately, summarise its details into an *ensemble,* and represent it as a portrait of character and expression.

It will be convenient to mention here those men of remarkable originality, whose development was apart from the influence we have been discussing. Entirely self-taught and detached from this influence, except in so far as it was in the air, and no one could escape some recognition of it, Ralph A. Blakelock remained a curiously isolated figure. The son of a New York physician, born in 1847, he would not follow in his father's profession, but determined to divide his studies between music and painting. In neither did he receive any instruction, and prepared himself for painting by a trip to the West, where he lived among the Indians and secured material that he afterwards introduced into

THE BROOK BY MOONLIGHT   RALPH A. BLAKELOCK

*T*HE *finest example of this artist. Nature no doubt inspired him, but he
was not a nature painter. The actual appearances of nature he trans-
posed into a convention of his own, which he employed for the purpose
of emotional expression. The latter was his motive; nature he used only as a
means.*

In the Collection of Catholina Lambert, Esq.

SIEGFRIED

ALBERT P. RYDER

*A*N *admirable example of this painter's poetic-dramatic manner, the whole conception and rendering of the scene being the reverse of naturalistic. The patterning of the tree-forms, the massing of light and shade, and, most of all, the coloring, have been arbitrarily assembled for the purpose of expressing the painter's own emotional conception.*

In the Collection of Sir William Van Horne

his pictures. He was a born colourist, and such men are usually musical, while the musician is conscious of colour-quality in sound. Indeed, the modern mind, in its subtle analysis of sensations, has added to the expressiveness of language by using interchangeably the terminology of these two arts. Thus, having by habit ceased to regard it as an affectation, we find, on the contrary, a usefulness and propriety in speaking, for example, of harmonies and tones of color, high key and low key of colour, and so on; similarly of shading of expression in music, of richness of colour and the like. Both sensations reach us by wave movements, and we may recognise a certain correspondence in the way in which they affect us. But Blakelock went further than a mere consciousness of correspondence, and worked out for his own use a chromatic scale of colour equivalent to that of music.

Unfortunately he had never learned the manual trick of painting, and in the details, notably the foliage, used his brush as a pencil, without, apparently, having acquired the trick of drawing. His trees are as hard, flat, and motionless, and often as dark and opaque in colour, as if cut out of japanned tin. Accordingly, considered as portraits of nature, they are unsatisfactory. But this is not the proper way to regard them. Rather they are pictorial arrangements founded upon a theme which he has borrowed from nature; as a musical composer may take some simple folk-tune and use it as the slender thread on which to string his harmonious inventions. If we will divest our minds for a moment of the habit of looking in a landscape for an intimate study of nature, and estimate Blakelock's simply as pictorial convention, a symphony of colour based upon nature *motif,* intended to affect us in a purely abstract way, we shall find the best of them extraordinarily original and inspiring.

This is also the best way to estimate the work of another isolated figure, Albert P. Ryder, although he himself is apt to confuse the issue by giving his pictures titles that have a literary suggestion. Among his subjects, for example, will be remembered *Jonah and the Whale, Siegfried, Temple of the Mind, Flying Dutchman.* This literary allusion is a source of weakness in his pictures. Their real strength consists in the way in which he makes the rendering of the landscape a pattern of colour and form, full of emotional appeal, or the ocean and sky contribute to a symphony of colour; in the *Jonah* as wild and whirling as a Hungarian Gipsy dance by torchlight, in the *Flying Dutchman* as weird as the squealing flight of witches. With no thought of nature in his mind, but intent on making every part of the picture beautiful in colour and texture, he embroiders every inch of the canvas, as

[218]

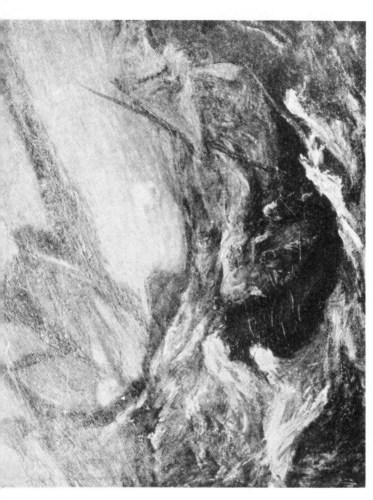

THE FLYING DUTCHMAN

ALBERT RYDER

A TUMULT of water, in the trough of which is a small boat with a few shipwrecked sailors. Beyond them passes the phantom ship, her sails confused with the sweep of cloud that hovers over the setting sun. The emotional suggestion of the picture is mainly the result of the color-scheme, a turbulence of gold-flecked splendor

In the Collection of John Gellatly, Esq.

ICE CUTTERS

Copyright, 1904, by N. E. Montross

HORATIO WALKER

T HE character of the action, as diversely excited by the horse and the men, is rendered with remarkable knowledge and skill. An admirable touch of romantic feeling is introduced by placing the solid
bulk of the hard-breathing, tugging horse in contrast with the ideal loveliness of the sky. Similarly,

if his brush were a needle, threaded with brilliant silks or strands of gold and silver, until the whole gleams like precious stones. All this is beautiful, very beautiful, pregnant with imagination.

Ryder has been likened to Monticelli, but scarcely with justice to the latter. For the Frenchman was a master in the rendering of light; his pictures are saturated with it; nay, more, they are constructed in light, creations of light; the figures moving or fixed in lighted atmosphere. Ryder's pictures are usually opaque, and radiant on their surfaces alone. But there is another fundamental difference—a racial one. Monticelli's pictures are creations of pure fancy, while Ryder exhibits the Anglo-Saxon tendency to supplement the music with ideas, and his literary additions are singularly ineffectual. The little figures, boats, fish, and architecture, appear ill-drawn, ill-placed, and curiously childish in conception, and suggest that their author has nothing of the saving grace of humour. His work, notwithstanding its emotional charm, gives the impression of its author being too much preoccupied with his own seriousness.

❧ ❧ ❧ ❧ ❧ ❧ ❧ ❧ ❧ ❧

The third of the independents, George Fuller, belongs to a generation earlier than that of Ryder and Blakelock, having been born in 1822, three years before the birth of Inness. Yet it was not until 1876 that the work by which he is now remembered was presented to the public gaze. It had been produced under circumstances that render his career a chapter of romance in the story of American painting, and a very unusual variation on the theme of "art for art's sake."

Up to 1859 it was not unlike the careers of other painters in those days of limited opportunity. Some instruction at home in Deerfield, Massachusetts, where his father was a farmer, was gained from a half-brother who had skill as a miniature-painter; later, a little instruction in drawing from the sculptor, Henry Kirke Brown, in Albany, and further help from another sculptor, John Ball. Portraits occupied him principally, though he made some efforts to break away from them and indulge himself in imaginative subjects. In 1857 he was elected an associate of the National Academy. The most notable feature of this period of his life was the determination he made, as expressed in a letter to his friend Brown: " I have concluded," he wrote, " to see nature for myself, through the eye of no one else, and put my trust in God, awaiting the result."

In 1859 the tenor of his life was changed by the death of his father and elder brother. In the interest of the younger children—his mother had died some years previously—his presence was needed on the farm. But before settling down he realised the long-cherished hope of visiting Europe.

THE WOOD CUTTERS HORATIO WALKER

By Courtesy of N. E. Montross

A FINE rendering of the characteristic action of the two bodies, the one about to pull, the other to push. The picture is filled with light, that strikes sharply on the edges and surfaces of the freshly cut wood and penetrates the shadows.

In the Collection of the Museum of Fine Arts, St. Louis

Copyright, 1902, by N. E. Montross

SHEEP WASHING

HORATIO WALKER

*A VERY striking example of artistic synthesis. Though one's attention is easily retained by the centre of the picture,
the impression of distance and spaciousness is equally received, while the feeling of energy in the foreground is*

EXAMPLES OF INDEPENDENCE

In London he made the acquaintance of Rossetti and Holman Hunt; passed on to Paris, and thence travelled from one to another of the principal cities of Belgium, Holland, Germany, and Italy, making sketches in the galleries, and being attracted especially by the works of the Colourists and Rembrandt.

Then he returned home, and went to work as a farmer; and for nearly sixteen years passed out of the ken of both makers and buyers of pictures. Only a few friends knew that in the intervals of superintending the farm he found time to paint; with no thought of selling or exhibiting his pictures, intent simply on trying to express some ideal of his own. It is likely that he would have continued in this voluntary seclusion had not a failure of his tobacco crop brought him to the verge of bankruptcy and compelled him to put some of his pictures on sale in Boston. They were received with acclamation, and during the eight remaining years of his life—he died in 1884—Fuller resumed his career as a professional painter.

He had determined to see nature for himself, and he saw it through the medium of his imagination, veiled with mist. Behind it, the landscape glimmers with subtle colours; the outlines of the figures are indistinct, their motionless forms scintillate with suppressed light; their large eyes gaze fixedly, as if trying to pierce the veil.

All these pictures, among the best of which may be reckoned *The Turkey Pasture, Winifred Dysart, The Romany Girl,* have a quality of distinction, due particularly to the rare quality of the feeling that inspires them. They are expressions of a singularly beautiful condition of soul. Considered, however, purely as painting, they are less satisfactory. In undertaking the technical problem of rendering light and atmosphere he anticipated what we shall see became a motive of the next generation, but, in comparison with modern pictures, his own lack elasticity and clarity of colour. He stood on the threshold of the New Movement, peering, like one of his own figures, through the veil.

It is this New Movement that is now to engross our attention.

Copyright, 1906, by N. E. Montross

VE MARIA   HORATIO WALKER

*T*HE *regular scene of this artist's work is the Island of Orleans in the St. Lawrence
River, where the inhabitants, descended from the first French settlers, have preserved
the religion, language, habits, and modes of farming of their forefathers. Walker's
*ndering of these folk, product of an intimate and sympathetic comprehension, is distinguished
y the technical qualities of virile drawing and of color, by turns splendid and subtle.*

In the Collection of the Corcoran Gallery of Art, Washington

DR. GROSS' SURGICAL CLINIC   Thomas Eakin

A *MODERN variant of Rembrandt's Dr. Tulp and the "Lesson in Anatomy."*

In the Collection of the Jefferson Medical College, Philadelphia

CHAPTER XI

A T the conclusion of the previous chapter we
spoke of the New Movement. It led up
finally to the wedding of art with life,
which, as we have more than once noted, was to be
the characteristic achievement of the nineteenth
century.

We have seen already what the painters of Barbizon did to accomplish this, and how their influence set the course of American landscape on a
firm road that has led alike to truth and to spiritual
expression. We have now to trace the corresponding development in the domain of figure painting.
It is true that Millet had already done for the
figure, what Rousseau and the other Barbizon
painters had done for landscape. He had reconciled what the Academicians regarded as contra-
dictory—art and nature. But, as yet, he was little
known outside of Barbizon. It was necessary that
someone of more belligerent spirit should carry
the war of realism into the enemy's stronghold—
into Paris. The man of the hour was Gustave
Courbet.

The reader may be reminded that in France the realistic movement was represented in literature by Flaubert, Daudet, the brothers Goncourt, and Zola. It was reflected in painting by Courbet. The latter, as early as 1855, had thrown down the gage of battle to the Academicians, proclaiming himself a realist, asserting that it was a ridiculous presumption for an artist to paint what he had never seen, that his province is limited to what is visible to the eye, and that it is the familiar facts of life with which he ought to be concerned. Courbet had passed off the stage before the later generation of American students reached Paris, but his turbulent personality had given an impulse to the Realistic movement that was carried forward by others. It even affected the Academy, Gérôme, for example, varying subjects of classic motive with the rendering of actual incidents; while Bonnat, who, as we have seen, had early imbibed the naturalistic tendencies of the old Spanish School, became a conspicuous instance of exact and analytical study. His portraits of men, by reason of their intense objective rendering of the external characteristics, are also, so far as the latter indicate what is below the surface, extraordinary representations of human personality. Of both these men Thomas Eakins was a pupil, and he stands out among our painters as at once the most analytical in his observation and the most representative of the influence of the Realistic movement upon the Academic training.

✖ ✖ ✖ ✖ ✖ ✖ ✖ ✖ ✖ ✖ ✖

Born at Philadelphia in 1844, he passed from the schools of the Pennsylvania Academy to the studios of Gérôme and Bonnat, and came back with an eye trained to precise observation, and a hand skilled in precision of drawing. In these particulars he is a master; beyond them he has shown no disposition to travel; he is as coldly and dispassionately analytical as Gérôme at his strongest, as unflinchingly exact as Bonnat. Under the former's influence he produced his masterpiece, which is owned by Jefferson College, Philadelphia. As Rembrandt, in his *Lesson in Anatomy,* portrayed the celebrated surgeon, Dr. Tulp, so Eakins has commemorated the personality of Professor Gross in this picture, representing a *Surgical Clinic.* It involves an effectively artistic composition, as well of lines and masses as of light and shade, and fine characterisation in the individual figures, but the inherent power of the picture is the product of the artist's own point of view.

He approached the incident in precisely the same kind of condition of mind as the surgeons engaged in the operation. The patient, for the time being at any rate, is but a " subject," toward which their attitude of mind is absolutely impersonal, but on which they concentrate all their knowledge and skill, so that their own personality declares itself masterfully in a complete control of the situation.

Equally objective are the portraits of men by Eakins, which represent a similarly impersonal point of view toward the sitter, and in his best ones an extraordinary display of the artist's own personality in his grip of the technical problems of the picture. One of the most remarkable examples is the *Portrait of Louis N. Kenton;* a lean, shambling figure, with the hands thrust into the waist-pockets of the trousers; the strong, intellectual head bowed in meditation. It suggests that the man has been pacing up and down the room, thinking out some matter, and has suddenly halted, all alert, as he finds himself near to its solution. It is a picture that in its matter-of-factness and in its disregard of the elegancies of line, and of the persuasiveness of colour and tone, might be charged with ugliness, but as the record of a human individual is extraordinarily arresting and satisfactory. Considered from the more general standpoint of a work of art, it might be the better for some of those tricks of grace in which our young students nowadays are drilled to be proficient. Let us grant it, but with the amendment, that here is an instance where a picture may be superior to a mere work of art; that there is in Eakins a capacity broader and deeper than that of simply being an artist. He has the qualities of manhood and mentality that are not too conspicuous in American painting.

❧ ❧ ❧ ❧ ❧ ❧ ❧ ❧ ❧ ❧ ❧

They appear again in Winslow Homer, the painter of the Ocean. He is our greatest exponent of Realism, with nothing, however, of the Academician in his make-up. Rather, one may see in him some traces of the Barbizon influence, and of other later influences yet to be described; but in the main he is a painter who has worked out for himself his own development.

Independence has been the ruling characteristic of his life. He began his career as an assistant in a lithographic shop in Boston, and there acquired a distaste for doing things according to the dictates of other people. The Civil War broke out, and the Harpers offered him a position as their illustrator at the front. He refused to bind himself by any contract, but joined the Army of the Potomac, and thence sent back to the office drawings of such incidents of camp life as caught his eye and interest, which appeared regularly in " Harper's Weekly." At the same time he practised oil-painting, and at length produced a picture to which the stirring emotions of the time lent a considerable popularity. In this *Prisoners from the Front* he represented a batch of Confederate troops passing to the rear through groups of Union soldiers. After the war he remained for a time in the South, painting rural scenes, especially of negro life. They reveal a keenness of observation and a certain straightforward method of representation, but are not yet essentially the work of a painter, nor of any considerable artistic merit. To-day they are chiefly interesting as evidence of their author's resolute intention to see and express things in his own way.

The turning point in his career was reached when he transferred his studies to the characteristics of the Maine coast. There the big, simple heroism of the fishermen and their womenfolk at once attracted him, and prompted a number of pictures, the very titles of which tell their own direct tale. In the *Life Line, Undertow, Danger, Eight Bells, All's Well,* and others he had caught the spirit of the life; the tragedy that underlies its faithful routine of duty; the unconscious bigness of it all, as Kipling did in his word-picture of the Gloucester fishermen in " Captains Courageous." To Homer the study of this life meant the enlargement of his own; a deepening of his motive, the gradual realisation of his own power as an artist.

Already these pictures are big work; big in their sympathy with and comprehension of the subject of his study. They were to be succeeded by work that was even bigger, because the interest that impelled it and the impression it produces is more abstract, of a more universal kind. For, it was no longer the ocean, mainly as a background to the

THE WEST WIND   WINSLOW HOMER

DREAR sand-dunes and green sea, swollen white and lashed into spray; a leaden sky, and, facing the turmoil of the elements, a solitary figure. The picture represents a fragment of the ocean's epic.

In the Collection of Samuel Untermyer, Esq.

THE CASTAWAY
WINSLOW HOMER

*T*HIS picture with its brilliant coloring, so different from the gray skies and water off the coast of Maine, is a product of the artist's visit to the West Indies. Here the vivid hues and the clarity of the light attracted him and were recorded in a number of very remarkable water colors—a medium in which he is singularly skilful. To many of his admirers

human tragedy, but the might and majesty of the ocean itself, that now attracted him supremely. Figures may be introduced, but only as a musician employs a theme in the composition of his fugue; and oftentimes the sole subject of contemplation is the ocean itself. In daily companionship with it, he has led for many years a solitary life upon a spit of coast near Scarboro. Its wild purple and brown rocks, the grey-green seething sea, and the immense skies, laden with wind and moisture, have been his constant and sole inspiration. Their solemn grandeur has entered into his soul, and the work which it has inspired is without any rival in American art for originality and impressiveness.

❧ ❧ ❧ ❧ ❧ ❧ ❧ ❧ ❧ ❧ ❧

But the Realism for which Courbet contended was only a transitionary phase of the Realistic movement. While it achieved an accuracy of form, it failed to render accurately the colour of form, and its true appearance as affected by light and atmosphere. In this further contribution to realistic painting Manet was the leader, and he drew his inspiration from Velasquez. It has so profoundly affected the painter's point of view and method that it must be comprehended by everyone who would understand the general trend of modern painting, and its particular bias in America. For it was enthusiasm for this new teaching that characterised the students who returned home in the late 'eighties and early 'nineties; and while some of them for a time displayed the extravagance of neophytes, the principles for which they stood have prevailed.

To state the matter as briefly as possible, the recovery of Velasquez, dating from 1857, gradually brought about the following changes:

Firstly, it affected the painter's way of seeing things. It substituted for a realism of observation such as is recorded by the camera, a painter's way of seeing; for a detailed analysis, a pictorial synthesis or summary. It was realised that Velasquez painted what he could see, not what he knew was present to his eyes. Meissonier, for example, in painting a charge of cavalry, because he knew that every horse had bit and bridle and buckles, every rider sundry buttons on his uniform, represented all and each with microscopic fidelity. Velasquez, on the contrary, making his eyes the standard, took in the figure, or scene, as a whole, with swift comprehensive glance, and then rendered the impression he had received. Following his example, the moderns began to paint " impressions," to be, as the phrase was coined, " impressionists." *

Secondly, it affected a change in the way painters regarded colour and their manner of lay-

---

* This original significance of the term impressionist, we shall find, was subsequently modified. See page 266.

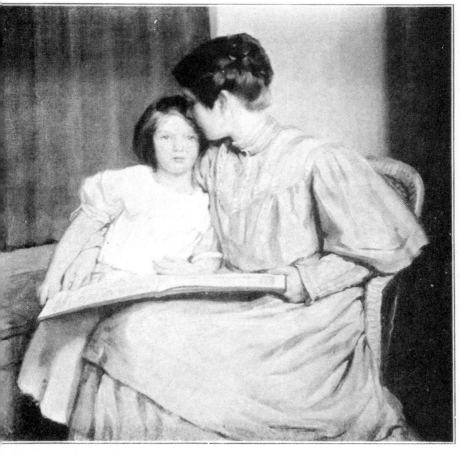

Copyright, 1906, by Sergeant Kendall

N INTERLUDE   SERGEANT KENDALL

*T*HIS *artist sees nature in a way peculiar to himself, with a sharpness of vision
    that seems to take little account of the subduing effects of atmosphere, yet he
    comprehends the mystery which underlies the obvious appearance.   The senti-
ment in his pictures always rings true.*

A MARINE VIEW

PAUL DOUGHERTY

NONE of the younger artists exhibits a bigger feeling for the elemental grandeur of rocks and ocean.

ing on the paint. Velasquez's subdued harmonies of blacks and greys, sparingly relieved with yellows, blues, and old rose, opened their eyes to the fascination of subtleties, as compared with the brilliance of strongly contrasted tints. The long, sweeping contours of his figures promoted a taste for the dignity of simple lines and massy compositions. His manner of relieving the monotony of the large coloured masses—black, grey, or otherwise—by breaking them into several tones, and giving them a character of distinction through the broad and virile handling of a brush, loaded with paint, taught the value at once of subtlety and of effective craftsmanship. It made it clear that the brush and not the crayon was the tool to be relied upon, and gave an impetus to the art of painting, as distinguished from the art of drawing a figure and subsequently tinting it.

Thirdly, the extraordinarily natural appearance of Velasquez's figures and scenes, summed up by Gautier when in front of the *Maids of Honour* he exclaimed, "Where is the picture?" set the painters to discovering its secret. It was found to be due to the fact that Velasquez placed his figures, as they appeared in nature, within a surrounding envelope of lighted atmosphere; and that his method of doing so had been the accurate rendering of the exact amount of light given off from every visible part of the figure or object represented. So now the painters, coining a new word to explain their intentions, began to occupy themselves with " values."

To sum up: these discoveries effected the emancipation of painting from the thraldom of Academic draughtsmanship. It restored the actual craftsmanship of the brush to an honourable standing, and gave the painter thereby an opportunity of developing and exhibiting his individuality. You may recognise a man's brushwork as you can another's handwriting. Further, it changed the method of painting. For now, instead of making an elaborate drawing of the figure, accurately shaded, and then laying on the paint with a careful, almost timorous intention not to lose touch with the original drawing, the painter, satisfied with a preliminary sketch that merely indicates the general form and its position on the canvas, builds up his figure from the start by successive layers of paint, so as to reproduce the successive planes of lighted surface which the figure presents. It is a vigorous method, but yet it admits of the fullest amount of subtlety of observation and representation. It involves also a much more realistic as well as vigorous rendering of the subject—an immense step in the direction of effecting a union of art and life.

From the beginning of the 'sixties this method of painting spread, until it has become a usual practice of painters and the basis of instruction for

CALM BEFORE A STORM   ALLEN B. TALCOTT

THIS artist at present makes his summer home on the Connecticut River, near Lyme.
His landscapes are characterized not less by a feeling for the vigorous aspects of nature
than by a sensitiveness toward the varying expressions of her moods of atmospheric change.

MRS. CARL MEYER AND CHILDREN John S. Sargent

ONE of the artist's most ravishingly dainty conceptions of femininity. The costume of the lady is a delicate shell-pink, and the whole color-scheme, notwithstanding the size of the canvas, has the exquisiteness of a morsel of Dresden china.

students. While Manet and many others influenced the vogue by their example, Carolus-Duran was the first and most distinguished of the regular teachers of it. His most important pupil, at any rate from the point of view of the present story, was John S. Sargent, whose work is in an eminent degree representative of what the most skilful of our modern portrait-painters are doing.

❧ ❧ ❧ ❧ ❧ ❧ ❧ ❧ ❧ ❧ ❧

Of New England stock, the son of a physician who had retired from practice in Philadelphia, John Singer Sargent was born in 1856, in Florence, where his boyhood and youth were spent. Brought up amid the advantages of cultured home-life and of early and constant familiarity with the artistic treasures of that beautiful city, he learned to draw and paint at the local Academy of Fine Arts. He was already skilful beyond the average of students and grounded in knowledge of great art and trained in taste, by the time that he went to Paris to study under Carolus-Duran. Having rapidly assimilated that master's teaching, he visited Madrid and studied Velasquez in the Prado, and afterwards moved to Holland, where the portraits of Hals attracted him. Later he was influenced by those of the Scottish artist, Raeburn. His style is a brilliant epitome of these various sources of technical inspiration.

Instead, however, of trying to trace his particular

obligation to each of these, it may be more practically useful to attempt a summary of what characterises his own style. Its charm is a combination of vivid impressions and of extraordinarily vital and effective technique.

As becomes a student of Velasquez, what he paints is the impression that the subject produces on his mind. It would seem as if the impression were generally one that had been immediately registered; but, even if he has had to wait for it, by the time it reaches him, it does so with such vividness that it appears to have all the freshness of immediacy. On rare occasions, however, his portraits are laboured and incompletely realised; it is then, we may conjecture, that he has failed to receive a strong impression.

As a rule, his portraits reveal no psychological analysis, or poetry of feeling, nor, except possibly in some of his portraits of children, any sympathy with the subject. Dispassionate as a mirror, for the most part, with equal fidelity and, at times, relentlessness, his mind reflects the surface characteristics of his sitter, the mannerisms of expression, evidence of social or professional caste, the individualities of dress and gesture, suggestions of temperament and of the atmosphere in which the person moves. No painter of the present day can better render the elegance of fashionable femininity. But while he revels in the opportunity of

BEATRICE

PORTRAIT OF MISS BEATRICE GOELET   JOHN S. SARGENT

*I*N his child-portraits, of which this is one of the most beautiful, Sargent
exhibits a sympathetic personal feeling that is ordinarily apart from his
work.   This one suggests a tenderness for the little subject amounting
almost to romance; and yet with what an assurance and virility it is painted,
and with what unerring taste and judgment the quaintness of the costume is
echoed in the bizarrerie of the bird-cage and the unusualness of the composition.

PORTRAIT OF HENRY G. MARQUAND   JOHN S. SARGENT

*T*HIS *portrait of the second president of the Metropolitan Museum (1890-1902), the collection of which his taste and munificence so materially enriched, is one of Sargent's greatest
successes in dignity and depth of characterization.*

In the Collection of the Metropolitan Museum of Art, New York

luxurious display, he is never carried away by it. It interests him as a problem for his brush. Consciously he never flatters, unconsciously he may sometimes do less than justice; sometimes also he fails to secure a likeness, for it is not as an individual, but as a type, that the sitter chiefly interests him.

As a matter of fact, his main interest is in his technique, and in the artistic problem that the subject offers. Because of this he is often, perhaps generally, puzzling to the public, and appreciated best by brother craftsmen, who speak of him as a " painter's painter." Knowing the difficulties of painting, they are alike astonished and enthusiastic at the audacity with which he attacks a problem, and at the masterful ease with which he solves it. Not that this is always the product of a magical facility, but often of exacting self-criticism, indomitable perseverance, and patient renewal of effort. Again and again, if necessary, he will scrape out, until he has realised his intention, by which time the labour of endeavour will have disappeared in the triumph of achievement. The latter, to speak of it in untechnical language, is characterised by a maximum of suggestion and a minimum of apparent means, the latter thrilling with animation.

As to the suggestion. When a painter copies exactly what he sees in front of him, as, for example, Meissonier did, and our own John G. Brown, you can peer into the canvas at close range and find every detail rendered with minute finish. But that is not how we view people in real life; we do not step close up to them and peer into their faces and scrutinise every particle of their costumes. We watch them from a little distance off, and get a general impression of their personality and appearance. It is this that Sargent strives to give us. When you are close to one of his canvases you are confronted with a number of bold dabs or sweeping strokes of paint that to the inexpert eye convey no meaning: but step back, so as to gain, as it were, a perspective, and those dabs and patches resolve themselves into modelling of features and hands, and the delineation of draperies and accessories. But, admitting it is so, you may ask in what consists the advantage of this method? The answer involves a psychological consideration, that this process demands a greater exercise of mentality on the part of both artist and spectator.

The exact imitation of a button gives you no more mental excitation than the original button would. Skill and patient precision were required to manufacture the original, and the same qualities, carried perhaps a little farther, were employed on its imitation; and, while we may exclaim, " How wonderful! " we do so because the wonder is that anyone could have such extraordinary patience. In-

PORTRAIT GROUP   JOHN S. SARGENT

*THE portraits in order from the spectator's left are of Dr. William H. Welch,
Dr. William S. Halsted (standing), Dr. William Osler, and Dr. Howard A.
Kelly. The heads are finely characterized. The background of brown wood-
work is not very happily rendered in the original, lacking depth of atmosphere. In
the reproduction it is worse than it should be, as the canvas was not properly
stretched and the photograph showed wrinkles.*

In the Collection of Johns Hopkins University

A PORTRAIT STUDY IRVING R. WILES

A DELIGHTFUL example of this artist's brilliant and yet refined brushwork, his skill in suggesting a spontaneous pose of the figure, thrilling with life, and his ability to render expression.

stead of stimulating the mind, it makes us tired to think of it; just as we have to disguise our boredom when a person insists on telling us every petty detail of some occurrence that to start with was not of much account. On the other hand, to analyse, as Sargent does, a certain effect, so absolutely that the essential of it is discovered, and then to determine just how that essential may best be rendered, and out of many possible methods to select unerringly the precise one which will put his mental conception into immediate shape—this represents a keen and vigorous mental exercise, the magnetism of which, if we study his work, will stimulate us. Moreover, since, as a rule, in the finished picture each stroke is there as it came hot and straight from his constructive imagination, the whole subject has the thrill of life. And this, you will observe, is something more than being life-like.

Sargent's eminence has had a great influence upon American painting. On the one hand, it has helped to popularise the new method of painting, and, on the other, to foster the idea that masterfulness of technique may justify a lack of ability or inclination to penetrate the character of the sitter. For, like Carolus-Duran, he is a brilliant exponent of the material and mundane, for the most part engrossed in his impression of externals.

❧ ❧ ❧ ❧ ❧ ❧

It is the purpose of this story to summarise results, and therefore it may be convenient to divide American portraiture into two classes.

Omitting from our present review a good many portraits which simply represent more or less honest mediocrity, we may sum up the more conspicuously skilful ones as either portraits of *ésprit* or portraits of character. The former with us, as elsewhere, are in the majority. They are distinguished by manifest dexterity of brushwork and by animated and piquant rendering of the sitter's exterior and of such hints of personality as lie near the surface and are expressed by individual mannerisms. The best of such portraits are those of women, which permit the added charm of attractive costumes and of surroundings that are pervaded with the atmosphere of refined elegance. We have elsewhere spoken of portraits of this kind by Chase, and may supplement them by the examples of Irving R. Wiles, J. J. Shannon, Cecilia Beaux, Adelaide Cole Chase, and Frank W. Benson. The work of each of these admirably represents the qualities above referred to, and in certain instances may seem to indicate a deeper appreciation of character. It is because of a still more marked intention in this direction that I mention separately the work of John W. Alexander. Nevertheless, he is perhaps more characteristically represented by what I have chosen to call the portrait of *ésprit,* in his case distinguished by a very decorative composition and a flat manner of

MISS KITTY   J. J. SHANNON

*T*HIS *painter, who lives in London, must not be confused with the English painter, Charles H. Shannon. The simple sincerity, both of feeling and technique, which distinguishes this early example, has scarcely been sustained in his later portraits.*

In the Collection of the Carnegie Art Institute, Pittsburgh

PORTRAIT OF ADELAIDE NUTTING   CECILIA BEAUX

*F*OR *the complete naturalness and simple dignity of its pose, for the brilliant directness and meaningfulness of its brushwork, and for its sincere expression of character in the head and hands and carriage of the body, this portrait represents Miss Beaux at her best.*

In the Collection of the Johns Hopkins Hospital

painting that enhances the decorative suggestion. He has been happily represented also by many purely figure subjects.

Foremost among the portraitists of character stands Wilton Lockwood, the example of whose work illustrated here exhibits the soundness, subtlety and imaginative insight of his present matured style. Another painter whose portraits, too rarely seen, possess the qualities of depth and force, is Joseph de Camp. They both work in Boston, as also does Frederic P. Vinton, whose portraits of men, while less dexterous in technique, are powerful records of the strong breed that is shaping the life of affairs in modern America.

Indeed, it is worth notice that where psychological insight appears in an American portrait, the subject will usually be a man. The same is true to-day in France, just as it was in England at the close of the eighteenth century. That the decline of the English Portrait School was due in a large measure to the excessive popularity of the portraits of women of fashion, with all its temptation to the artist of pre-occupying himself with furbelows and finery in lieu of stronger and deeper qualities, can scarcely be doubted; and equally in modern America the same cause is at work, retarding the lustier growth of our art.

Parallel with this tendency to lack of character

in portraiture runs a poverty of imagination in figure-painting generally. With a few exceptions, it is very apparent in American painting, and for a while was equally characteristic of French art. It has been a perhaps not unnatural result of the attention paid to technique. The new methods were so fascinating that painters became too much enamoured of the skill with which they could render the appearances of things. Many lost sight of the fact that technique is but the means to expression, and extolled it as an end in itself. Hence was started in Paris, and thence imported to America, the confession of faith in " art for art's sake."

It had, as other such rallying cries, a modicum of sanity and much extravagance. It was in its best sense a protest against the dependence of painting upon literature, and against the tendency to consider the subject of more importance than the method of representation. It was an assertion never out of place, that the quality of the artistic form must be the final test of a work of art. But it ran to extravagance in assuming that the artistic form was the only test; that what it might embody was of no account at all; that the method of presentation was the first, last, and only important concern of the artist. It put asunder the twain that should be one flesh—the form and the expression. The result was for a time, sterility; much

PORTRAIT OF MRS. THOMAS HASTINGS   John W. Alexander

*I*N *this charmingly vivacious characterization the artist has exhibited to a marked
degree the appearance of brilliant improvisation that his particular technique
suggests.*

PORTRAIT WILTON LOCKWOOD

*T*HOUGH *he subsequently studied in Paris, Lockwood's early training was under John La Farge, by whose influence his own temperament was confirmed in its preference for profound and subtle study. It is the spiritual rather than the physical ego that he tries to compass; and his portraits, enveloped in atmosphere and elaborated into a very subtle orchestration of color, while their suggestion of the figure is sufficiently real, excel as evocations of the inner personality of the sitter. His portrait of John La Farge is another most distinguished work.*

REALISM

cry and little wool; plenty of good workmanship, but a poverty of emotional or spiritual significance.

Meanwhile, landscape painting, for the most part unaffected by this tendency, kept steadily on its path of progress. We resume its story in the next chapter.

CHAPTER XII

WE have already seen how American painting has been affected by the influence of Velasquez. By an age that had become enamoured of realism he was discovered to have been the most distinguished of realists; not only in his way of seeing his subject, but of representing it. Modern painters imitated his impressionistic way of comprehending and summarising the subject, and his method of painting the "values," or varying quantities and qualities of light given off from every part of the figure and scene. In one respect, however, they carried the realism of painting a step further than Velasquez. He had painted for the most part in the grey light of Philip the Fourth's palace; they, however, extended their studies of light into the open air and experimented in the representation of all kinds and degrees of light. This has been the special contribution of modern times to the art of painting.

It represents the final emancipation of the painter not only from the restrictions of Academic draughtsmanship, but also from subservience to

LADY IN BLACK Robert Henri

*A PORTRAIT beautiful in feeling and particularly
distinguished for the breadth and expressiveness of
the brushwork. The influence of Velasquez is notice-
able in his work. He is a leader of the younger men, who are
bent upon making sound brushwork and virility of vision the
basis of their art. An able technician, he is also a man of
fine qualities of mind and imagination.*

Copyright, 1907, by N. E. Montross

AGAINST THE SKY

FRANK W. BENS[

O NE *of the daintiest conceptions of this Boston artist, who has made a close study of Americ*
  femininity and effects of pure sunlight.

the Old Masters in the picture galleries. He would be free of all conventions and see the world for himself; no longer through the medium of varnish and the dirt and discoloration of time that disfigured the old pictures, but in all the freshness of its real colouring. It was, on the one hand, a logical extension of the nature-study of the Barbizon men; and, on the other, the painter's conformity with the realistic and scientific tendency of the time.

Manet's study of sunlight started the vogue of *plein air.* Men began to paint in the open air. Among the earliest and best of the pictures produced under this condition were those of Alexander Harrison, a native of Philadelphia. *In Arcady,* for example, represents a fragment of a meadow, interspersed with gnarled trunks and slender tree stems, among which, in easy natural attitudes, are grouped three nude girls. The sunlight filters through the canopy of leaves, dappling the grass and gilding here and there a leaf or blade of grass, glancing over the human forms and touching the delicate flesh tones with shafts of radiance. It was the product at once of keen observation and of sure and dainty craftsmanship, while it breathed a spirit of poetry that lifted the whole scene into an idyl. Even more decisive, however, both in its virtuosity and in its effect upon contemporary painting, was his later picture, *The Wave,* which is now in the galleries of the Pennsylvania Academy of the Fine Arts. For the first time the true colouring of the blue water, curling over a smooth, sandy shore, had been searched into and recorded; the light that glinted on its crest, lay on the shining curve of the swell, or nestled in the hollow of the trough—each aspect had been rendered in its true relation. And the result of this truthful rendering of the passage of light over the wave was to increase the suggestion of the latter's movement. The picture was a beautiful lesson in colour, light, and movement.

This trinity of qualities became the faith of the moderns. It is literally a three in one: light the source, colour the product, movement the spirit or expression. Let the Academicians be satisfied to keep to a convention in which art is divorced from life. It was the aim of the new men to effect a union of the two, to make art an expression of nature and of human life, and, incidentally, of their own temperaments, or souls. The secret of this they had discovered in the study of that element wherein things live and move and have their being. It was no longer form alone that had to be considered; but form in relation to and as affected by the surrounding, that it has in nature, of lighted atmosphere. And this study gave a more definite meaning to Impressionism. It is realism extended by study of what the French call the *milieu*—the

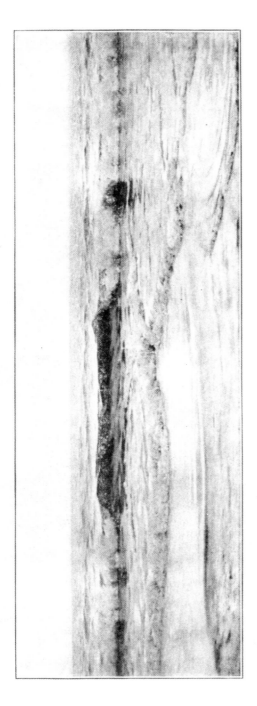

THE WAVE

*T*HIS large canvas, measuring 40 by 109 inches, still justifies the enthusiasm that its original appearance aroused. For it was among the earliest of the plein air pictures, in which the actual appearance of sunlight upon moving water was recorded, and with such extraordinary subtlety of rendering that the truth of it has never been surpassed.

ALEXANDER HARRISON

In the Collection of the Pennsylvania Academy of Fine Arts, Philadelphia

Copyright, 1905, by N. E. Montross

CALM MORNING

F. W. BENS

A GOOD example of this Boston artist's charming way of representing children and of skill in rendering the vivid effects of high sunlight. It is painted with a facile and dir brushwork that is full of suggestion and preserves the spontaneity of the impression.

surrounding conditions, through which the subject is viewed. And this is the principle that distinguishes the newer realism from such realistic pictures as those, for example, of the Düsseldorfians. The latter represented scenes of peasant life, in which the characters are playing more or less natural parts; but the realism is confined to the forms, and does not embrace a representation of the actual conditions of light and atmosphere in which they would appear in nature. They painted realistic pictures, but they did not represent the real manifestations of life.

The latter, in all their infinite degrees from seriousness to triviality, became the study of the moderns. The result has been a general extension of skilful craftsmanship, of a painter-like way of seeing and rendering the subject, which has not always been put to any very interesting purpose. A vast majority of modern pictures, including many American ones, are nothing more than studies of light as it filters through muslin curtains, creeps between the slats of Venetian blinds, or in full sunshine pours over the lace caps of peasant women or the white gowns of first communicants. These devices, multiplied a thousandfold, have engrossed the attention of the painter. He has been applauded by his brother painters, because they recognise the subtlety of his observation, and his manual dexterity, but to the laymen, who regard such excellences as, after all, but a means to an end, these pictures have become more than a little wearisome. It is as if a speaker should utter an interminable string of well-turned phrases, with not one idea involved in them to stir either one's intelligence or imagination—vacant chaff.

The best fruits of this new method of study and practice have been furnished, at any rate in America, by the landscape painters. It is to their advantage that they do not have to hunt up or invent subjects for pictures. Nature offers them an inexhaustible choice, and their own love of nature keeps their sympathies active. The fascination of technical proficiency seldom monopolises their interest; they feel constantly the stirring of emotion in themselves, and delight to express it in their pictures. The latter are rarely without some quality of idealism.

The modern landscape, as a rule, is characterised by an absence of strong contrasts. The colours of shadows have been carefully analysed, and found to contain more light and a greater variety of colour than had previously been suspected. The shadow is regarded no longer as a dark spot, but as a spot from which more or less light has been intercepted. Therefore, it varies in density according to the quality of light that pervades the scene, as well as according to the amount of light that is intercepted. The colours of shadows also

By Courtesy of N. F. Montross

LS READING   EDMUND C. TARBELL

N what modern genre consists is admirably shown in the work of this Boston artist. It is the character
of the scene as a whole that he represents, the sum total of the impression recorded by the eye. Further, the
parts are seen in their variety of relations to one another and the ensemble, everything also in its proper
of lighted atmospheres and with reference to the latter's diverse effects on form, color, and texture.

A GENTLEWOMAN

J. ALDEN W

*O*NE *of the artist's delicately expressive interpretations of femininity. Though the ten*
and spiritual feeling culminates in the rendering of the head, it pervades the whole can
being echoed in the subtle color-tones of the dress and in the sensitive repose of
shadowed hands

In the Collection of the National Gallery, Washing

are not uniform; they depend upon the local colour of the object on which they lie; the shadow on grass, for instance, differing from that on snow. Moreover, the colour may be affected in tone by the reflections from other adjacent objects. For instance, the shadow on a girl's face, if she is seated in the sunshine upon grass, may receive from the latter a green tone. In this discrimination of the colour and tones of shadows, the quality of the prevailing light, as we have remarked, is a most essential ingredient.

It is, in fact, in analysing the different kinds and degrees of light that modern painters have made a new and important contribution to art. They have not been satisfied with general distinctions between bright and dull light, or cold and warm, but have pushed their investigations into its varying aspects, under different conditions of weather, season, locality, and, even, time of day.

In this close analysis of the varying manifestations of light, no one has surpassed the Frenchman, Monet. He carried forward the study begun by Manet; and there are few modern landscapes that do not owe something to his example, although they may not follow his method. The latter represents a manner of laying on the paint to which the French have given the name *pointilliste,* since it covers the canvas with innumerable little *points* or dabs. This method was suggested to him and his friends, Seurat and Pissarro, by the writings of the late Professor Rood of Columbia University. For they recognised that in this study of light the discoveries of scientists might aid the vision of the artist. Among the experiments described by Rood was the following:

Two or three pigments having been selected, they were first mixed together, as a painter would mix them on his palette, and applied to a white card. Secondly, each pigment, in the same proportion as before, was painted directly on to a white disc, so that the latter was covered with the two or three segments of pure colour. When this disc was revolved rapidly, these blended into one tint, that corresponded in hue with that obtained by mixing the pigments on the palette, but was found to be more intense, for it contained more light. Monet and his friends, whose prime end was to represent light, derived a hint from this experiment. Instead of mixing their colours on the palette, they would lay them separately on the canvas, very close together, and rely upon the eye of the spectator, at the requisite distance, to effect the blending. For an actual mingling they substituted a visual impression of it.

Some eyes, however, seem to be physically unable to effect this blending; many more are offended by the spottiness of the method; moreover, a great many of Monet's canvases suggest experiment

By Courtesy of N. E. Montrose

E FARM IN WINTER   J. ALDEN WEIR

N his landscapes this artist exhibits a virile comprehension of the actualities of the scene, together with a refined appreciation of the subtleties of light and tone.

Copyright, 1905, by N. E. Montross

LISTENING TO THE ORCHARD ORIOLE   CHILDE HASSA

*T*HIS *well illustrates the artist's method of painting in separate points or dabs of color whic
 even in the black and white reproduction, suggests that the whole scene palpitates with light.
         is a charming example also of the strain of lyric feeling that underlies his keen study of t
natural and artistic aspects of the scene.*

rather than realisation, and are embarrassing even to those who admire his best work. Consequently his method has not been popular either with painters or with the public.

The latter, however, have made the mistake, since Monet is an impressionist, of confounding this method with impressionism, with which it has absolutely nothing to do. It would be just as reasonable to conclude that every impressionist painter wears a sweater, and loose trousers turned up over strong shoes. The one is Monet's method of dressing, as the other is of painting; neither has anything to do with the principles which underly his motive as an artist. He is an impressionist because, to quote the definition given above, he has " extended realism by a study of the *milieu*." He is a leader among impressionists because he has been foremost in pushing the study, so as to include an extended variety of surrounding conditions, and to discriminate between them with such subtle refinement. It is chiefly due to his influence that modern landscapes are so pure and fresh in colour, and exhibit such a subtlety of observation and expression.

Among the very few Americans who have directly followed his method the most distinguished is Childe Hassam. His earlier efforts are marked by the crudity that is inseparable from experimentation; but of late years he has mastered the difficulties of the process, and his pictures now present a unity of effect, a vibrancy of colour, and a delicate *ésprit* both of style and feeling, that render them almost unique in American art.

Courbet in the early days of realism used to affirm that the main thing for each painter to aim at was the emancipation of the individual; and in modern landscape this has certainly been achieved. The close study of the actual phenomena of nature, seen necessarily through the painter's own eyes and affected by his own peculiarity of temperament, has produced over the wide field of landscape a great variety, and in the pictures of each man an equally notable individuality. This latter fact makes it impossible to enumerate examples. Any attempt to characterise our landscape painters in batches, according to some assumed similarity of motive or method, would be arbitrary as well as inexact. To single out a few names would work injustice to many others, and be outside the purpose of our story, which has been to note the progress of our painting, in hope that the reader may find in the general statement a clue to the appreciation of particular individuals.

Nevertheless, I will conclude this summary of modern American landscape with a particular instance. It is that of the late John H. Twachtman, whose work revealed a quality of idealism that may be said to represent the most modern note in painting. Earlier in our story we touched upon the

Copyright, 1905, by N. E. Montross

LORELEI   CHILDE HASSAM

A PICTURE of exquisitely contrasted effects: the pure grace of the human form and the rugged outlines and formations of the cliffs; warm, clear sunshine, respectively, on the blue water, the creamy smoothness of the flesh, and the pinks, violets, and greens of the indented rock; lastly, the air and water, brisk and alert, the figure in pensive repose.

Copyright, 1905, by N. E. Montross

CHILDE HASSAM

A RAINY NIGHT

A RATHER early example of Childe Hassam's use of the pointilliste method, to give an impression of the momentary aspect of a scene. Only what the trained eye of the artist can comprehend, a part more and a part less definite, is represented. Imagine the same scene rendered, not as the artist saw it, but as he knew it to be — the cabs, the figures, drawn with a scrupulous regard for their exact appearance, if studied as separate items. What landscape painter's study of the forms of nature, as a basis for any subsequent expression of sentiment. It is not the least of the enjoyment to be derived from many pictures that they make one conscious of the strong-ribbed substance of the earth, the force and vigour of the trees and vegetation, the reach of sky, the volume and buoyancy of clouds, and the weight and movement of water. Before such pictures we experience that stir of blood and suggestion to the imagination which we may feel in the presence of nature itself, and often in a heightened form.

On the other hand, there may be pictures in which the artist has so thoroughly comprehended the facts of nature that for his own need and ours he can lay aside the consideration of them. He has extracted from them their essential abstract significance, so that he interprets that highest kind of sentiment, which is not a product of the individual and personal, but a whisper from the universal. To anyone who esteems of highest value the abstract expression in a picture, some of John H. Twachtman's landscapes are of superlative interest.

Living upon a farm near Greenwich, Connecticut, he absorbed the facts of his surroundings so completely that their very spirit entered into him, and it was the spirit that he strove to render on canvases that are marvels of delicate tonality. In examples like the *Brook in Winter* (for he seems to have had a partiality for winter scenes), it is the soul, as it were, of the still, cold, dormant world that he has rendered. Never has been better expressed through the subtle resources of modern methods of painting the suggestion of the abstract. For Twachtman, in technical matters, was a modern of the moderns, and ahead of all but a few of them in what he sought to express. He realised, as Whistler, for example, did, that if painting in the future is to hold its own alongside the developments of modern music, it can only be by finding its motive in the abstract.

His best work, like Whistler's, has in it the latest modern note of idealism. It represents the effort of the artist to free himself from the encumbrance of the material, by giving expression to the spirit that abides in matter.

HE HEMLOCK POOL

JOHN W. TWACHTMAN

A SPOT among the hills near Greenwich, Conn., seen and felt and rendered in the artist's most characteristic way.   The snow, faintly blue, fringes the cold, motionless water, and lies sprinkled on the slopes, over the dead vegetation of which seems to hover the spent breath of late autumnal coloring in faintest suggestion of tawny yellow, rose, and violet.   In the dry, white, sty atmosphere the slender tree-stems stand, as if silent.   Fecundity is checked; nature is inert; and e soul of nature is stilled in the grip of Winter.   The whole scene is an emanation of nature's spirit, erpreted through the spiritual emotion of the artist.

In the Collection of John Gellatly, Esq.

FEBRUARY   JOHN H. TWACHTMAN

ONE half the picture given up to the bare desolation of snow, the other to the scarcely less desolate diversity of a frost-

CHAPTER XIII

THE previous chapter concluded with a reference to Whistler. He has been reserved until the close of the story, since his art in a very striking way reflected the various influences of the Impressionistic movement. To those influences which we have already discussed must be added one more—that of Japanese art.

It was in the early 'sixties that the Japanese prints and paintings began to find their way into Paris studios and attract the interest of certain artists, notably of Manet, Monet, and Whistler. To men who had already learned to appreciate Velasquez's impressionistic way of seeing his subject, his dignity of line and the subtlety of his colour harmonies, the Japanese work came as a corroboration of the lesson. Here, too, were miracles of harmony in blacks and greys, and in addition a range of tonal effects of an infinite variety and extraordinary subtlety, that opened up to the imagination of the colourist a new world of motives. They offered also a new principle of composition. The old method of building up and balancing, invented by the great Italians and preserved by the Academicians, did not suit the purpose of the Impressionists who were bent on achieving a union of art and life.   In real life people do not dispose themselves in formal groups, and affect set poses; the suggestion is rather of spontaneity, unexpectedness, and movement.   How to reconcile these with unity of effect, and grace and dignity of composition?   The answer was discovered in the art of the Japanese.

It appeared that they, too, were Impressionists; not interested in form for its own sake, but in the suggestion that it afforded to the artist's imagination, and that they had developed a principle of composition suitable to their needs.   The aim of the artist was to make his painting or drawing decorative, but instead of arranging his lines and masses in a geometric pattern, suggested by the formality of architecture, he had gone to nature for inspiration.   In nature it is not order but irregularity that prevails, and yet this disorder presents appearances of unity of effect.   The masses of hills against the sky, the contours of coastline as it pushes its way sharply into the sea, or recedes in swelling curves, the windings of rivers and streams, the free growth of vines, and the spotting of trees against the hillside, of labourers working in the rice-fields, or fishing boats dotting the distant waters—these and countless other phenomena had gradually taught the Japanese to find a new kind of symmetry. It was the result of careful calculation, and gratified the eye with a sense of unity; yet it had the appearance of being the result of accident. It was characterised by spontaneity, unexpectedness, and movement.

The fitness of this to the purpose of investing the appearance of reality with artistic charm was immediately apparent to artists like Manet, Degas, Monet, and Whistler. From their hands it passed to others, until now you cannot open an illustrated magazine without finding the evidence of it.

But, while countless men have adopted this technical principle, some few have discovered the psychological motive underlying it. In the best periods of Japanese art, religion and art were inseparable. The philosophy of religion taught the supremacy of spirit over matter; and the joy and the duty of the artist was to interpret this truth. So by him perishable matter was regarded as only the outward and visible sign of the indwelling, eternal, universal spirit. Form for its own sake did not occupy his attention; as far as possible, he eliminated from it all its grossness, all its suggestion of matter, striving to extract its essence and to interpret it in terms of spirit. Like the old Byzantine art, Japanese art was symbolical.

Now, the growth of realism in Europe corresponded with a loosening of religious beliefs.

The old foundations of spirituality were being swept away by materialism. In art, both the Academic and the Realistic schools were materialistic; each in its own way magnified the importance of form, and matter, as such, was the object of its worship. But here and there appeared an artist to whom the representation of the material was of less moment than the expression of the spiritual and universal, and such found in the symbolism of Japanese art an inspiration and a clue. One of these was James MacNeill Whistler.

He was born at Lowell, Massachusetts, in 1834. His father, Major George Whistler, an eminent engineer, having accepted a commission in Russia to lay out the St. Petersburg and Moscow Railroad, continued to occupy an influential position under Emperor Nicholas. After the father's death the mother returned to America to educate her son, who in time was entered at West Point. His stay there, however, was short, and his next move was to Paris, where he became the pupil of Gleyre, in whose studio he associated with Degas, Bracquemond, Fantin-Latour, and Legros. Yet this period of Academic instruction was but an incident in his career.

His art was a product of most delicate selection: a hybrid derived from the intermingling of many strains—Velasquez, Rossetti, the Impressionists, and Japanese—with his own rarely gifted person-

WHISTLER

ality, itself a curious mingling of aristocratic *hauteur* and spiritual sensibility.

From Velasquez he learned the value of the grand line, and of the variously defined and vanishing outlines; the placing of the figure in cool, real atmosphere, and the dignity and refinement of tones of black and grey; from Rossetti, the fascination of his woman with " the star-like sorrows of immortal eyes "; from the Impressionists, the renunciation of form, as such by means of lines, and the rendering of its effect by chromatic values of colour, harmonised in the medium of natural light, instead of the golden atmospheres created by the older masters. And by the Japanese he was inspired to more ravishing harmonies of tone, harmonies of sumptuous sobriety, of tender or sparkling sprightliness, and was taught the secret of their composition, the fanastic balancing of irregular forms and spaces, with continual surprise of detail, and the arbitrary choice of a point of view, such as looking at the scene from below or from a point higher up than the spot from which one would normally expect to view it. Lastly, the Japanese helped him to find in form a symbol of the spiritual.

These various strands of motive he wove into the warp of his own creation, and the result was a fabric which had the faded splendour of old Gobelin tapestry.

But, after all, it is the character of the warp, the personal expression of himself, that is the element of salient interest in his art. He was *par excellence* a " painter "; one, that is to say, who did not view nature as a collection of forms to be delineated by lines and filled in afterwards with colour, but as an accord of coloured masses. By means of these coloured masses he rendered the *effect* of form. He mocked at the uncompromising reproduction of the model, as he did at the idea that nature is always beautiful.

" Nature indeed," he wrote, " contains the elements in colour and form of all pictures, as the keyboard contains the notes of all music. But the artist is born to pick and choose and group with science these elements, that the result may be beautiful—as the musician gathers his notes and forms chords, until he brings forth from chaos glorious harmonies." Again he wrote: " And when the evening mist clothes the riverside with poetry, as with a veil, and the poor buildings lose themselves in the dim sky, and the tall chimneys become campanili, and the warehouses are palaces in the night, and the whole city hangs in the heavens, and fairyland is before us—then the wayfarer hastens home; the workingman and the cultured one, the wise man and the one of pleasure, cease to understand, as they have ceased to see; and Nature, who for once has sung in tune, sings her exquisite song to the artist alone, her son and her master—her son in that he loves her, her master in that he knows her. To him her secrets are unfolded; to him her lessons have become gradually clear. He looks at her flower, not with the enlarging lens, that he may gather facts for the botanist, but with the light of the one who sees in her choice selection of brilliant tones and delicate tints, suggestion of future harmonies."

In this last sentence he betrays the *ultima ratio* of his artistic purpose, which was to extract from Nature her abstract appeal to the sense of sight, even as the chemist distils from flowers the fragrance that will appeal to the sense of smell, or as a musician from the throbbing of his brain brings forth the abstract harmonies of sound. In the pride of his art he claimed for it an independent value that needed no bolstering up with words. He would, if possible, have made it entirely independent of ideas. For a while he tried the experiment of leaving out forms and relying solely on tones of colour, calling his canvases "nocturnes," "symphonies," or "harmonies," because he was trying by means of colour to emulate the musician's use of sounds. Of course the public did not understand these efforts, and expended much thin witticism over the experiment. For it was merely an experiment; re-establishing the truth, very generally disregarded in those days, that colour, when used harmonically, makes an independent, abstract impression on the imagination; but otherwise unavailing, for the painter cannot get away permanently from what is at once the strength and the disability of his art—the necessity of representing the appearances of objects. This Whistler realised.

He did not ignore form—very far from it; but it was the effect of form, in its relation to the character of the subject and in its relation to considerations of abstract beauty, that alone seemed to him to be worth interpretation. In a material age he made his artistic protest against the accepted axiom that " seeing is believing "; teaching and proving in his works that it is not what the average man sees that counts for much in art, but what, for the most part, he omits to see, since he sees only with the ocular vision and is prone to peer through spectacles.

So, in that masterpiece, *The Portrait of the Artist's Mother,* he did not picture a lady as she would appear to the indifferent gaze of strangers, but as she was known to the heart of her son in the spiritual communion of their mutual love. And the son being a great master, the picture becomes the noblest tribute to motherhood that painting can show, and to everyone who has known the blessing of a good mother the most wonderful interpretation of his own devotion, if he have eyes to see it.

TRAIT OF THE ARTIST'S MOTHER   JAMES A. McNEILL WHISTLER

RIGINALLY exhibited under the title "An Arrangement in Black and Gray;" for the composition, to use Whistler's own phrase, is essentially "an accord of colored masses." The black and gray are relieved by the delicate flesh tints, the white of the cap and kerchief, and the dull green of the curtain. The suggestion of the color-arrangement mingles ty with tenderness, reticence with austerity, solemnity with graciousness.

In the Collection of the Luxembourg, Paris

PORTRAIT OF CARLYLE   JAMES A. McNEILL WHIST

*A*N *arrangement in black and gray.* *The abrupt angularities in the pose of the figure*
characteristic of the impetuous and uncompromising nature of the great preacher-histor
but the fire has died out of him and the pale face with its mane of gray locks shows wea
against the gray of the wall. *A wonderful example of impressionism, lifted to the high plan*
spiritual expression.

In the Collection of the Corporation Art Galleries, Glas

WHISTLER

In *The Portrait of Carlyle* the figure is entirely in black, the pallid face and grey hair silhouetted against a grey wall, the whole enveloped in a dull, dreary atmosphere. It is, indeed, a colour arrangement of slightly different tones of black and grey, forming a sombre harmony that Richard Müther, the German critic-historian, has likened to a funeral march. The prevailing expression is one of weariness of soul and mind. The volcanic fire that used to glow white-hot in this bitter opponent of all world-shams has burned itself to blackness and grey ash. Whether or not this truly represented, at the time the portrait was painted, the personality of Carlyle, work-worn though he was and a chronic sufferer from dyspepsia, may be doubted. The making of a likeness was seldom in Whistler's thoughts; it was the impression that the subject made upon his imagination that he strove to render; and in this case it is a pathetic one, consistent with itself, and most poetically wrought. It reveals, moreover, that aloofness so characteristic of this master's work. The figure dwells apart in an atmosphere of its own, far from the glare and din of the world, wrapt in the calm that follows after passion. In the *Sarasate,* however, another study in black and greys only relieved by the whiteness of the shirt, the figure is represented as emerging from darkness, but only into a half light. The magic of his genius is still suspended, only a suggestion of it being hinted at in the nervous delicacy of the hands.

The value of elusiveness in a work of art was one of the great truths that Whistler's example teaches. It is this quality which gives it pungency of suggestion and enduring interest; just as a woman, to hold the heart of a man, must preserve some savour of inaccessible mystery. Of what is obviously and fully realised, if it yield no further suggestion, human nature soon tires.

The *Nocturne-Bognor* is penetrated with this quality of elusiveness; phantom shapes glimmering in misty, ethereal light, a spirit picture, rendering the impressions which such a scene in nature gently makes upon the imagination. So gently, that, while we are filled with sensations, they are vague, unrealisable; our spirit is allured to infinite longings in the very unattainableness of which there is a poignancy of cleansing sadness. If you have come under the spell of this enchantment in the actual presence of Nature, you recognise it instantly in this picture; if you have not, the picture may lead you to find it.

What the artist has given us is not the facts of nature, but their effect upon the spirit; interpreting the dream or spirit world, of which the actual is the solid basis. " The landscapes of Whistler are places of dreamland," says Müther; " landscapes of the mind, summoned with closed eyes and

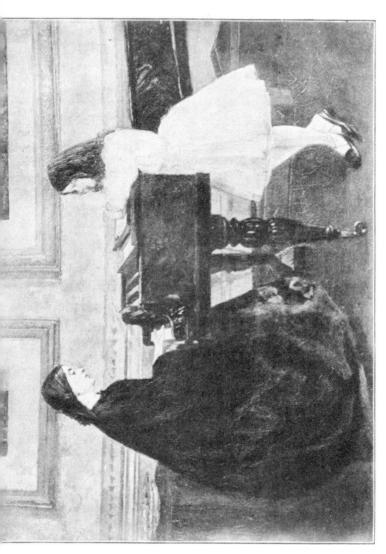

AT THE PIANO   JAMES A. McNEILL WHISTLER

ONE of the artist's earliest examples, painted probably in 1860. An arrangement in black, gray, and white. In its directness of composition and yet subtlety of feeling and expression a prelude to those great portraits of his mother and Carlyle.

PORTRAIT OF
MISS ALEXANDER

JAMES A. McNEILL WHISTLER

*A*N *early work, combining the influence of Velasquez and of the
Japanese.*

set free from everything coarse and material,
breathed upon the picture and encompassed with
mysteries." It was not the forms of nature *per se*
which interested him, but their significance to the
spirit; the suggestion of beauty which they yielded
to the imagination. To quote Müther again:
" Like the Japanese, but with brilliant refinements
such as never occurred even to the greatest painters, this wonderful harmonist has the art of simpli-
fying and of spiritualising, retaining the mere
essence of forms, and of colours; only what is transient, subtle, musical."

If you set that wonderful portrait, *The White
Girl,* or, as Whistler called it to distinguish it from
another corresponding motive, *Symphony in White,
No. 1,* before a young girl the fragrance of
whose nature is still fresh, who still has the sanc-
tity of maidenhood in her soul, undesecrated by
precocious contact with the world, it will be strange
if she does not find in the picture an echo of her own
heart and thinkings. Nor can anyone to whom the
exquisitely delicate flower of maidenhood is precious fail to discover therein an interpretation of
his own feelings.

Again, in *The Little Lady Sophie of Soho,* what
tenderness of spiritual insight! This child of un-
toward chances, dwelling in an unsavoury district
of a great city, carrying her girlhood in and out of
studios! The great master has dipped beneath ex-

ternals; has looked beyond what she was to what she might have been, to what indeed she may, in a measure, still have been, and spied a flicker of pure flame within her tarnished soul. There is a pitiful tenderness in the rendering of the girl's face, as it peers at us from its frame of elf-locks, out of the mystery of the dim, dark background. It is treated also with a touch of irony, with that mingling of pity and mockery with which the gods, themselves not free from Fate, are fabled to have watched the lives of fate-distraught mortals; and withal it is full of mystery, pregnant with the cry of why such things must be and the wonder as to whither they tend.

Nor in Whistler's paintings, despite the mystery and spirituality, and notwithstanding the elusiveness of the brushwork, is there any lack of virility. Dignity of line and mass and tone proclaims the master; and the actual laying-on of the pigment something greater than the skilful audacity of a magician of the brush. We do not see the stroke of hand which dazzles and bewilders. It is rather as if the presence on the canvas had been invoked by a supreme effort of will, so that, by the side of one of his portraits, the work of the brilliant brush-technist is apt to seem commonplace. Perhaps one reason is that such legerdemain is for the most part associated with a keen fondness for the actual, the artist being enamoured of externals, the coquetries of costume, the intrinsic desirableness of fine fabrics. So that it may be due to inferiority of motive, rather than to the difference of technique, that he seems to suffer by comparison.

Not that Whistler ignored the fascination of textures and fabrics. No artist could. But it was not their mere appearance of valuableness per yard with which he concerned himself, but their sentiment of æsthetic suggestion. I recall, for example, the curtains in *The Music Room,* creamy white, with sprigs of flowers. What a sense of freshness and purity they give to the room! And the costume in which he represents some *grande dame* will offer little comfort to a milliner, nor much to the lady, if it were her gown on which she depended to be attractive. Whistler, indeed, made the dignity of the woman superior to and independent of the costume.

Besides enforcing the need of selection in art and that the spiritual and æsthetic significance of things is more worthy of the artist's study than the mere appearances, Whistler waged war against the preference of the Philistine for what he calls a "finished picture." He had a fine scorn for the tailor-kind of mind which yearns to see each button, tag, and furbelow reproduced precisely, as well as for that furnishing and upholstering propensity which desires a picture to be as crowded with details as the average parlour, and every detail highly polished. With him a picture was finished when he had succeeded, as far as might be, in reproducing the impression that he had in mind, and in disguising the means by which he had created it.

It was in his etchings that he reached the maximum of expression by the smallest expenditure of means; for the medium admits a greater possibility of omission and suggestion. In the hands of a master, that is to say, for the ordinary etcher will load his plate with lines. But the mental superiority of Whistler, as an artist, was in no way more demonstrated than in his power of forming a conception of the scene and then in a few flexible, pregnant lines, executed with apparent ease, giving its character and expressiveness.

It has been remarked that he created no school. It was neither possible nor necessary. The finest quality of his art was personal to himself, an emanation of genius, not transferable; the principles that he adopted were diversely used by others; his tenets too simple and universal to found or need a school for their propagation. He did better than attract a few followers and imitators; he influenced the whole world of art. Consciously or unconsciously, his presence is felt in countless studios; his genius permeates modern artistic thought.

It may be equally an inspiration to ourselves. We are overmuch drilled from childhood to catch

at the form and miss the substance; to substitute
words and phraseologies for thinking and ideas;
to estimate life by material standards and to
sharpen our wits at the expense of what is spiritual; to have little reverence or habit of quiet
thoughtfulness, and too soon to lose the fragrance
of our natures in the withering heat of worldliness.
With Whistler, we may do well to enter at times
into the tranquil half-light of the soul, and ponder
upon the things of the Spirit.

CHAPTER XIV

IN 1817 Congress gave Trumbull a commission for four paintings to adorn the Capitol. The intention of Congress in appropriating $32,000 for this work was to commemorate certain important events in the history of the new Republic, and the artist conceived and treated his subjects in the manner of historical pictures. It was fidelity to the incident rather than any ideas of making his paintings decorative, that influenced him. Though intended for wall spaces, they were not in the true sense mural paintings. Why they were not, may perhaps be understood by a comparison of the first commission in this country, given and accepted as advisedly a work of mural decoration. The date was 1876; the building, Trinity Church, Boston, and the immediate principals in the transaction were H. H. Richardson, the architect, and the painter, John La Farge.

Two points are of importance: first, that it was the architect then, engaged in building the church, who realised that its interior effect would be improved by a scheme of painted decoration; secondly, that although the scheme might involve the representation of certain persons or incidents of the Bible, its primary and final purpose was to be complementary to the architecture. To these points another may be added, not perhaps essential, but certainly conducive to a successful result, that the whole scheme of interior colouring, its smallest details as well as the important figure compositions, was entrusted to one man.

Here we get an inkling of what mural painting really is. It is not the affixing of a picture to the walls, as we hang a picture on the wall of a living-room to embellish it, or for the separate interest and value of the picture. It becomes an integral part of an architectural unit. Trinity Church, for example, is in design an adaptation of the Romanesque style which in addition to vaulted roofs has an excess of wall over window space. These surfaces in the mediæval churches were frequently overlaid with marble veneer and mosaic. Richardson determined to substitute a painted decoration, that should at once relieve the barrenness of the interior and unite all its parts into an *ensemble* of rich harmoniousness. It is indeed as a whole that the interior affects us. Within, as outside, the culmination of the design is the centre tower, crowned with a low spire. To it converge the short nave and side aisles, the transepts and apse-ended chancel. The plan, in fact, is more apparent inside than without, and while the stained-glass windows make intervals of brilliant splendour, the general effect is one of subdued dignity of tone, out of the mystery of which, if you are minded to look for them, the details of the decoration may be discerned. But as I have said, the first and chief impression is of an organic unity of colour growing out of the architecture, the very dimness of the effect seeming characteristic of this particular architectural style, which in its origin belonged to the South and was designed to exclude rather than to admit the light.

Moreover, the Romanesque style of Southern France, which was the particular brand of the Romanesque that Richardson had adopted, had been itself an adaptation by comparatively unskilled Western builders of various influences, only partly digested—the Byzantine, the Roman, and the Greek. There was a peculiar fitness, that probably presented itself to Richardson's mind and was certainly present in La Farge's, in choosing this character of construction for the first attempt in the New Western World to combine the labours of the architect and decorator in some scheme that might emulate the traditions of the past. In La Farge's own words: "It would permit, as long ago it has permitted, a wide range of skill in artistic training; the rough bungling of the native and the ill-digested culture of the foreigner. I could think myself back to a time when I might have employed some cheap Byzantine of set habits, some ill-equipped Barbarian, some Roman, dwelling near by for a time—perhaps even some artist, keeping alive both the tradition and culture of Greece." And it was under similar conditions of limited experience on the part of the artist, of habits comfirmed in a wrong direction on the part of available workmen, of low trade ideals and indifferent materials, that the beginnings of a new movement in America were inaugurated. For, although La Farge had been giving some attention to decorative problems, especially to those of colour, his opportunities of practical experience had been small indeed as compared with the magnitude of this one. He was at a moment's notice launched into what was, under the circumstances, a huge experiment; the subordinates on whom he had to rely were inexperienced, and, as a climax to these limitations, he was compelled to work amid the discomfort and confusion of a windowless, unfinished building, under the severe strain of having to conceive, elaborate, and conclude this big scheme in a short space of time.

This tendency to " rush " the artist, which is not infrequently characteristic of decorative commissions in our country, was illustrated again two years later in the case of W. M. Hunt. He was requested to paint two decorations of considerable size for the Capitol at Albany, the time allotted him for their inception and completion being thirteen weeks! He produced the *Flight of Night* and *The Discoverer,* but at what cost! The mental and physical strain proved too much for him; the work completed, he noticeably declined, and died the following year. The work, too, has perished, for the plaster had not been allowed to dry out; it was still " green," and the paintings have since decayed and crumbled away.

La Farge, having completed the work in Trinity Church, was almost immediately commissioned to decorate the apse of St. Thomas' in New York. Here he worked in collaboration not only with the architect, but with the sculptor, thus for the first time in this country asserting practically the interdependence and kinship of these three arts of construction and decoration. The reredos was modelled by Saint Gaudens, and on each side of it the painter installed a scene from the Resurrection, enshrining all three in a scheme of colour and of moulded and carved work, designed and partly executed by himself, though the design in its entirety was never completed. Nevertheless, as it stood, it was the most completely noble of La Farge's schemes of decoration, and its destruction in 1904 by fire was a national calamity. For there is lost to us, not only a great artistic achievement, but one that in the course of years would have had increasing historic interest as a landmark in the progress

THE ASCENSION   JOHN LA FARGE

A Mural Painting in the Church of the Ascension, New York

CONSIDERED by many the noblest example of mural decoration in the country. The student of painting will note with interest how the composition is founded, with considerable variation, on that of Raphael's Disputá.

THE FEET WASHERS

W. B. VAN INGEN

One of a Series of Mural Decorations in the Pennsylvania Capitol

*T*HE artist's intention was twofold: to fill fourteen spaces with decorations and also to commemorate something characteristic of the State. He chose, as his theme, the various religious groups, represented among the early settlers. Many of
these have survived to the present time, and this ceremony of feet washing is still practised

of American art. It might also eventually have had an influence in checking what I venture to call the "department store tendencies" that characterise so largely the present manifestations of our decorative movement.

For, as we pursue the study of the latter, we shall find that instead of the mind of a master-decorator, such as La Farge is by instinct and training, being not only permitted but encouraged to control the whole scheme of internal embellishment, circumstances bring it about that the architects, whose talent and *metier* are primarily of the constructive order, have become also the decorative designers of the interiors, deputing the execution of their schemes to a variety of subordinates. It is a highly organised system, capable of turning out an immense quantity of work, creditable in quality, but of little personal distinction. Yet, if we study the matter, we shall find that the system has grown inevitably out of existing conditions.

Little more than a quarter of a century ago the ground in our development now occupied by architecture and decoration was a prairie wilderness, spotted here and there with beautiful survivals of a past taste, such as the examples of Colonial mansions and churches, and of later public edifices, like the White House and the Capitol. For the rest it was a waste upon which modern disfigurements had encroached. Then two men appeared as pioneers: H. H. Richardson,* already mentioned, and Richard Morris Hunt; both architects who, like some of our painters, had studied in Paris at the famous *École des Beaux Arts.*

ж ж ж ж ж ж ж ж ж ж ж

The movement they inaugurated was, from its inception, one of architecture, Hunt representing the constructive, logical phase of the art, Richardson its more notably æsthetic possibilities. The latter, as we have seen, hastened to secure the co-operation of La Farge. But decorators such as he are not to be found by the wayside. There was no other painter in the country to whom an architect could safely have entrusted an important scheme of decoration in its entirety. Moreover, La Farge has always been too much of an investigator and experimentor to adapt himself to the " driving hurry " of American methods, and, furthermore, he very soon turned aside into a special department of decoration, that of decorated windows. How in this direction he proved himself to be an original genius, substituting for the usual stained glass the use of opalescent glass, thereby inventing a new kind of window, distinguished by extreme richness and subtlety of colour, has already occupied our

* Is it not rather characteristic of American attitude toward artistic genius that the " Universal Cyclopædia," published in New York, 1901, a *newly revised* and *enlarged* edition, omits the name of this architect?

notice in a previous chapter. It interfered with his continuing the rôle in which he had already qualified, as a painter who could undertake and carry through an *ensemble* of mural decoration. There was still another reason. When he was in the prime of his vigour, the period of opportunity in the shape of great public buildings had scarcely begun, and, by the time that it was fairly afoot, the architects were from the circumstances of the case, not only the initiators, but the controllers of the movement.

The event from which this movement has gone on advancing with steadily increasing bulk and momentum was the World's Fair at Chicago. Previously to this there had been divers instances of mural decoration in the private houses of the rich, and at least one public building, the new Hotel Ponce de Leon at St. Augustine, had been elaborately decorated, while the Trustees of the Boston Public Library had already given commissions for mural paintings to the French artist, Puvis de Chavannes, and to Sargent and Abbey. But the effect of this and other sporadic efforts was multiplied *ad infinitum* by the consolidated grandeur of the " White City." It was an object lesson, the virtue of which, though it has been frequently described, may well be continually enforced.

It taught, in the first place, the desirableness, even

the commercial value, of beauty. The shrewd, large-minded citizens of a city that is essentially the product and assertion of commerce discovered that they could give expression to their own local pride and attract business from outside, not only by following the old crude idea of attempting " the biggest show on earth," but by trying to make it the most beautiful. They succeeded; for, while millions of tired bodies testified to the former motive, as many hearts were gladdened and as many imaginations stimulated by the presentation of the latter.

In the second place, it exhibited the mutual inter-dependence of the arts of construction and design; the value of combination. Buildings which might have been constructed solely with a view to sepa-rate utility were treated also as monuments of architectural design, enriched by sculpture and painting, borrowing extra dignity from one an-other, and placed in a worthy setting by the co-operation of the landscape designer. In a word, the natural beauties of the spot had been utilised and increased; formal features, such as terraces, fountains, and bridges, had been added, and the cul-minating motive had been the creation of a series of magnificent or alluring *ensembles*. The result was a triumph, alike for the architects and land-scape designers, for the various painters and sculp-tors who co-operated in the details of the plan, and for the citizens of Chicago who permitted its inception and provided for its completion.

Scarcely more than a decade has elapsed since the passing of that temporarily realised dream of artistic beauty, yet already in thousands of instances throughout the country its influence has borne fruit. It is true that its biggest lesson has scarcely yet been recognised. Municipalities either are not yet aroused to the value of a combination of efforts into an *ensemble,* or have not had the courage or opportunity to realise it. There have been certain notable exceptions, as in the laying out of the water fronts in Chicago, Philadelphia, and New York, and in attention given to the regulation of the sky-line of buildings, as in Boston. Yet, notwithstanding these indications of a civic sense of pride and responsibility, little or nothing has been done toward an organic alleviation of the dire monotony of our gridiron street-plans, or toward a systematic treatment of such open spaces as they niggardly present. In failing to realise the value of *ensembles,* whether regarded as conveniences or embellishments, we are still far behind the modern activities of the Old World cities. On the other hand, in respect of the separate building, asserting itself as an independent unit, the activities in this country during the past ten years have been phenomenal.

It would be very interesting, if space permitted,

to sketch the story of what our architects have accomplished; how in Federal and State buildings, in City Halls and libraries, in churches, hotels, office and trade buildings, and in city and country residences, the motives of utility and beauty have jointly inspired the design; how the skill of the architects, trained in the knowledge of the Old World, has displayed itself both in adapting the various styles and principles to the American requirement, and in inventing new methods of construction to comply with the special conditions that exist here. If adequately told, the story would have the interest and surprise of a romance. But for our present purpose we can only note that the trend of the movement has been toward a superior logic and dignity in the character of the whole building, and toward a more sumptuous and, at the same time, more tactful use of embellishments in the details; and that in these latter the architects have more and more enlisted the co-operation of the painters.

During the past ten years the practice of mural painting in America has spread rapidly. At first it found the majority of the painters unprepared for the particular requirements of this kind of painting. They had been trained in the principles of the easel-picture, within the frame of which the painter may adopt any method of treatment that he chooses, intent solely upon making his picture; and one, not necessarily decorative. But mural

BURNING OF THE PEGGY STEWART AT ANNAPOLIS IN 1774

A Mural Decoration in the Federal Court House, Baltimore

C. Y. TURNER

THIS is one of the best examples in the country of an historical incident adapted to the purpose of a mural decoration.

Copyright, 1907, by Curtis Bell

PITTSBURGH PERSONIFIED   JOHN W. ALEXANDER

Part of the Mural Decoration in the Carnegie Institute

THIS panel is a part of an elaborate scheme of decoration. The spirit of the City of Steel Foundries is represented as a warrior in mediæval armor, but the figure which crowns him, those which announce his triumph, and the others, flying in from the four corners of the earth with rich gifts, are lovely types of modern girlhood.

painting does not fulfil the purposes of its existence unless it be decorative and at the same time
subsidiary to the general scheme of its surroundings, in which it should occupy the position not of
a separate unit but of an integral factor. The
character of its subject will partake of that of the
building: solemn, serious, elegant, or sportive, according to the spirit in which the architecture, following the purpose of the building, has been
planned. The character of its composition will be
determined by the shape and position of the space
that it is intended to adorn; the choice of its colour
regulated to the prevailing colour scheme of the
interior. In a word, the mural painting, besides
being decorative, should be functional.

The meaning of this may be readily grasped if
one remembers that the various parts of the architectural structure are not used arbitrarily, but that
each has its separate function to perform in the
complex arrangement of supports and resistances
that make up the whole system. For example, in
the Rotunda of the Library of Congress the eight
ribs of the dome sweep upward until they termi-
nate in the broad, smooth surface of the " collar,"
whose function is to clamp them all together and
at the same time to form a support for the super-
incumbent cupola. Recognising this, the decorator
of the " collar," Edwin H. Blashfield, devised a
composition which should form a compact and

continuous circle of decoration and simultaneously, by the introduction of eight principal figures, recall the eight ribs which the circle terminates. On the other hand, in the Delivery Room of the Boston Public Library, Edwin A. Abbey, commissioned to decorate the frieze and choosing for the subject the *Quest of the Holy Grail,* has ignored the function of a frieze, which is to counteract the various interruptions down below, of windows, doors, and fireplaces, by an effect above of continuity. Whereas he might have treated the space as a continuous whole, by dividing it into a series of panels that should succeed one another in a rhythmic sequence, he has chopped it up into a variety of different measurements.

The more strictly functional treatment of a frieze may be studied in the same building, in the fine example of John S. Sargent's *Prophets.* In them there is a collective effect of continuity, a rhythmic sequence of handsome masses and striking lines. Moreover, the choice of the subject is readily comprehensible, which is a considerable virtue, since it offers no interference with one's immediate appreciation of the painting as a decoration. The panels above them, however, in the lunette and soffit of the arch, are not so simple. The pattern of their composition presents an exuberance of interwoven forms. It may be quite appropriate to the idea of turmoil involved in the subject of Polythe-

THE TRIUMPH OF MINNESOTA

Copyright, 1894, by E. H. Blashfield

A Mural Decoration in the Capitol of Minnesota

*A*N *allegory of Minnesota, represented as the "Granary of the World." While the ox-cart typifies the earlier conditions of the State, the later development of her resources is suggested by the modern reaper; nor is her share in the battles of the Union overlooked. The painting illustrates the fragrant beauty which the artist gives to his ideals of American womanhood and childhood, and also the admirable skill with which he combines allegorical figures with types of persons drawn from actual life. Here as elsewhere his work represents the academic and scholarly point of view, adjusted to the realities of our modern conditions.*

EDWIN H. BLASHFELD

Copyright, 1903, by the Trustees of the Boston Public Library.   From a Copley Print, Copyright, 1903, by Curtis and Cameron

THE DOGMA OF REDEMPTION

JOHN S. SARGENT

A Mural Decoration in the Boston Public Library

A REMARKABLE *example of modern religious symbolism, in its feeling and method,
and conventionalized figures recalls the Byzantine tradition; the central composition
of painting uniting the present and the past.   The upper portion in its flat tone
imitates, though in much higher relief, the applied raised ornament of the Renaissance, while
the lower figures, holding the symbols of the Passion, are rendered in the modern technique.
The inscription, copied from a mediaeval original, may be translated so as to reproduce the
curious play upon words: "Made man, though myself the maker of man and Redeemer,
what I have made, I redeem in my body their bodies and souls, being God."*

ism and Apostasy from the Faith in the One God that they are intended to represent, but it is confusing to the eye. Moreover, the forms are associated with a great deal of abstruse symbolism, unintelligible to most people, so that all but a few visitors miss the decorative intention of the paintings and devote the greater portion of their study to the printed key.

Sargent himself would seem to have realised that he has here overdone the literary allusiveness of his subject, for in his latest work, *The Dogma of Redemption,* the symbolism is comparatively simple, and he has reverted also to simplicity of forms, partly basing his composition upon the examples of the Byzantine decorators, in many respects the finest in the Old World.

For their forms were very simple, and simply handled; not modelled into relief, but kept as a pattern of masses, of coloured masses harmonised into a rich tone, so that the whole painting was very flat. It clung to the wall, proclaimed the fact of the wall beneath, and was in a very strict sense mural.

A consciousness of the value of such principles of painting for the purpose of mural decoration is one of the distinguished characteristics of the panels by Puvis de Chavannes in the Boston Library. In the Library of Congress it has also prompted the method of Kenyon Cox. But the

latter, while an excellent draughtsman, is no colourist. His panels of the *Arts* and *Sciences,* with
their pale tinting not drawn into harmonic relation, give the impression of a good design not yet
completed.

The design itself is a formal arrangement of
female figures, each bearing an emblem of the
particular art or science which it is intended to
symbolise. Were the colour as effective as the
drawing, the result would be exceedingly decorative; though, in other respects, as impoverished as
the present tinting. For the conception displays
no imagination and offers little interest to the visi-
tor. In this threadbare affectation of classicalism
there is evidence neither of American inspiration
nor of the painter himself having any participation
in the fulness of our modern life. His aim has
been solely decorative.

No doubt the painter himself would admit it,
and very likely would defend the position that the
whole end of decoration is to be decorative. That,
however, was not the characteristic of the great
days of Mural Decoration. Many of the finest
examples were more or less frankly illustrations, as
well as decorations, intended to bring home the
truths and doctrines of Christianity to the masses;
while those of a more purely decorative character
were of a kind not only to appeal to the taste of
cultivated people, but to stimulate their imag-

ination and their personal and local pride. In either case the decoration was significant of the habit of mind and feeling of its era. So far, however, in American Mural Painting there has been little indication even of the modern spirit, much less of the particular genius of America. It is still an exotic, imperfectly acclimatised, and not yet adapted to our soil.

Nevertheless, there have been numerous attempts to make the subject interpret our special conditions. C. Y. Turner, for example, in the Manhattan Hotel, New York, has represented the City as a queenly maiden surrounded by other maidens, typifying the arts and sciences; while in attendance are realistic figures of Indians, Colonials, and portrait-groups of scientists and other distinguished persons. A similar mingling of allegory and fact appears in Albert Herter's panels of *Agriculture* and *Commerce* in a New York bank; and in panels by Edwin H. Blashfield: at Baltimore of *Washington Relinquishing Office;* at the Capitol of St. Paul, commemorating the agricultural triumphs of the West, and at Pittsburg, celebrating the steel industries. This last subject has been treated anew, and again with a mingling of allegorical figures and of more or less realistic accessories, in the recent paintings, executed by John W. Alexander, for the Carnegie Institute.

On the other hand, panels illustrating actual

incidents and treated with regard for historical accuracy have been painted for the Boston State House by Robert Reid and Edward Simmons, while a corresponding motive influenced the treatment of F. D. Millet's *Treaty of the Traverse des Sioux,* for the Capitol of St. Paul, and C. Y. Turner's *Opening of the Erie Canal,* for the De Witt Clinton High School, New York.

So far, therefore, as the character of the subject is concerned, we find our painters following the example of the old Italians. Sometimes they treat an incident with the fidelity to facts of an illustration; sometimes they unite allegorical and realistic elements. Evidently, then, neither of these methods is absolutely right or absolutely wrong. The character of the subject, in fact, is only a part of the matter. Of even more importance is the manner in which the subject is represented. In the first place, whether the motive is allegorical or realistic, the treatment must be decorative: the painting must be a pattern of colour, adorning the space and harmonising with the form and spirit of the surrounding architecture. But is this all that is desirable?

Are we to be satisfied merely with an agreeable or sumptuous impression? Shall we not look to receive some stir to our imagination, some fresh insight into or encouragement of the principles we believe in, some enlargement of our mental and

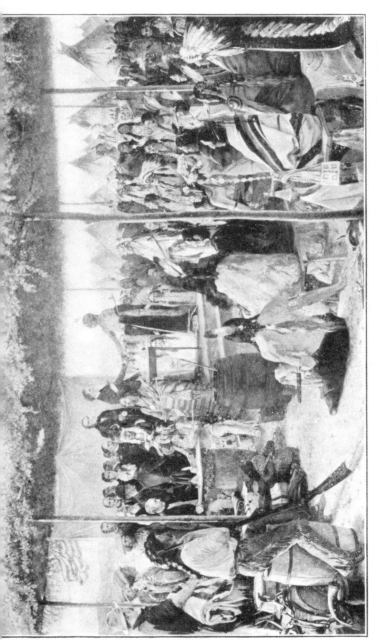

THE TREATY OF THE TRAVERSE DES SIOUX

FRANK D. MILLET

A Mural Decoration in the Capitol of Minnesota

A NOTHER example of the twofold motive: to record an historic incident and at the same time decorate a space.

ROME

A Mural Decoration in the Walker Art Gallery, Bowdoin College

ELIHU VEDDER

R ECOGNIZING Rome as the main source of modern culture, the artist has expressed the latter under personifications of the physical, intellectual, spiritual, and emotional qualities. Wisdom, typified by a globe, a plan, and an anatomical figure; Thought prompted by Spirit; Nature, the alpha of whose purpose is life that has its roots in death, her omega the fruit of fulfilment; the Arts of

spiritual horizon? It is futile to say that the times are changed; that now, since the majority of people can read, pictures have ceased to be a necessary or suitable way of reaching the imagination and conscience. It is, on the contrary, extraordinary how little essential conditions are changed. Our present age, it is true, is a reading one, of an insatiable hunger for reading; yet was there ever a time when there was so much illustration? Those whose business it is to keep a touch upon the public pulse and diagnose the symptoms of its taste, assert that it craves illustrations and must have them. Certainly it gets them, and one hears no protest.

No, the fault is not with the public, but with the painters themselves. They are, for the most part, out of touch with the vital forces at work in the community, nor possessed of that vigour and originality which characterises the leaders in other departments of life. Too few of them can strike out a truth on the anvil of facts, as Vedder has done in his decorations at Washington, particularly in the one that, with a mingling of allegory and realism, embodies the idea of *Corrupt Government*. The sleek respectability of the pious-faced briber, the slatternly wantonness of the women whom he prostitutes, the mute protest of the smokeless chimney-stack, the piteous appeal of the destitute, haggard child—at a glance is revealed the hideous loathsomeness of the whole dirty business. It is the work of a man who has a mind to comprehend the fact, and an imagination that can invest it with a new force of meaning, and who, moreover, is a born decorator.

These are unusual qualities, especially in combination, and it is the lack of them that is most conspicuous in American Mural decoration. Nowhere do conditions, present and past, offer more abundant suggestions to the imagination, and nowhere are mural painters receiving so much encouragement of opportunity. Yet, with slight exceptions, they have not yet risen to the occasion. If we seek further reasons, we may find them, first of all, in the fact that most of them are not decorators. The latter are born, not made; the gift is primarily one of exuberant inventiveness. Now, American Art, in all its branches, is so far singularly barren of this quality. Its present phase involves a more or less tactful application of eclecticism. Again, the painters have been trained in a good school; but one which did not include any separate consideration of mural decoration; nor in this direction is any real provision being made even now for younger students, notwithstanding that this offers them a very large field and a rich one. Moreover, our older men have not recovered from the paralysing effects of the " art for art's sake " formula. Taught in their youth to be afraid of an idea, their ability to conceive or express one has been stunted.

NOTES ON MURAL PAINTING

They have nothing of the dare-devil in their conception. And there is another reason. The best development in our painting has been along the lines of the small canvas, intimately treated. The excessive influence of the Barbizon pictures, the preciosity that Whistler's example fostered, and the mild domesticity of American fiction, only now just yielding place to the romantic imagining of the red-blooded writers, have helped to confine our painting within very sincere but very limited methods of expression.

As compared with this propriety, which is the distinguishing feature of American art, both literary and pictorial, the country itself presents a crudity of contrasts. A virility, not without its flavour of brutality, characterises the active life of the community, while its leisure is gilded and brocaded with a luxuriousness that recalls the splendour of Monarchical France or of Imperial Rome. But deep beneath the myriad lights and shadows of the surface is an earnestness of pride in the past and present of the race, and of confidence in the future, that in its reasonableness is without a parallel in history.

Some day, upon the walls of the buildings that embody this grandeur, we may hope that there will be mural decorations which in magnitude of conception and splendour of decorative treatment will adequately represent the theme.

CHAPTER XV

HAVING traced the various influences which have affected the development of American painting during the past fifty years, we may reasonably attempt a summary of the results. Since our art has aligned itself with that of other countries, how does it stand in comparison with theirs?

Frequently one hears the question asked in a somewhat different form. Is there yet a distinctly American school of painting; and, if so, how does it compare with other schools? But, strictly speaking, there are no longer distinct schools anywhere, since the reasons which accounted for their existence in the past no longer exist to-day. As we have seen in the previous pages, the whole trend of modern art has been toward a free-trade in motives and methods, the clearing-house of which for all the world has been Paris. Yet, while the age of close communities of artists, following some distinct tradition or influenced by some one leader, and producing work which bears the stamp of a common sentiment and manner of expression, is past, it is unquestionably true that the local con-

[332]

ON THE CANAL

By Courtesy of N. E. Montross

W. L. LATHROP

THIS artist is pre-eminently an interpreter of nature in her gentlest and least obtrusive moods, represented generally by subjects to which it is only sympathetic observation and delicate rendering of tonality that lend interest.

PITTSBURGH

COLIN CAMPBELL COOPER

*T*HE *local characteristics of Pittsburgh, and particularly its wonderful atmospheric conditions, interest the numerous artists who visit the city. But none have been able to reproduce them so truthfully or in a way so finely pictorial as*

ditions of race temperament and natural environment do still stamp with a certain general distinction the work of each country. It is not difficult, for example, in the presence of a given picture, to be secure in the conclusion that it is Dutch or German, French or English. Is there, then, any corresponding mark by which we could feel equally sure that such and such a picture was by an American painter? I believe there is; but let us try to make this question answer itself.

The Dutch picture is readily identified; firstly, because the subject in almost every case is drawn from the natural and human life of Holland, the externals of which are so distinctly characteristic; and, secondly, because the spirit as well as the external is reproduced. The country, in fact, is small enough to have a spirit that is recognisable as characteristic. Its low-lying land and immense skies, the richness of vegetation due to the prevalence of moisture, both in rain-laden clouds overhead and in the canals and ditches that interthread the soil, the fitfulness of sunshine, now glinting crisply between the showers or lambent over the polders, now chastened by the silky atmosphere or shrouded in vapour till its light and warmth are chilled to greyness—all these and many other conditions, so frequent and expressive, give a distinction to Holland and form the most affectionate study of her artists. They are all in love with the same mistress, and she shows to each the same changes of moods, so that their various renderings of her spirit bear a likeness to one another.

Recognising this, we see at once that there can scarcely be a similar unity of feeling in the work of American artists. Even if the devotion to the pictorial aspects of their own country were as single-hearted, the country itself presents no such compact synthesis of suggestion. Both in topographical features and in the still more significant matter of atmospheric conditions, wherein reside the moods and changes, the actual expression and spirit of the scene, the country offers a wide range of differences. The intelligent student of pictures, especially if he is also, as he should be, a student of nature, can recognise at once this scene drawn from California, that from the Middle West, another from Pennsylvania, and still another from the East. These are broad distinctions; nor are closer ones less recognisable. We use the general term New England, but the landscapes from each State in the group, both in form and feeling, differ from those of the others. When we realise this, and the further fact that it is in the subtle differentiation of these variations of natural and spiritual manifestations that the best art of to-day is displayed, we are admitting the impossibility of there being such family resemblance among American pictures as among the Dutch.

SOLITUDE

CHARLES MELVILLE DEWEY

I MAGINE the foliage of a juicy grayish green, the sky a greenish gray, and you begin to realize the feeling of the picture. It is removed from the warmth of sunlight, withdrawn into a "solitude" of feeling.

In the Collection of John Gellatly, Esq.

THE CLOUD   ALBERT L. GR

*A*N *Arizona landscape by one of the ablest of our younger painters. His work is distinguished by technical skill with which he suggests the structure as well as the forms of nature, and by expressional quality.*

SUMMARY OF RESULTS

Then, again, there is the general resemblance that may characterise the work of painters of one country through idiosyncrasy of racial temperament. We recognise, for example, in the artists grouped about Munich, a prevalence of exuberant and original imagination, and a direct and often somewhat exaggerated mode of expression; traits of the Teutonic temperament, sufficiently prevalent to make it almost possible to speak of a Munich school. But you will find no counterpart of this among American painters. If anything they are rather distinguished for the opposite: a certain kind of cosmopolitanism of feeling, and an independence of one another in their methods.

On the other hand, although it might be impossible to discover any positive indications of uniformity, certain negative resemblances are notable. It did not escape the notice of careful observers at the Paris Exposition of 1900, when there was ample opportunity of comparing the art of different countries, that that of the United States made a very separate impression. Trying to analyse it, one found one's self recurring to phrases: capability, moderation, sanity, and perhaps a lack of individualism. There was a general high standard of craftsmanship, the equivalent of which was to be found perhaps only in the French and Dutch exhibits. But, unlike the French, our artists seldom, if ever, seemed to use their technical skill with ostentation, either to display mere prowess with the brush or to attract attention by the meretricious device of a startling subject; while, on the other hand, unlike the Dutch, they failed, as a group, to suggest a marked individuality. I say as a group; for, of course, there were particular examples of notable individuality. But the general impression of the *ensemble* was of a moderation, grateful in comparison with the ostentation and vagaries that abounded elsewhere, but in itself open to the suggestion of being too negative a virtue, a little fibreless and lacking in marrow. To be candid, a similar lack of positive moderation may be charged against our annual exhibitions of native work. For there is all the difference in the world between a strong man, adjusting his output of strength to the work in hand, while holding a portion in reserve, and another whose moderation seems to be the result of not having an abundance of either force or conviction.

One may find a counterpart of this in American fiction. Publishers are fond of preaching moderation. Both in illustration and in writing they discourage much that is original, vital, and born of convictions, fearing that it may shock the sensibilities of their public. Since the latter is overwhelmingly composed of young girls, they may exhibit an appropriate canniness, but the result upon a great deal of our literature is to confuse purity

Copyright, 1907, N. E. Montross

AY NIGHT   WILLARD L. METCALF

*T*HIS *artist was one of the group of men who first brought from Paris the practice of
the* plein air *motive.* .*The study of light in its effects upon open-air nature has been
his constant theme. The present example is one of much reverence and spiritual-
y of feeling.*

In the Collection of the Corcoran Gallery of Art

THE ROAD TO THE OLD FARM   J. FRANCIS MURPHY

*I*MPELLED *perhaps by popular demand for his "characteristic" work, this artist
  has confined his observation to a limited phase of nature. The present example, with
  its stretch of meadow, sprinkling of delicate tree forms, and distant hillside, enveloped
in a smoky haze of atmosphere, well represents him. Within this restricted range of
expression he is a master.*

with prudishness and sincerity with dilettanteism
—to crush conviction on the part alike of author
and of reader. The actual plague spot of this
disease centres around the relation of the sexes in
literature and the use of the nude in art, but its
morbid effects spread through the whole body of
fiction and painting, inducing a flacid condition of
self-consciousness and insincerity. It has taken
such grip of artists and public that to a considerable extent moderation has been supplanted by
repression, and tamely to hold back is esteemed
worthier than to put forth with a reserve of power.

The effect of this condition which has become
fluent in the public conscience is to be discovered
in our painting. For its prevalence one can
scarcely blame the painters. They represent a
comparatively small number of men and women,
in the midst of a community impregnated with
this insincerity. With a few exceptions they are
unable to resist the effect of what is in the atmosphere around them; and the less so because, as
illustrators, a majority of the figure-painters, at
any rate, have become directly infected with the
prevailing pseudo-ethics of the publishers. The
necessity of prettiness, of not giving offence to
"the most fastidious," and of exploiting the obvious, has been urged upon them, until it is small
wonder that a great deal of American painting is
characterised, if I may be allowed the expression,

by irreproachable table-manners rather than by salient self-expression; by a desire to be amiable rather than convincing. The portrait-painter, for example, if he would make a living, is tempted by the vogue of the pretty face in periodicals to sacrifice truth of art and of human character to the glib exploitation of prettiness of face and form and flashiness of costume. The figure-painter will meet his readiest reward if he confine himself to subjects of trite propriety, represented with insistent regard for the obvious; while even the painter of landscape is lured into the pleasant moods of innocuous sentimentality. The taste of our time, in fact, runs to superficial sentimentality, and consciously or unconsciously the painter is apt to respond to it.

Among those who have maintained a vigorously independent course and whose pictures, whenever they appear in exhibitions, create a pronounced interest, none is more conspicuous than Gari Melchers. To a French cleverness of brushwork he has added from his frequent sojourning in Holland, a conscientiousness truly Dutch. Yet, although he has spent many years in depicting subjects of the Dutch peasantry, he has, unlike many others who have been similarly drawn to Holland, avoided all imitation of the modern Dutch technique. His own, indeed, has more kinship with that of the old Flemish painters in its enforcement

EARLY SPRING

LEONARD OCHTMAN

A MONG the artists of this country who have taken the lead in studying nature in the light of the open air, Ochtman has won a foremost position. He is keenly sensitive to the quiet moods of nature and to the manifestations of subtlest quality. Few canvases equal his in refinement of observation and delicate tonality.

In the Collection of Louis A. Lehmaier, Esq.

THE VALLEY

EDWARD W. REDFIELD

*T*HIS artist, one of most vigorous and sympathetic of our younger landscape painters, makes his home upon
the Delaware River, which he has rendered under a great variety of seasonal and atmospheric aspects. He is
essentially an impressionist, whose canvases invariably convey a remarkable interpretation of the feeling of the
scene.

of character, elaboration of detail, and fondness for the qualities of texture. Avoiding alike the summariness of much modern impressionism, and the perfection of finish which in a Bourguereau, for example, is so tame and unlifelike, he recognises the importance of detail in the make-up of the whole, and by his frank and resolute rendering of it gives to all his pictures a markedly individual personality. In this respect he might be ranged alongside of Thomas Eakins, for his insight of observation and fidelity of statement are correspondingly sure; but he differs from the older painter in having essentially a modern point of view. This leads him to study his figures and accessories under the effect of real light, for the most part a cool, evenly diffused light which admits of little shadow and avoids any spots of heightened piquancy. Again, it draws him into sympathy with his subject. He has put himself in touch with the lives of the people, the young peasant women and men, whom he represents, and recognises the sweetness and sadness that underly its ruggedness. His expression of this sentiment is marked by the same comprehension and fidelity to truth that distinguish his method of painting. It is as far as possible from the sentimentality that mars the work of so many painters of the peasant-subject, just as his technique is equally devoid of sloppiness and superficiality.

This distinction, one should observe, is a measure of Melchers' own character. It is the personality of his own mental distinction, investing everything he does with original directness and scrupulous truth. The importance of this fact cannot be overstated: that character counts in painting as much as in any other department of life. But how few people seem to realise this! Because a painter must be sensitive to certain aspects, such as those of colour and form, beyond the habit of men engaged in other pursuits, they take it for granted that he must be an emotionalist at the mercy of his sensibilities, and make allowances accordingly. Yet, if we study the lives and works of artists, not in painting only, but in music, sculpture, and literature, we shall find, perhaps without exception, that the greatest results, those, I mean, that endure and most appeal to the largest number of thoughtful students, are those which are the product of sensibility controlled. Not by any means has all strong work been the output of artists physically strong; indeed, the balance, if one carefully reckoned it, might be found on the other side; but whether physically weak or strong, they have been strong in character. They have had a mental poise that sustained them, and set the standard of their endeavour and accomplishment. And the mental poise is the product of a clear and vigorous mind remaining true to itself and enlarging its scope

THE SLUICE   FREDERICK BALLARD WILLIAMS

*T*HE *landscapes of this artist are distinguished by largeness of feeling combined with a close observation of nature. While all the forms are strongly contrasted, he excels in the drawing of turbulent water. His coloring is full of quality, and the lighting effects are admirably done.*

THE SHEPHERDESS   GARI MELCHERS

*W*ITH no meretricious appeal in the way of prettiness, the picture compels admiration through its downright acceptance
of the facts and sincerity of sympathetic comprehension.

by contact with what is sane and true in surrounding art and life.

It is on this ground that art and morality really meet; namely, in the person of the artist himself. For I will not admit that view held by many, that art must be moral in its purpose and suggestion; by which, apparently, it is meant that art must directly assist the cause of morality by presenting subjects in which the virtue of morality is explicitly set forth. Although, at one time, art did splendid service for the church in picturing the truth of doctrine and the beauty of the Bible story and of holy living, that was only one of the glorious incidents in its career. But the real domain of the arts is not that of the preacher, the philosopher, or the moralist. It is to make known, not the beauty of holiness, but the holiness of beauty, to a world overmuch occupied with the material or purely intellectual sides of life. It is, if you will, to sanctify the senses by drawing them off from merely carnal and material gratification, to a realisation of the abstract essence of beauty that pervades nature and human life. Viewed in this light, it is as important a factor in the betterment of the whole man, the body, mind, and soul that are in all of us, as are the labours of the preacher, the philosopher, the moralist, and the purveyors of the material necessaries and embellishments of life. The labours of all are necessary to the nurturing of the whole man, of the full life. They work mutually, and often in aim and result impinge upon one another's domains. But each is separate.

Yet, even if this be so, there is a definite alliance between art and morality, if by the latter we understand the being true to what is best in us and the reaching after the best of which we are capable. And the highest form of this, as I have already hinted, is based upon superior mental qualities, controlled by strength of mind. A man may be faithful unto death, but unless his acts are prompted and controlled by strength of mind, his faithfulness differs in degree, perhaps, but not in quality, from that of a dog. It would be idle to affirm that mental form is of small account in the qualification of a preacher, a philosopher, or a business man. All our experience is to the contrary. Yet in an artist we customarily overlook both the need and the lack of it, and are content to regard him as a chartered emotionalist. His training tends to affirm the emotionalist in himself. Early discovering an aptitude for drawing and a peculiar sensitiveness to beauty, he enters upon a course of instruction, too much limited to the promotion of these qualities, and escapes from rough contact with men and things and the discipline which it involves. He learns, not to repress, but to express himself; to take his feelings as a guide to conduct, and to nurse and pamper them as his most

MOTHER AND CHILD   GARI MELCHERS

THE face of the mother recalls that of The Shepherdess, *only now it is not heavy with toil, but alert with the contentment of motherhood.*

In the Collection of the Pennsylvania Academy of Fine Arts, Philadelphia

THE SAILOR AND HIS SWEETHEART   GARI MELCHERS

THE abstract gaze of the fisherman, stolid with much looking on sky and water; the personal straining gaze of the

valuable assets in life. But in art, as in other vocations of life, it is the man who is endowed with intellectuality and by self-discipline preserves the integrity of this endowment, that accomplishes the vital thing. He is in his treatment of himself a moral man, and his morality is declared in the poise and vigour of his art.

It would be obviously out of place in a work of this kind to cite all the men who seem to one's self, as Gari Melchers does, to represent this union of artistic sensibility with intellectual integrity. To attempt such a thing would be to pass a very serious slight upon the names omitted; and it has been my intention to avoid as far as possible all personalities. Yet, because of the general comment that it suggests, I will cite one other instance, that of a younger painter, whose work so far has not received the consideration to which it seems to me entitled. He is Robert David Gauley, a pupil of F. W. Benson and Edmund C. Tarbell in Boston, and of Bouguereau and Ferrier in Paris. Subsequently he studied Velasquez in Madrid, and worked and studied in Holland. This variety of influences and the resolute personality of Gauley himself may account in part for the slowness of his acceptance by the public.

The latter is more readily attracted to a painter whose style it can identify immediately, whereas this one has been assimilating his impressions with deliberation, experimenting in various methods of technique, and holding himself back from the acquisition of any formula or fixed mode of painting. Thus the public is thwarted in its quite intelligible satisfaction of being able to exclaim, as it visits an exhibition: "Look, that is a Gauley!" On the other hand, he may fail to attract general attention because there is nothing of the obvious in his pictures, none of those elegant little irrelevances of costume or pose which so gladden the superficial amateur of art. The ideal toward which he is working is by contrast a severe one. It involves in the matter of composition a search for choiceness as well as dignity of line, and for a movement or pose of the figure that unites subtlety with simplicity. A corresponding subtlety and choiceness distinguish the expression of the whole. The jealousy with which he tries to keep his art pure of any meretriciousness determines his attitude toward his sitter. Whether the latter be a man or woman, he approaches his subject with a reverence none too usual in the portrait painter.

For, in the presence of so many portraits, especially of women, one is conscious of a lack of reverence in the mental attitude of the painter. Frequently the subject, for all her finery, or possibly because so much stress has been put upon it, does not even look like a lady. She has been made to flaunt her person and costume upon one's notice

PORTRAIT OF A LADY   ROBERT DAVID GAULEY

A PORTRAIT *of rarely choice distinction.*

LADY WITH MUFF   Robert David Gauley

A^N *unusually alluring and distinguished portrait.*

after the fashion of those who go to market with their personal wares. This blatant form of vulgarity, not uncommon in the portraits by foreigners, is, it must be acknowledged, rarely seen in those by Americans. Their tendency in this direction is confined for the most part to a preoccupation with frippery and to an exploitation of skill of painting for its own sake. The result may be not so blatantly vulgar, but it none the less indicates irreverence. And, mark you, irreverence on the part of a painter toward the manhood or womanhood of his subject is irreverence toward what at least should be sacred to him—his own art. For peculiarly true of the painter's case is that old saying of Novalis: " There is but one temple in the universe, and that is the body of man." Human nature, its fabric of flesh and its indwelling spirit, is the highest object of the artist's study, the richest treasury of his artistic ideals. If he hold it in little honour, the price he pays is the prostitution of his art. But for this prostitution, to the existence of which in American painting the thoughtful student cannot shut his eyes, the American public is in part responsible. One could name painters whose ideals were true enough at the start, but who have been driven on to the streets of easy virtue by hard conditions. The public demand for honest art is so small, the reward it offers to meretriciousness so cordial and handsome. Why not? You cannot make a silk purse out of a sow's ear. A society sprawling on materialism and wallowing in ostentatious display —what should it care for, or even know of, choiceness of taste and reverence for what is true in art? Naturally, since it pays the piper, it calls the kind of tune it likes; and the piper accordingly must debauch his art or step aside and rot. Under such circumstances the artist needs to have a more than commonly stout heart to continue to be true to himself and to preserve confidence in a saving residue of taste in the public.

For that there is such a residue one knows. While present American conditions in the gross are not favourable to the highest possibilities of native art, here, there, and everywhere throughout the country knowledge and taste are growing, and the still, small voice of true appreciation is gathering volume. It is on people with knowledge enough to dare to have opinions of their own, and with the taste that can distinguish between what is meretricious and what is sterling, that the future of American art depends.

CHAPTER XVI

IN the previous chapter I touched upon some of the insidious effects of the popular taste for prettiness. These, it is to be anticipated, will pass away as the American public grows in serious appreciation of what is truly beautiful in art. But even then there will remain another phase of the matter which is likely to be of perennial interest, since it strikes at the roots of our conceptions of beauty. Stated bluntly, it involves the question: How far is the conception of beauty in art compatible with ugliness?

At the outset the two ideas seem to be mutually antagonistic, and so they are reckoned by those who narrow their conceptions of beauty to the ideal purity of Greek sculpture of the golden age, and to the subsequent work of Roman, Rennaissance, and later times that tried to emulate it. With all such the ideal is to render form and feeling in the harmony of a perfect poise, to exclude the individual or irregular, and to imagine and suggest an abstract ideal of perfection. But in actual life absolute perfection of form is not to be found, still less a complete harmony of poise between the physical, the intellectual, and the emotional. Exception both to one and to the other is the rule. So the question eternally cropping up, eternally unsolved, arises out of the artist's attitude toward life. Does he regard life itself as the end and object of his study, or merely as a rich mine from which he may extract ore to fashion it into creations of his own imagination? In the latter case he will strive to improve upon nature, in the former to represent it as it is. These two ideals of art differ so widely that it is difficult for the artists who embrace the one to have much sympathy with those in the opposite camp. For the layman, however, there need be no such difficulty, because his detachment from any preoccupation with technique enables him to view the matter from outside. Doing so, he may, if he has clear eyes, find truth in both directions. Many a layman will reach his conclusions somewhat in this fashion:

To him it seems that life is the thing of supreme importance; art being but one of the sources of higher living. He thinks of art as a magic mirror in which life is reflected, and looks to find in it a heightened impression of the things of sight, as a suggestion to the spirit or sense-imagination of the things not seen. If the mirror only gives back a repeated vision of what he can see with his own eyes, he is disappointed, for in this case art has added nothing to nature. There is no heightening of impression, no stimulus to imagination or spirit.

THE SILVER GOWN HOWARD J. CUSHING

A GOOD example of a young painter whose work is characterized by originality of feeling, a refined color sense, and a distinguished quality of line.

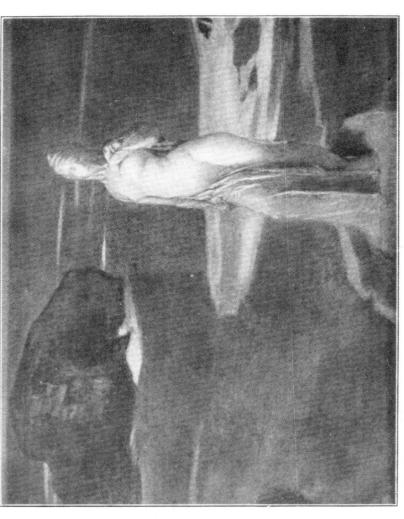

THE MYSTERIES OF NIGHT

J. HUMPHREYS JOHNSTON

IMAGINE the color of the water a violet-blue, luminous with moonlight that whitens the eddies and invests the figure

He may admire the skill or fidelity with which this vision has been produced, even as he admires the craftsmanship involved in the mechanism of a piece of machinery, but for him in neither case is there any evidence of creation. The mechanic, whether his tool be the brush or turning lathe, is but engaged in reproducing; he is not an inventor. And the painter is only an inventor, a creator, if he has the artist's vision, by means of which our own may be kindled to a heightened sense of beauty.

By the time that we have learned to demand this of a painter, and to refuse him the higher title of artist, unless he comply with it, our whole attitude toward pictures is changed. Especially do we cease to concern ourselves much with the subject of the picture. The most exalted subject will not of itself impress us. It is not the subject, but the artist's vision of it, which affects us. A pumpkin, rendered by that great French master of still-life, Vollon, may move us deeply, where an elaborate figure composition leaves us cold. And why? Because Vollon's pumpkin becomes, as it were, a symbol through which we receive a heightened impression of the sumptuousness and subtlety of nature's colouring, the vitalising power of light, and the opulence of nature's productive vigour. Our own sensibility is enriched; for the moment, at least, we live more abundantly. And for this effect upon ourselves we are indebted to the artist's vision, which he has enabled us to share through his power to give it technical expression.

But if he is endowed with these qualifications of vision and expression, the artist can look upon nature and life and find in them occasions of beauty, overlooked by ordinary eyes. He will even discover beauty lurking in ugliness, or by his treatment of the latter will transmute it into a form of beauty. For, in the first place, what do we ourselves understand by ugliness? Have we in mind some such exaggerated type of physical formation as that of a toad or spider-crab, or, to take another extreme instance, that of a man of the slums who is morally as well as physically deteriorated, offensive alike to our senses and our conscience? But, as to nature's form of so-called ugliness, I doubt if there be one, however abnormal in comparison with our ordinary standards of comeliness, but has some quality of colouring or of movement that to the searching eye of the artist's vision may not be able to yield suggestion of beauty, which his technical skill will evolve into expression. The Japanese, in their carvings, lacquers, and prints, have abundantly illustrated this. As to the slum-man, we may turn from him with repugnance, but it is precisely to him that the Salvation Army turns, in its conviction that somewhere latent in him is still a possibility of goodness. Similarly an artist may turn to him as a source of artistic inspiration. If

Copyright, 1906, by Hugo Ballin

UROPA SIBYL   HUGO BALLIN

N allegorical subject represented in a spirit that is essentially, even if not too ob-
viously, academic, for the idealism scarcely pervades the feeling of the picture.
It is, rather, the result of costumes and accessories that are out of the usual.

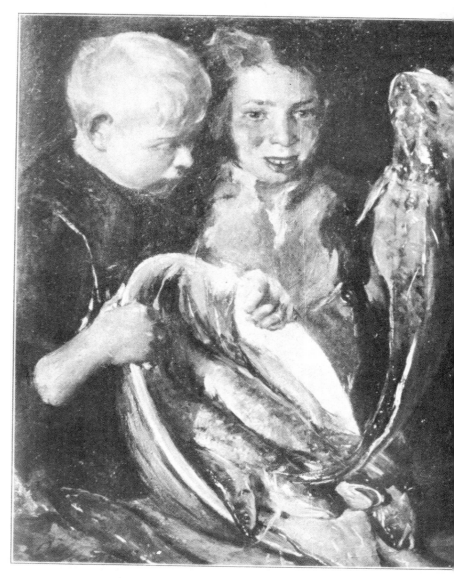

BOYS WITH FISH

Charles W. Hawthe

*W*HAT *may seem in the reproduction a brutality of effect is alleviated in the o
nal by the dexterity with which the colors and slippery forms of the fish
rendered. The painter is perhaps the best of Chase's pupils, but has ye
find himself. That he will do so is probable, through his study in Italy, where men disc
that brushwork does not constitute the whole art of painting.*

he does so, he has the excellent precedent, among others, of Rembrandt and Velasquez. Shall we venture to deny to those artists a sense of beauty, or shall we reconstruct our notion of beauty so as to include their example? I think the latter will seem the wiser plan. The notion, then, of beauty, so extended, involves character; both expression of character and character of expression. Character implies something distinctive, individual, so far abnormal that it is a deviation from the general run, and still more so from the abstract type. It is, for example, the quality conspicuous in a locust tree, so unexpectedly original in its growth, as compared with the exquisitely balanced grace of an American elm. Really one might venture to illustrate the difference between the academic understanding of beauty, and the extended acceptation of it to include character, by the comparison of these two trees.

But it must be remembered that the artist comprehends character as a functional quality. He deals primarily with externals, and, while he may not be unconscious of the psychological import of character, it is primarily its effect upon the physical aspect that he notes and renders. If he is really a nature-student, it is character in a human being, affecting the latter's form, the functions of the limbs and joints, the disposition and texture of the flesh, the very kind and carrying of the clothes, that form a large portion of his study. Or, if he is a landscape painter, the effect of permanent environment and temporary conditions upon the forms of objects. Always he feels the forces working through nature and declaring themselves in form. It is the beauty of nature's law of cause and effect, illustrated in a myriad aspects, that attracts him, rather than man's invention of an abstract perfection of beauty. And it is because that law is working in the slum-man that he claims the right, if he will, to make him the subject of artistic study. We may shudder at the evidences of functional degradation presented in the picture, but do not let us forget that there are the physical and moral counterparts of this in the tragedies of Œdipus and Othello. But, you will say, these are clothed in a splendour of diction that dignifies the theme. Quite so, and it is precisely a corresponding splendour of technical presentation that justifies the treatment of horrible subjects in pictures. There should be character of expression as well as expression of character.

The foregoing analysis of the place of so-called ugliness in art has been suggested by the effort of a few of our younger painters to shake themselves free from the fetters of prettiness and sentimentality in which much American art is confined. They are men who are interested in life as well as art, and who use the one to interpret the other.

SPANISH FÊTE

F. LUIS MORA

*T*HIS clever young painter, who first made his mark as an illustrator and is now painting pictures, is of Spanish extraction and has studied much in Spain. He has here chosen the costume period of the early nineteenth century, but more usually, his subjects are drawn from modern life, and are distinguished by vivid characterization, easy and vivacious action, and sparkle of color. Their weakest point hitherto has been a lack of atmosphere and real appearance of light.

EASTER EVE

JOHN SLOAN

*A*N *excellent example of impressionism. The subject has been felt as well as seen, and is rendered with a vigorous generalization that selects for emphasis just what is needed to impress the spectator with the effect produced on the artist's own mind*

SUMMARY OF RESULTS

One of these is John Sloan, a native of Philadelphia, and a pupil of the Pennsylvania Academy of the Fine Arts. He is now a resident of New York, whose crowded avenues, especially on the West Side, supply the subjects of his choice. For it is what the Japanese call the " Ukiyoye " that attracts him—the " passing show " of shops and streets, overhead and surface traffic, and the moving throngs of people, smart and squalid, sad and merry —a phantasmagoria of changing colour, form, and action. Out of the multiplied features of the scene, by eliminating some and emphasising others, he produces a synthesis of effect, in which confusion has disappeared, but the suggestion of vivid actuality remains. His pictures are excellent examples of modern impressionism; but, while the rendering of the spectacle presented to the eye is his first concern, his mind also is busy with the human comedy and tragedy that beats below the surface. It is the humanity of the scene, as well as its pictorial suggestions, that interests him. Not, however, in the way of telling a definite story, but by inference and suggestion. It is an impression of the human interest that he has received, and he renders it impressionistically. A writer, for example, if he were attracted by one of these scenes with its incidental suggestion, might make it the subject of a story, inventing a past and present for the personages and a sequel to what they are engaged in; investing them and the situation with detailed motive and conduct, and elaborating a dénouement. Many a painter also, mostly of the old-fashioned kind, might attempt to force upon your attention a corresponding definition of detailed incident. But he would operate under the serious limitation of being able to represent only one single phase of the story. Sloan, like other impressionists, recognising this limitation, avoids all competition with the verbal artist, and renders exclusively a painter's impression both of the scene and of its underlying human interest. He grasps the actual moment of appearance and suggestion.

In the rendering of these scenes line is superseded by masses; the whole is viewed as a collection of coloured patches, differing in hues, in the amount of light which they receive, and in the quantity of atmosphere which intervenes between them and the eye of the observer. Is it necessary to add that this impressionistic vision is, after all, the normal way in which the eye receives impressions of a scene? We are not conscious of hard lines enclosing objects, but of contours more or less blurred and blending; forming masses of light and dark, or of light and less light, of various hues and shapes. But in the actual scene, especially if it be laid in a crowded thoroughfare, flanked by the irregularities of buildings, the masses, both in their variety and shape, will present a good deal of the

DUMPING SNOW GEORGE LUKS

*T*HERE *is a brutal side to life, when the necessities of existence force themselves upon one. It is
such a scene that is here represented. A lowering sky, a city choked with snow — the only
receptacle for it the dark, swirling water of the river. The conditions are monstrous, a modern
revival of the fight of the earth-folk with the Titans. In a very remarkable way the young painter has
comprehended the significance of what to the average eye might seem a very ordinary scene.*

EAST SIDE PICTURE

JEROME MYERS

Copyright, 1906, by James Speyer

THE rare color-sense of this artist is not suggested in the reproduction. His pictures are a bouquet of subdued colors. The reproduction does, however, give an idea of the character of his subjects. They are drawn from the life of New York's streets, on the East Side, in their shifting aspects of color and movement. Every figure in the group of children, dancing variously to the one tune, is a bit of genuine characterization.

In the Collection of James Speyer

bizarrerie of a crazy quilt. It is a part of the artist's vision to draw these conflicting elements into a harmony of colour, lighting, tone, and atmosphere; so that the impression rendered may be one of artistic *ensemble*. By the time that the work has gone through the artist's two processes of receiving and rendering his impressions, it will partake of the unity of his own individuality and temperament. It will still give a suggestion of variety and busy action, but the different features of activity will be busy toward a common end, the modes of variety will be harmonised. The scene itself, composed of a great number of independent units, will have become unified into a picture that represents the impression of a single mind.

Now, our appreciation of the picture will depend, not only upon the artist's ability to create this *ensemble* of impression, but upon our own willingness to accept it. We may fail of the latter for two reasons: a general dislike of the impressionistic method, or a particular one of the kind of subject affected by Sloan and others. With neither is it any use to argue, since likes and dislikes are largely the product of temperament. Yet, if possible, they should be fortified by judgment, based upon understanding. Especially should this be the case in the matter of impressionism, since it plays so large a part in modern art.

Our understanding and possible appreciation of

it depends entirely—to go back to the point from which we started—upon our attitude toward the relation between art and life. For some painters the call of life is so urgent and alluring that they are not satisfied to make pictures about life, but try to render life in their pictures. The distinction is an important one. In the one case the scene within the frame, having had its origin in the desire to make a picture, continues to affect us as a picture, while in the other case we may be made to forget the canvas, paint, and frame, and find ourselves looking, as through a window, out upon a pageant of real life. Has this a fascination for us, as it had for the painter? We may agree that it has, and yet demur to the kind of life that the painter has chosen to render. If so, we are again brought back to the attitude of art toward life. Shall the painter confine his study to idealising life, or at least to presenting only its comely aspects, or may he have the whole run of life for his field, as the writer has; trusting to the sincerity of his purpose and the beauty of his technique to justify the ugliness of his theme? Whatever may be our individual answer to this question, let us recognise that the work of Sloan and a few others, such as Robert Henri, C. W. Hawthorne, William G. Glackens, Jerome Myers, and George Luks, is a natural and wholesome reaction from the vogue of frippery, tameness, and sentimentality. It has, however, its

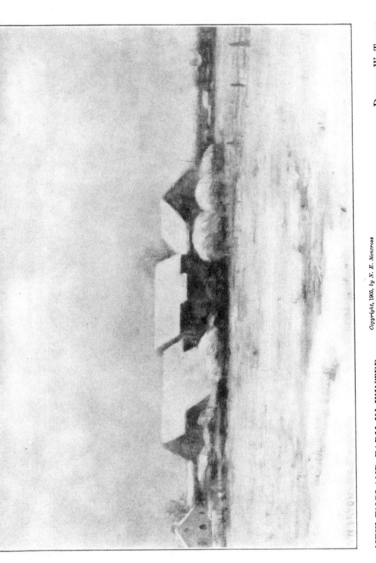

NEW ENGLAND FARM IN WINTER   Dwight W. Tryon

Copyright, 1905, by N. E. Montross

*B*ORN *in New York, 1849, Tryon went abroad in 1876, studying under Daubigny, and painting also in Holland, Italy, and the Channel Islands. His style is a very personal one, based upon a rigidly conscientious observation of the physical facts of nature. But these he penetrates with a poetical imagination that veils the fact with a suggestion of spirituality.*

TWILIGHT — AUTUMN

DWIGHT W. TRYON

Copyright, 1906, by N. E. Montross

CHARACTERISTIC subject — the foreground strong and rigid; slender trees, with foliage sprayed against an
aërial distance of luminous vibrations; the sentiment organically enabling its men shot the the

own inherent shortcoming when it reveals a tendency to be overoccupied with the appearances of life, and makes little or no appeal to the imagination or spirit. Based practically, if not avowedly, upon the assumption that "seeing is believing," that the painter's domain is that of the eye, it may easily ignore the at least equally important aspect of life which is made up of things not seen. It may take no account of the mystery that is in us and everywhere about us. It may be in its own superior way an exploitation of the obvious.

One should understand that its appearance in American painting is rather belated; for it is but repeating what Courbet and Manet did for the refreshment and invigoration of French art forty years ago. They, however, were the leaders in painting of the theories and practices entertained by the writers of the period; and painters and writers alike were a part of the realistic movement that was affecting the thought of the time. But since then the wheel has revolved; realism is no longer a motive; it is now only one of other means to an end. People, indeed, have grown a little weary of the diet, discovering that they cannot live by bread alone. Once more the spiritual needs of man are awake and calling to be fed. Abroad, especially in Germany, the more progressive of the painters have realised this reaction from materialism, and are responding to it. It is for a similar recognition and response on the part of the painters of this country that we are waiting.

Not that American painting can show no example of such progress. In a previous chapter we have noted that, while Whistler may be studied under many aspects, the most important and abiding one was his habit of evolving from material appearances their essence, the intangible element in them—in fact, the spirituality inherent in matter. The same is true of Thayer, Dewing, Lockwood, and some others among figure-painters. In their diverse ways these artists have treated the actual appearance as a symbol of moods and apprehensions of the imagination and spirit. A similar tendency may also be detected in a few of our landscape painters, notably in Twachtman, Winslow Homer, Dwight W. Tryon, Edward T. Steichen, and Ben Foster. Broadly speaking, however, the prevailing characteristic of American painting is materialistic rather than spiritual.

That the latter quality is necessary for the highest form of expression in modern art seems to me undeniable. For there was a time when spirituality and religion were practically one. The cravings of the spirit grew out of and found expression in the religious consciousness; and those were the great days of painting. The common and collective need of the people was to have its faith and soul-experiences bodied forth by art in terms of

MOONLIGHT   DWIGHT W. TRYON

By Courtesy of N. E. Montross

A PICTURE full of the mystery of night, the great hush of nature, and its tender invocation to the spirit.

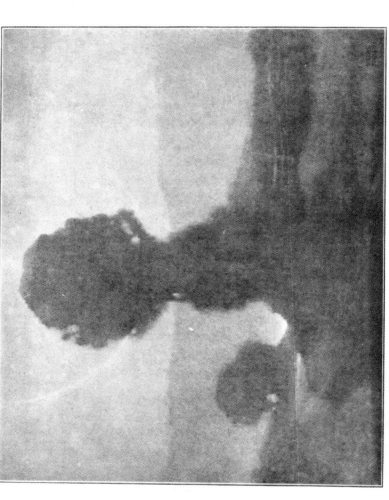

LAKE GEORGE

EDUARD T. STEICHEN

*T*HIS young painter, a remarkable photographer also, who stands in the first rank of the American and
European artists who practise that medium of expression, is distinguished by the originality and spirituality

religion; and the artists, whether as men they were religious or not, responded to the need with a nobility of design and execution, the influence of which extended also to the portrayal of subjects not religious. But in our time religion and spirituality, if not exactly divorced, are at least very far from being one. Much religion is mainly a system of doctrine and ethics; a great deal of spirituality exists among people not attracted to any specific formula of religion. This general lack of union between spirituality and religion is of itself quite sufficient to account for the absence of noble religious art in these days. There exists no common and collective need demanding it and making it possible. Since, then, modern art is debarred by circumstances from revealing the great art of the past along the latter's own lines, the question arises: Can it find some new motive growing out of the conditions of the present? Only, I feel assured, if a common and collective recognition of the claims of the spirit results in a need on the part of the public, so strong as to encourage and compel its realisation in art.

Belief in humanity is the practical religion of to-day, and it works for man's physical, material, and intellectual uplifting. But, as a motive for art, its influence is almost purely materialistic and sensuous. It is only when this new religion shall become impregnated with a correspondingly prac-

tical belief in the facts of spirit, that the possibilities of a great art in modern times will arise.
Symptoms of this new movement, as I have said,
can already be detected in American painting.
Whether they shall multiply and replenish the earth
depends in a final analysis upon the public.

INDEX

INDEX

INDEX

[389]

INDEX

INDEX

INDEX

INDEX

INDEX

INDEX

In Philadelphia, 24
Influence in Düsseldorf, 104
Thomas, Church of Saint, mural
decoration, 308
Tiffany, Louis C., 163
*Treaty of the Traverse des
Sioux,* Frank D. Millet, 327
Trial of Katherine of Aragon,
Edwin A. Abbey, 195
Trinity Church, Boston, mural
decoration, 305
Trumbull, John, early life, 49
Studies with West, 50
Estimate as painter, 50
Portrait of Hamilton, 51
Battle of Bunker Hill, 52
Mural Decoration, 304
Tryon, Dwight W., 382
New England Farm in Winter,
379
Twilight—Autumn, 380
Moonlight, 383
Turner, C. Y., 186
Burning of the Peggy Stewart,
317
Mural decoration, 325
Opening of the Erie Canal, 326
Twachtman, J. H., 163, 382
Characteristics analysed, 278
Career, 281
Hemlock Pool, 283
February, 284
Twilight—Autumn, Dwight Tryon,
380
Two Men, Eastman Johnson, 111

Universal Geometry, 149

Valley, The, Edward W. Redfield,
346
Values, 242, 262
Vanderlyn, John, 64
Estimate of paintings, 65
Portrait of the Artist, 61
Ariadne, 62
Van Ingen, *The Feet Washers,* 310
Vedder, Elihu, 163
Analysis of method, 171

Illustrations, 171
Symbolism, 172
Rome, 328
Corrupt Government, 329
Keeper of the Threshold, 175
Velasquez, 238, 262, 285, 289
View of the Seine, Homer Martin, 208
Vinton, Frederick P., 163, 257
Virgin Enthroned, Abbot H.
Thayer, 183
Volk, Douglas, 163, 186
Vollon, 365

Wagner, professor at Munich, 113
Walker, Horatio, *Ice Cutters,* 220
Wood Cutters, 223
Sheep Washing, 224
Ave Maria, 227
Washington, Crossing the Delaware, E. Leutze, 107
Washington, Portrait of, Charles
Wilson Peale, 33
Washington, Portrait of, Gilbert
Stuart, 39
Washington, D. C., Library of
Congress, 319, 323, 329
Wave, The, A. Harrison, 267
Webster, Daniel, Portrait of,
Chester Harding, 92
Weir, J. Alden, 163
A Gentlewoman, 272
The Farm in Winter, 275
Weir, Portrait of Mrs. Robert,
Unknown, 3
Well and Water Tank, F. Duveneck, 112
Wentworth, Lady, 17
West, Benjamin, 10
Birth and early training, 10
Earliest portraits, 11
Residence in England, 11
Visited by Copley, 21
Visited by Stuart, 36
Teacher of Trumbull, 50
Hagar and Ishmael, 8
Portrait of C. W. Peale, 13
Teacher of Sully, 89

[395]

INDEX